YOUR 15-MO
COMPLETE AND IN

VIRGO

August 22 - September 22

1990 SUPER HOROSCOPE

ARROW BOOKS LIMITED
62-65 Chandos Place
London WC2N 4NW

CONTENTS

THE PUBLISHERS REGRET THAT THEY CANNOT ANSWER INDIVIDUAL LETTERS REQUESTING PERSONAL HOROSCOPE INFORMATION.

FIRST PUBLISHED IN GREAT BRITAIN BY ARROW BOOKS 1989

THIS EDITION PUBLISHED BY AGREEMENT WITH THE BERKLEY PUBLISHING GROUP

PRINTED IN GREAT BRITAIN BY
THE GUERNSEY PRESS CO. LTD
GUERNSEY C.I.
ISBN 0 09 962640 3

NOTE TO THE CUSP-BORN

First find the year of your birth, and then find the sign under which you were born according to your day of birth. Thus, you can determine if you are a true Virgo (or Leo or Libra), according to the variations of the dates of the Zodiac. (See also page 7.)

Are *really* a Virgo? If your birthday falls during the fourth week of August, at the beginning of Virgo, will you still retain the traits of Leo, the sign of the Zodiac before Virgo? And what if you were born late in September—are you more Libra than Virgo? Many people born at the edge, or cusp, of a sign have great difficulty determining exactly what sign they are. If you are one of these people, here's how you can figure it out, once and for all.

Consult the following table. It will tell you the precise days on which the sun entered and left your sign for the year of your birth. If you were born either at the beginning or the end of Libra, yours is a lifetime reflecting a process of subtle transformation. Your life on earth will symbolize a significant change in consciousness, for you are either about to enter a whole new way of living or are leaving one behind.

If you were born at the beginning of Virgo, you may want to read the horoscope book for Leo as well as Virgo, for Leo holds the key to much of your complexity of spirit, reflects certain hidden weaknesses and compulsions, and your unspoken wishes. Your tie to Leo symbolizes your romantic dilemma and your unusual—often timid—approach to love. You are afraid of taking a gamble and letting everything ride on your emotions. You may resist giving up the rational, logical, clear-minded approach to life, but you can never really flee from your need for love.

You symbolize the warmth and fullness of a late summer day, a natural ripeness and maturity that is mellow and comfortable to be near.

If you were born sometime after the third week of September, you may want to read the horoscope book for Libra as well as Virgo, for Libra is possibly your greatest asset. Though you are eager to get involved with another person and you crave warmth and companionship, you may hover between still, mental analyzing and poetic romanticism. You have that Garboesque desire to be secluded, untouched—yet you want to share your life with another. You are a blend of monastic, spartan simplicity with grace, harmony and gentle beauty. You combine a profound power to sift, purify and analyze with the sensibilities of recognizing what is right, beautiful and just. You can be picky and fault-finding, inconsistent and small, needing someone desperately but rejecting the one you love most. Yet you are fundamentally a thoughtful, loving person with the sincere wish to serve and make someone happy.

Developing your capacity to share will aid you in joint financial ventures, bring your values into harmony and create a balance in your life.

DATES SUN ENTERS VIRGO (LEAVES LEO)

August 23 every year from 1900 to 2000, except for the following:

August 22:			August 24:	
1960	1980	1992	1903	1919
64	84	93	07	23
68	88	96	11	27
72	89	97	15	
76				

DATES SUN LEAVES VIRGO (ENTERS LIBRA)

September 23 every year from 1900 to 2000, except for the following:

September 22:				September 24:
1948	1968	1981	1992	1903
52	72	84	93	07
56	76	85	96	
60	77	88	97	
64	80	89		

HISTORY AND USES OF ASTROLOGY

Does astrology have a place in the fast-moving, ultra-scientific world we live in today? Can it be justified in a sophisticated society whose outriders are already preparing to step off the moon into the deep space of the planets themselves? Or is it just a hangover of ancient superstition, a psychological dummy for neurotics and dreamers of every historical age?

These are the kind of questions that any inquiring person can be expected to ask when they approach a subject like astrology which goes beyond, but never excludes, the materialistic side of life.

The simple, single answer is that astrology works. It works for tens of millions of people in the western world alone. In the United States there are 10 million followers and in Europe, an estimated 25 million. America has more than 4000 practicing astrologers, Europe nearly three times as many. Even down-under Australia has its hundreds of thousands of adherents. The importance of such vast numbers of people from diverse backgrounds and cultures is recognized by the world's biggest newspapers and magazines who probably devote more of their space to this subject in a year than to any other. In the eastern countries, astrology has enormous followings, again, because it has been proved to work. In countries like India, brides and grooms for centuries have been chosen on the basis of astrological compatibility. The low divorce rate there, despite today's heavy westernizing influence, is attributed largely to this practice.

In the western world, astrology today is more vital than ever before; more practicable because it needs a sophisticated society like ours to understand and develop its contribution to the full; more valid because science itself is confirming the precepts of astrological knowledge with every new exciting step. The ordinary person who daily applies astrology intelligently does not have to wonder whether it is true nor believe in it blindly. He can see it working for himself. And, if he can use it—and this book is designed to help the reader to do just that—he can make living a far richer experience, and become a more developed personality and a better person.

Astrology is the science of relationships. It is not just a study of planetary influences on man and his environment. It is the study of man himself.

We are at the center of our personal universe, of all our relationships. And our happiness or sadness depends on how we act, how we relate to the people and things that surround us. The emotions that we generate have a distinct affect—for better or worse—on the world around us. Our friends and our enemies will confirm this. Just look in the mirror the next time you are angry. In other words, each of us is a kind of sun or planet or star and our influence on our personal universe, whether loving, helpful or destructive, varies with our changing moods, expressed through our individual character.

And to an extent that includes the entire galaxy, this is true of the planetary bodies. Their radiations affect each other, including the earth and all the things on it. And in comparatively recent years, giant constellations called "quasars" have been discovered. These exist far beyond the night stars that we can observe, and science says these quasars are emitting radiating influences more powerful and different than ever recorded on earth. Their effect on man from an astrological point of view is under deep study. Compared with these inter-stellar forces, our personal "radiations" are negligible on the planetary scale. But ours are just as potent in the way they affect our moods, and our ability to control them. To this extent they determine much of the happiness and satisfaction in our lives. For instance, if we were bound and gagged and had to hold some strong emotion within us without being able to move, we would soon start to feel very uncomfortable. We are obviously pretty powerful radiators inside, in our own way. But usually, we are able to throw off our emotion in some sort of action—we have a good cry, walk it off, or tell someone our troubles—before it can build up too far and make us physically ill. Astrology helps us to understand the universal forces working on us, and through this understanding, we can become more properly adjusted to our surroundings and find ourselves coping where others may flounder.

Closely related to our emotions is the "other side" of our personal universe, our physical welfare. Our body, of course, is largely influenced by things around us over which we have very little control. The phone rings, we hear it. The train runs late. We snag our stocking or cut our face shaving. Our body is under a constant bombardment of events that influence our lives to varying degrees.

The question that arises from all this is, what makes each of us act so that we have to involve other people and keep the ball of activity and evolution rolling? This is the question that both science and astrology are involved with. The scientists have attacked it from different angles: anthropology, the study of human evolution as body, mind and response to environment; anatomy, the study of bodily structure; psychology, the science of the human mind; and so on. These studies have produced very impressive classifications and valuable information, but because the approach to the problem is fragmented, so is the result. They remain "branches" of science. Science generally studies effects. It keeps turning up wonderful answers but no lasting solutions. Astrology, on the other hand approaches the question from the broader viewpoint. Astrology began its inquiry with the totality of human experience and saw it as an effect. It then looked to find the cause, or at least the prime movers, and during thousands of years of observation of man and his *universal* environment, came up with the extraordinary principle of planetary influence—or astrology, which, from the Greek, means the science of the stars.

Modern science, as we shall see, has confirmed much of astrology's foundations—most of it unintentionally, some of it reluctantly, but still, indisputably.

It is not difficult to imagine that there must be a connection between outer space and the earth. Even today, scientists are not too sure how our earth was created, but it is generally agreed that it is only a tiny part of the universe. And as a part of the universe, people on earth see and feel the influence of heavenly bodies in almost every aspect of our existence. There is no doubt that the sun has the greatest influence on life on this planet. Without it there would be no life, for without it there would be no warmth, no division into day and night, no cycles of time or season at all. This is clear and easy to see. The influence of the moon, on the other hand, is more subtle, though no less definite.

There are many ways in which the influence of the moon manifests itself here on earth, both on human and animal life. It is a well-known fact, for instance, that the large movements of water on our planet—that is the ebb and flow of the tides—are caused by the moon's gravitational pull. Since this is so, it follows that these water movements do not occur only in the oceans, but that all bodies of water are affected, even down to the tiniest puddle.

The human body, too, which consists of about 70 percent water, falls within the scope of this lunar influence. For example the menstrual cycle of most women corresponds to the lunar month; the period of pregnancy in humans is 273 days, or equal to nine lunar months. Similarly, many illnesses reach a crisis at the change of the moon, and statistics in many countries have shown that the crime rate is highest at the time of the full moon. Even human sexual desire has been associated with the phases of the moon. But, it is in the movement of the tides that we get the clearest demonstration of planetary influence, and the irresistible correspondence between the so-called metaphysical and the physical.

Tide tables are prepared years in advance by calculating the future positions of the moon. Science has known for a long time that the moon is the main cause of tidal action. But only in the last few years has it begun to realize the possible extent of this influence on mankind. To begin with, the ocean tides do not rise and fall as we might imagine from our personal observations of them. The moon as it orbits around the earth, sets up a circular wave of attraction which pulls the oceans of the world after it, broadly in an east to west direction. This influence is like a phantom wave crest, a loop of power stretching from pole to pole which passes over and around the earth like an invisible shadow. It travels with equal effect across the land masses and, as scientists were recently amazed to observe, caused oysters placed in the dark in the middle of the United States where there is no sea, to open their shells to receive the non-existent tide. If the land-locked oysters react to this invisible signal, what effect does it have on us who not so long ago in evolutionary time, came out of the sea and still have its salt in our blood and sweat?

Less well known is the fact that the moon is also the primary force behind the circulation of blood in human beings and animals, and the movement of sap in trees and plants. Agriculturists have established that the moon has a distinct influence on crops, which explains why for centuries people have planted according to moon cycles. The habits of many animals, too, are directed by the movement of the moon. Migratory birds, for instance, depart only at or near the time of the full moon. Just as certain fish, eels in particular, move only in accordance with certain phases of the moon.

Know Thyself—Why?

In today's fast-changing world, everyone still longs to know what the future holds. It is the one thing that everyone has in common: rich and poor, famous and infamous, all are deeply concerned about tomorrow.

But the key to the future, as every historian knows, lies in the past. This is as true of individual people as it is of nations. You cannot understand your future without first understanding your past, which is simply another way of saying that you must first of all know yourself.

The motto "know thyself" seems obvious enough nowadays, but it was originally put forward as the foundation of wisdom by the ancient Greek philosophers. It was then adopted by the "mystery religions" of the ancient Middle East, Greece and Rome, and is still used in all genuine schools of mind training or mystical discipline, both in those of the East, based on yoga, and those of the West. So it is universally accepted now, and has been through the ages.

But how do you go about discovering what sort of person you are? The first step is usually classification into some sort of system of types. Astrology did this long before the birth of Christ. Psychology has also done it. So has modern medicine, in its way.

One system classifies men according to the source of the impulses they respond to most readily: the muscles, leading to direct bodily action; the digestive organs, resulting in emotion, or the brain and nerves. Another such system says that character is determined by the endocrine glands, and gives us labels like "pituitary," "thyroid" and "hyperthyroid" types. These different systems are neither contradictory nor mutually exclusive. In fact, they are very often different ways of saying the same thing.

Very popular and useful classifications were devised by Dr. C. G. Jung, the eminent disciple of Freud. Jung observed among the different faculties of the mind, four which have a predominant influence on character. These four faculties exist in all of us without exception, but not in perfect balance. So when we say, for instance, that a man is a "thinking type," it means that in any situation he tries to be rational. It follows that emotion, which some say is the opposite of thinking, will be his weakest function. This type can be sensible and reasonable, or calculating and unsympathetic. The emotional type, on the other hand, can often be recognized by exaggerated language—everything is either marvelous or terrible—and in extreme cases they even invent dramas and quarrels out of nothing just to make life more interesting.

The other two faculties are intuition and physical sensation. The sensation type does not only care for food and drink, nice clothes and furniture; he is also interested in all forms of physical experience. Many scientists are sensation types as are athletes and nature-lovers. Like sensation, intuition is a form of perception and we all possess it. But it works through that part of the mind which is not under conscious control—consequently it sees meanings and connections which are not obvious to thought or emotion. Inventors and original thinkers are always intuitive, but so, too, are superstitious people who see meanings where none exist.

Thus, sensation tells us what is going on in the world, feeling (that is, emotion) tells us how important it is to ourselves, thinking enables us to interpret it and work out what we should do about it, and intuition tells us what it means to ourselves and others. All four faculties are essential, and all are present in every one of us. But some people are guided chiefly by one, others by another.

Besides these four types, Jung observed a division into extrovert and introvert, which cuts across them. By and large, the introvert is one who finds truth inside himself rather than outside. He is not, therefore, ideally suited to a religion or a political party which tells him what to believe. Original thinkers are almost necessarily introverts. The extrovert, on the other hand, finds truth coming to him from outside. He believes in experts and authorities, and wants to think that nature and the laws of nature really exists, that they are what they appear to be and not just generalities made by men.

A disadvantage of all these systems of classification, is that one cannot tell very easily where to place oneself. Some people are reluctant to admit that they act to please their emotions. So they deceive themselves for years by trying to belong to whichever type they think is the "best." Of course, there is no best; each has its faults and each has its good points.

The advantage of the signs of the Zodiac is that they simplify classification. Not only that, but your date of birth is personal—it is unarguably yours. What better way to know yourself than by going back as far as possible to the very moment of your birth? And this is precisely what your horoscope is all about.

What Is a Horoscope?

If you had been able to take a picture of the heavens at the moment of your birth, that photograph would be your horoscope. Lacking such a snapshot, it is still possible to recreate the picture—and this is at the basis of the astrologer's art. In other words, your horoscope is a representation of the skies with the planets in the exact positions they occupied at the time you were born.

This information, of course, is not enough for the astrologer. He has to have a background of significance to put the photograph on. You will get the idea if you imagine two balls—one inside the other. The inner one is transparent. In the center of both is the astrologer, able to look up, down and around in all directions. The outer sphere is the Zodiac which is divided into twelve approximately equal segments, like the segments of an orange. The inner ball is our photograph. It is transparent except for the images of the planets. Looking out from the center, the astrologer sees the planets in various segments of the Zodiac. These twelve segments are known as the signs or houses.

The position of the planets when each of us is born is always different. So the photograph is always different. But the Zodiac and its signs are fixed.

Now, where in all this are you, the subject of the horoscope?

Your character is largely determined by the sign the sun is in. So that is where the astrologer looks first in your horoscope.

There are twelve signs in the Zodiac and the sun spends approximately one month in each. As the sun's motion is almost perfectly regular, the astrologers have been able to fix the dates governing each sign. There are not many people who do not know which sign of the Zodiac they were born under or who have not been amazed at some time or other at the accuracy of the description of their own character. Here are the twelve signs, the ancient zodiacal symbol, and their dates for the year 1990.*

ARIES	Ram	March 20–April 20
TAURUS	Bull	April 20–May 21
GEMINI	Twins	May 21–June 21
CANCER	Crab	June 21–July 22
LEO	Lion	July 22–August 23
VIRGO	Virgin	August 23–September 23
LIBRA	Scales	September 23–October 23
SCORPIO	Scorpion	October 23–November 22
SAGITTARIUS	Archer	November 22–December 22
CAPRICORN	Sea-Goat	December 22–January 20
AQUARIUS	Water-Bearer	January 20–February 18
PISCES	Fish	February 18–March 20

The time of birth—apart from the date—is important in advanced astrology because the planets travel at such great speed that the patterns they form change from minute to minute. For this reason, each person's horoscope is his and his alone. Further on we will see that the practicing astrologer has ways of determining and reading these minute time changes which dictate the finer character differences in us all.

However, it is still possible to draw significant conclusions and make meaningful predictions based simply on the sign of the Zodiac a person is born under. In a horoscope, the signs do not necessarily correspond with the divisions of the houses. It could be that a house begins halfway across a sign. It is the interpretation of such combinations of different influences that distinguishes the professional astrologer from the student and the follower.

However, to gain a workable understanding of astrology, it is not necessary to go into great detail. In fact, the beginner is likely to find himself confused if he attempts to absorb too much too quickly. It should be remembered that this is a science and to become proficient at it, and especially to grasp the tremendous scope of possibilities in man and his affairs and direct them into a worthwhile reading, takes a great deal of study and experience.

*These dates are fluid and change with the motion of the Earth from year to year.

If you do intend to pursue it seriously you will have to learn to figure the exact moment of birth against the degrees of longitude and latitude of the planets at that precise time. This involves adapting local time to Greenwich Mean Time (G.M.T.), reference to tables of houses to establish the Ascendant, as well as making calculations from Ephemeris—the tables of the planets' positions.

After reading this introduction, try drawing up a rough horoscope to get the "feel" of reading some elementary characteristics and natal influences.

Draw a circle with twelve equal segments. Write in counterclockwise the names of the signs—Aries, Taurus, Gemini etc.—one for each segment. Look up an ephemeris for the year of the person's birth and note down the sign each planet was in on the birthday. Do not worry about the number of degrees (although if a planet is on the edge of a sign its position obviously should be considered). Write the name of the planet in the segment/sign on your chart. Write the number 1 in the sign where the sun is. This is the first house. Number the rest of the houses, counterclockwise till you finish at 12. Now you can investigate the probable basic expectation of experience of the person concerned. This is done first of all by seeing what planet or planets is/are in what sign and house. (See also page 72.)

The 12 houses control these functions:

1st.	Individuality, body appearance, general outlook on life	(Personality house)
2nd.	Finance, business	(Money house)
3rd.	Relatives, education correspondence	(Relatives house)
4th.	Family, neighbors	(Home house)
5th.	Pleasure, children, attempts, entertainment	(Pleasure house)
6th.	Health, employees	(Health house)
7th.	Marriage, partnerships	(Marriage house)
8th.	Death, secret deals, difficulties	(Death house)
9th.	Travel, intellectual affairs	(Travel house)
10th.	Ambition, social standing	(Business and Honor house)
11th.	Friendship, social life, luck	(Friends house)
12th.	Troubles, illness, loss	(Trouble house)

The characteristics of the planets modify the influence of the Sun according to their natures and strengths.

Sun: Source of life. Basic temperament according to sun sign. The will.
Moon: Superficial nature. Moods. Changeable. Adaptive. Mother.
Mercury: Communication. Intellect. Reasoning power. Curiosity. Short travels.
Venus: Love. Delight. Art. Beautiful possessions.
Mars: Energy. Initiative. War. Anger. Destruction. Impulse.
Jupiter: Good. Generous. Expansive. Opportunities. Protection.
Saturn: Jupiter's opposite. Contraction. Servant. Delay. Hardwork. Cold. Privation. Research. Lasting rewards after long struggle.
Uranus: Fashion. Electricity. Revolution. Sudden changes. Modern science.
Neptune: Sensationalism. Mass emotion. Devastation. Delusion.
Pluto: Creates and destroys. Lust for power. Strong obsessions.

Superimpose the characteristics of the planets on the functions of the house in which they appear. Express the result through the character of the birth (sun) sign, and you will get the basic idea of how astrology works.

Of course, many other considerations have been taken into account in producing the carefully worked out predictions in this book: The aspects of the planets to each other; their strength according to position and sign; whether they are in a house of exaltation or decline; whether they are natural enemies or not; whether a planet occupies his own sign; the position of a planet in relation to its own house or sign; whether the planet is male, female or neuter; whether the sign is a fire, earth, water or air sign. These are only a few of the colors on the astrologer's pallet which he must mix with the inspiration of the artist and the accuracy of the mathematician.

The Problem of Love

Love, of course, is never a problem. The problem lies in recognizing the difference between infatuation, emotion, sex and, sometimes, the downright deceit of the other person. Mankind, with its record of broken marriages, despair and disillusionment, is obviously not very good at making these distinctions.

Can astrology help?

Yes. In the same way that advance knowledge can usually help in any human situation. And there is probably no situation as human, as poignant, as pathetic and universal, as the failure of man's love.

Love, of course, is not just between man and woman. It involves love of children, parents, home and so on. But the big problems usually involve the choice of partner.

Astrology has established degrees of compatibility that exist between people born under the various signs of the Zodiac. Because people are individuals, there are numerous variations and modifications and the astrologer, when approached on mate and marriage matters makes allowances for them. But the fact remains that some groups of people are suited for each other and some are not and astrology has expressed this in terms of characteristics which all can study and use as a personal guide.

No matter how much enjoyment and pleasure we find in the different aspects of each other's character, if it is not an overall compatibility, the chances of our finding fulfillment or enduring happiness in each other are pretty hopeless. And astrology can help us to find someone compatible.

History of Astrology

The origins of astrology have been lost far back in history, but we do know that reference is made to it as far back as the first written records of the human race. It is not hard to see why. Even in primitive times, people must have looked for an explanation for the various happenings in their lives. They must have wanted to know why people were different from one to another. And in their search they turned to the regular movements of the sun, moon and stars to see if they could provide an answer.

It is interesting to note that as soon as man learned to use his tools in any type of design, or his mind in any kind of calculation, he turned his attention to the heavens. Ancient cave dwellings reveal dim crescents and circles representative of the sun and moon, rulers of day and night. Mesopotamia and the civilization of Chaldea, in itself the foundation of those of Babylonia and Assyria, show a complete picture of astronomical observation and well-developed astrological interpretation.

Humanity has a natural instinct for order. The study of anthropology reveals that primitive people—even as far back as prehistoric times—were striving to achieve a certain order in their lives. They tried to organize the apparent chaos of the universe. They had the desire to attach meaning to things. This demand for order has persisted throughout the history of man. So that observing the regularity of the heavenly bodies made it logical that primitive peoples should turn heavenwards in their search for an understanding of the world in which they found themselves so random and alone.

And they did find a significance in the movements of the stars. Shepherds tending their flocks, for instance, observed that when the cluster of stars now known as the constellation Aries was in sight, it was the time of fertility and they associated it with the Ram. And they noticed that the growth of plants and plant life corresponded with different phases of the moon, so that certain times were favorable for the planting of crops, and other times were not. In this way, there grew up a tradition of seasons and causes connected with the passage of the sun through the twelve signs of the Zodiac.

Astrology was valued so highly that the king was kept informed of the daily and monthly changes in the heavenly bodies, and the results of astrological studies regarding events of the future. Head astrologers were clearly men of great rank and position, and the office was said to be a hereditary one.

Omens were taken, not only from eclipses and conjunctions of the moon or sun with one of the planets, but also from storms and earthquakes. In the eastern civilizations, particularly, the reverence inspired by astrology appears to have remained unbroken since the very earliest days. In ancient China, astrology, astronomy and religion went hand in hand. The astrologer, who was also an astronomer, was part of the official government service and had his own corner in the Imperial Palace. The duties of the Imperial astrologer, whose office was one of the most important in the land, were clearly defined, as this extract from early records shows:

> "This exalted gentleman must concern himself with the stars in the heavens, keeping a record of the changes and movements of the Planets, the Sun and the Moon, in order to examine the movements of the terrestial world with the object of prognosticating good and bad fortune. He divides the territories of the nine regions of the empire in accordance with their dependence on particular celestial bodies. All the fiefs and principalities are connected with the stars and from this their prosperity or misfortune should be ascertained. He makes prognostications according to the twelve years of the Jupiter cycle of good and evil of the terrestial world. From the colors of the five kinds of clouds, he determines the coming of floods or droughts, abundance or famine. From the twelve winds, he draws conclusions about the state of harmony of heaven and earth, and takes note of good and bad signs that result from their accord or disaccord. In general, he concerns himself with five kinds of phenomena so as to warn the Emperor to come to the aid of the government and to allow for variations in the ceremonies according to their circumstances."

The Chinese were also keen observers of the fixed stars, giving them such unusual names as Ghost Vehicle, Sun of Imperial Concubine, Imperial Prince, Pivot of Heaven, Twinkling Brilliance or Weaving Girl. But, great astrologers though they may have been, the Chinese lacked one aspect of mathematics that the Greeks applied to astrology—deductive geometry. Deductive geometry was the basis of much classical astrology in and after the time of the Greeks, and this explains the different methods of prognostication used in the East and West.

Down through the ages the astrologer's art has depended, not so much on the uncovering of new facts, though this is important, as on the interpretation of the facts already known. This is the essence of his skill. Obviously one cannot always tell how people will react (and this underlines the very important difference between astrology and predestination which will be discussed later on) but one can be prepared, be forewarned, to know what to expect.

But why should the signs of the zodiac have any effect at all on the formation of human character? It is easy to see why people thought they did, and even now we constantly use astrological expressions in our everyday speech. The thoughts of "lucky star," "ill-fated," "star-crossed," "mooning around," are interwoven into the very structure of our language.

In the same way that the earth has been created by influences from outside, there remains an indisputable togetherness in the working of the universe. The world, after all, is a coherent structure, for if it were not, it would be quite without order and we would never know what to expect. A dog could turn into an apple, or an elephant sprout wings and fly at any moment without so much as a by your leave. But nature, as we know, functions according to laws, not whims, and the laws of nature are certainly not subject to capricious exceptions.

This means that no part of the universe is ever arbitrarily cut off from any other part. Everything is therefore to some extent linked with everything else. The moon draws an imperceptible tide on every puddle; tiny and trivial events can be effected by outside forces (such as the fall of a feather by the faintest puff of wind). And so it is fair to think that the local events at any moment reflect to a very small extent the evolution of the world as a whole.

From this principle follows the possibility of divination, and also knowledge of events at a distance, provided one's mind were always as perfectly undisturbed, as ideally smooth, as a mirror or unruffled lake. Provided, in other words, that one did not confuse the picture with hopes, guesses, and expectations. When people try to foretell the future by cards or crystal ball gazing they find it much easier to confuse the picture with expectations than to reflect it clearly.

But the present does contain a good deal of the future to which it leads—not all, but a good deal. The diver halfway between bridge and water is going to make a splash; the train whizzing towards the station will pass through it unless interfered with; the burglar breaking a pane of glass has exposed himself to the possibility of a prison sentence. Yet this is not a doctrine of determinism, as was emphasized earlier. Clearly, there are forces already at work in the present, and any one of them could alter the situation in some way. Equally, a change of decision could alter the whole situation as well. So the future depends, not on an irresistible force, but on a small act of free will.

An individual's age, physique, and position on the earth's surface are remote consequences of his birth. Birth counts as the original cause for all that happens subsequently. The horoscope, in this case, means "this person represents the further evolution of the state of the universe pictured in this chart." Such a chart can apply equally to man or woman, dog, ship or even limited company.

If the evolution of an idea, or of a person, is to be understood as a totality, it must continue to evolve from its own beginnings, which is to say, in the terms in which it began. The brown-eyed person will be faithful to brown eyes all his life; the traitor is being faithful to some complex of ideas which has long been evolving in him; and the person born at sunset will always express, as he evolves, the psychological implications or analogies of the moment when the sun sinks out of sight.

This is the doctrine that an idea must continue to evolve in terms of its origin. It is a completely non-materialist doctrine, though it never fails to apply to material objects. And it implies, too, that the individual will continue to evolve in terms of his moment of origin, and therefore possibly of the sign of the Zodiac rising on the eastern horizon at his birth. It also implies that the signs of the Zodiac themselves will evolve in the collective mind of the human race in the same terms that they were first devised and not in the terms in which modern astrologers consciously think they ought to work.

For the human race, like every other kind of animal, has a collective mind, as Professor Jung discovered in his investigation of dreams. If no such collective mind existed, no infant could ever learn anything, for communication would be impossible. Furthermore, it is absurd to suggest that the conscious mind could be older than the "unconscious," for an infant's nervous system functions correctly before it has discovered the difference between "myself" and "something else" or discovered what eyes and hands are for. Indeed, the involuntary muscles function correctly even before birth, and will never be under conscious control. They are part of what we call the "unconscious" which is not really "unconscious" at all. To the contrary, it is totally aware of itself and everything else; it is merely that part of the mind that cannot be controlled by conscious effort.

And human experience, though it varies in detail with every individual, is basically the same for each one of us, consisting of sky and earth, day and night, waking and sleeping, man and woman, birth and death. So there is bound to be in the mind of the human race a very large number of inescapable ideas, which are called our natural archetypes.

There are also, however, artificial or cultural archetypes which are not universal or applicable to everyone, but are nevertheless inescapable within the limits of a given culture. Examples of these are the cross in Christianity, and the notion of "escape from the wheel of rebirth" in India. There was a time when these ideas did not exist. And there was a time, too, when the scheme of the Zodiac did not exist. One would not expect the Zodiac to have any influence on remote and primitive peoples, for example, who have never heard of it. If the Zodiac is only an archetype, their horoscopes probably would not work and it would not matter which sign they were born under.

But where the Zodiac is known, and the idea of it has become worked into the collective mind, then there it could well appear to have an influence, even if it has no physical existence. For ideas do not have a physical existence, anyway. No physical basis has yet been discovered for the telepathy that controls an anthill; young swallows migrate before, not after, their parents; and the weaverbird builds its intricate nest without being taught. Materialists suppose, but cannot prove, that "instinct" (as it is called, for no one knows how it works) is controlled by nucleic acid in the chromosomes. This is not a genuine explanation, though, for it only pushes the mystery one stage further back.

Does this mean, then, that the human race, in whose civilization the idea of the twelve signs of the Zodiac has long been embedded, is divided into only twelve types? Can we honestly believe that it is really as simple as that? If so, there must be pretty wide ranges of variation within each type. And if, to explain the variation, we call in heredity and environment, experiences in early childhood, the thyroid and other glands, and also the four functions of the mind mentioned at the beginning of this introduction, and extroversion and introversion, then one begins to wonder if the original classification was worth making at all. No sensible person believes that his favorite system explains everything. But even so, he will not find it much use at all if it does not even save him the trouble of bothering with the others.

Under the Jungian system, everyone has not only a dominant or principal function, but also a secondary or subsidiary one, so that the four can be arranged in order of potency. In the intuitive type, sensation is always the most inefficient function, but the second most inefficient function can be either thinking (which tends to make original thinkers such as Jung himself) or else feeling (which tends to make artistic people). Therefore, allowing for introversion and extroversion, there are at least four kinds of intuitive types, and sixteen types in all. Furthermore, one can see how the sixteen types merge into each other, so that there are no unrealistic or unconvincingly rigid divisions.

In the same way, if we were to put every person under only one sign of the Zodiac, the system becomes too rigid and unlike life. Besides, it was never intended to be used like that. It may be convenient to have only twelve types, but we know that in practice there is every possible gradation between aggressiveness and timidity, or between conscientiousness and laziness. How, then, do we account for this?

The Tyrant and the Saint

Just as the thinking type of man is also influenced to some extent by sensation and intuition, but not very much by emotion, so a person born under Leo can be influenced to some extent by one or two (but not more) of the other signs. For instance, famous persons born under the sign of Gemini include Henry VIII, whom nothing and no-one could have induced to abdicate, and Edward VIII, who did just that. Obviously, then, the sign Gemini does not fully explain the complete character of either of them.

Again, under the opposite sign, Sagittarius, were both Stalin, who was totally consumed with the notion of power, and Charles V, who freely gave up an empire because he preferred to go into a monastery. And we find under Scorpio, many uncompromising characters such as Luther, de Gaulle, Indira Gandhi and Montgomery, but also Petain, a successful commander whose name later became synonymous with collaboration.

A single sign is therefore obviously inadequate to explain the differences between people; it can only explain resemblances, such as the combativeness of the Scorpio group, or the far-reaching devotion of Charles V and Stalin to their respective ideals—the Christian heaven and the Communist utopia.

But very few people are born under one sign only. As well as the month of birth, as was mentioned earlier, the day matters, and, even more, the hour, which ought, if possible, to be noted to the nearest minute. Without this, it is impossible to have an actual horoscope, for the word horoscope means literally, "a consideration of the hour."

The month of birth tells you only which sign of the Zodiac was occupied by the sun. The day and hour tell you what sign was occupied by the moon. And the minute tells you which sign was rising on the eastern horizon. This is called the Ascendant, and it is supposed to be the most important thing in the whole horoscope.

If you were born at midnight, the sun is then in an important position, although invisible. But at one o'clock in the morning the sun is not important, so the moment of birth will not matter much. The important thing then will be the Ascendant, and possibly one or two of the planets. At a given day and hour, say, dawn on January 1st, or 9:00 p.m. on the longest day, the Ascendant will always be the same at any given place. But the moon and planets alter from day to day, at different speeds and have to be looked up in an astronomical table.

The sun is said to signify one's heart, that is to say, one's deepest desires and inmost nature. This is quite different from the moon, which, as we have seen, signifies one's superficial way of behaving. When the ancient Romans referred to the Emperor Augustus as a Capricornian, they meant that he had the moon in Capricorn; they did not pay much attention to the sun, although he was born at sunrise. Or, to take another example, a modern astrologer would call Disraeli a Scorpion because he had Scorpio rising, but most people would call him Sagittarian because he had the sun there. The Romans would have called him Leo because his moon was in Leo.

The sun, as has already been pointed out, is important if one is born near sunrise, sunset, noon or midnight, but is otherwise not reckoned as the principal influence. So if one does not seem to fit one's birth month, it is always worthwhile reading the other signs, for one may have been born at a time when any of them were rising or occupied by the moon. It also seems to be the case that the influence of the sun develops as life goes on, so that the month of birth is easier to guess in people over the age of forty. The young are supposed to be influenced mainly by their Ascendant which characterizes the body and physical personality as a whole.

It should be clearly understood that it is nonsense to assume that all people born at a certain time will exhibit the same characteristics, or that they will even behave in the same manner. It is quite obvious that, from the very moment of its birth, a child is subject to the effects of its environment, and that this in turn will influence its character and heritage to a decisive extent. Also to be taken into account are education and economic conditions, which play a very important part in the formation of one's character as well.

However, it is clearly established that people born under one sign of the Zodiac do have certain basic traits in their character which are different from those born under other signs. It is obvious to every thinking person that certain events produce different reactions in various people. For instance, if a man slips on a banana skin and falls heavily on the pavement, one passer-by may laugh and find this extremely amusing, while another may just walk on, thinking: "What a fool falling down like that. He should look where he is going." A third might also walk away saying to himself: "It's none of my business—I'm glad it wasn't me." A fourth might walk past and think: "I'm sorry for that man, but I haven't the time to be bothered with helping him." And a fifth might stop to help the fallen man to his feet, comfort him and take him home. Here is just one event which could produce entirely different reactions in different people. And, obviously, there are many more. One that comes to mind immediately is the violently opposed views to events such as wars, industrial strikes, and so on. The fact that people have different attitudes to the same event is simply another way of saying that they have different characters. And this is not something that can be put down to background, for people of the same race, religion, or class, very often express quite different reactions to happenings or events. Similarly, it is often the case that members of the same family, where there is clearly uniform background of economic and social standing, education, race and religion, often argue bitterly among themselves over political and social issues.

People have, in general, certain character traits and qualities which, according to their environment, develop in either a positive or a negative manner. Therefore, selfishness (inherent selfishness, that is) might emerge as unselfishness; kindness and consideration as cruelty and lack of consideration towards others. In the same way, a naturally constructive person, may, through frustration, become destructive, and so on. The latent characteristics with which people are born can, therefore, through environment and good or bad training, become something that would appear to be its opposite, and so give the lie to the astrologer's description of their character. But this is not the case. The true character is still there, but it is buried deep beneath these external superficialities.

Careful study of the character traits of different signs can be immeasurable help, and can render beneficial service to the intelligent person. Undoubtedly, the reader will already have discovered that, while he is able to get on very well with some people, he just "cannot stand" others. The causes sometimes seem inexplicable. At times there is intense dislike, at other times immediate sympathy. And there is, too, the phenomenon of love at first sight, which is also apparently inexplicable. People appear to be either sympathetic or unsympathetic towards each other for no apparent reason.

Now if we look at this in the light of the Zodiac, we find that people born under different signs are either compatible or incompatible with each other. In other words, there are good and bad interrelating factors among the various signs. This does not, of course, mean that humanity can be divided into groups of hostile camps. It would be quite wrong to be hostile or indifferent toward people who happen to be born under an incompatible sign. There is no reason why everybody should not, or cannot, learn to control and adjust their feelings and actions, especially after they are aware of the positive qualities of other people by studying their character analyses, among other things.

Every person born under a certain sign has both positive and negative qualities, which are developed more or less according to his free will. Nobody is entirely good or entirely bad, and it is up to each one of us to learn to control himself on the one hand, and at the same time to endeavor to learn about himself and others.

It cannot be repeated often enough that, though the intrinsic nature of man and his basic character traits are born in him, nevertheless it is his own free will that determines whether he will make really good use of his talents and abilities—whether, in other words, he will overcome his vices or allow them to rule him. Most of us are born with at least a streak of laziness, irritability, or some other fault in our nature, and it is up to each one of us to see that we exert sufficient willpower to control our failings so that they do not harm ourselves or others.

Astrology can reveal our inclinations and tendencies. Our weaknesses should not be viewed as shortcomings that are impossible to change. The horoscope of a man may show him to have criminal leanings, for instance, but this does not mean he will definitely become a criminal.

The ordinary man usually finds it difficult to know himself. He is often bewildered. Astrology can frequently tell him more about himself than the different schools of psychology are able to do. Knowing his failings and shortcomings, he will do his best to overcome them, and make himself a better and more useful member of society and a helpmate to his family and friends. It can also save him a great deal of unhappiness and remorse.

And yet it may seem absurd that an ancient philosophy, something that is known as a "pseudo-science," could be a prop to the men and women of the twentieth century. But below the materialistic surface of modern life, there are hidden streams of feeling and thought. Symbology is reappearing as a study worthy of the scholar; the psychosomatic factor in illness has passed from the writings of the crank to those of the specialist; spiritual healing in all its forms is no longer a pious hope but an accepted phenomenon. And it is into this context that we consider astrology, in the sense that it is an analysis of human types.

Astrology and medicine had a long journey together, and only parted company a couple of centuries ago. There still remain in medical language such astrological terms as "saturnine," "choleric," and "mercurial," used in the diagnosis of physical tendencies. The herbalist, for long the handyman of the medical profession, has been dominated by astrology since the days of the Greeks. Certain herbs traditionally respond to certain planetary influences, and diseases must therefore be treated to ensure harmony between the medicine and the disease.

No one expects the most eccentric of modern doctors to go back to the practices of his predecessors. We have come a long way since the time when phases of the moon were studied in illness. Those days were a medical nightmare, with epidemics that were beyond control, and an explanation of the Black Death sought in conjunction with the planets. Nowadays, astrological diagnosis of disease has literally no parallel in modern life. And yet, age-old symbols of types and of the vulnerability of, say, the Saturnian to chronic diseases or the choleric to apoplexy and blood pressure and so on, are still applicable.

But the stars are expected to foretell and not only to diagnose. The astrological forecaster has a counterpart on a highly conventional level in the shape of the weather prophet, racing tipster and stock market forecaster, to name just three examples. All in their own way are aiming at the same result. They attempt to look a little further into the pattern of life and also try to determine future patterns accurately.

Astrological forecasting has been remarkably accurate, but often it is wide of the mark. The brave man who cares to predict world events takes dangerous chances. Individual forecasting is less clear cut; it can be a help or a disillusionment. Then welcome to the nagging question: if it is possible to foreknow, is it right to foretell? A complex point of ethics on which it is hard to pronounce judgment. The doctor faces the same dilemma if he finds that symptoms of a mortal disease are present in his patient and that he can only prognosticate a steady decline. How much to tell an individual in a crisis is a problem that has perplexed many distinguished scholars. Honest and conscientious astrologers in this modern world, where so many people are seeking guidance, face the same problem.

The ancient cults, the symbols of old religions, are eclipsed for the moment. They may return with their old force within a decade or two. But at present the outlook is dark. Human beings badly need assurance, as they did in the past, that all is not chaos. Somewhere, somehow, there is a pattern that must be worked out. As to the why and wherefore, the astrologer is not expected to give judgment. He is just someone who, by dint of talent and training, can gaze into the future.

Five hundred years ago it was customary to call in a learned man who was an astrologer who was probably also a doctor and a philosopher. By his knowledge of astrology, his study of planetary influences, he felt himself qualified to guide those in distress. The world has moved forward at a fantastic rate since then, and in this twentieth century speed has been the keyword everywhere. Tensions have increased, the spur of ambition has been applied indiscriminately. People are uncertain of themselves. At first sight it seems fantastic in the light of modern thinking that they turn to the most ancient of all studies, and get someone to calculate a horoscope for them. But is it *really* so fantastic if you take a second look? For astrology is concerned with tomorrow, with survival. And in a world such as ours, those two things are the keywords of the time in which we live.

HOW TO USE THESE PREDICTIONS

A person reading the predictions in this book should understand that they are produced from the daily position of the planets for a group of people and are not, of course, individually specialized. To get the full benefit of them he should relate the predictions to his own character and circumstances, co-ordinate them, and draw his own conclusions from them.

If he is a serious observer of his own life he should find a definite pattern emerge that will be a helpful and reliable guide.

The point is that we always retain our free will. The stars indicate certain directional tendencies but we are not compelled to follow. We can do or not do, and wisdom must make the choice.

We all have our good and bad days. Sometimes they extend into cycles of weeks. It is therefore advisable to study daily predictions in a span ranging from the day before to several days ahead; also to re-read the monthly predictions for similar cycles.

Daily predictions should be taken very generally. The word "difficult" does not necessarily indicate a whole day of obstruction or inconvenience. It is a warning to you to be cautious. Your caution will often see you around the difficulty before you are involved. This is the correct use of astrology.

In another section, detailed information is given about the influence of the moon as it passes through the various signs of the Zodiac. It includes instructions on how to use the Moon Tables. This information should be used in conjunction with the daily forecasts to give a fuller picture of the astrological trends.

THE MOON

Moon is the nearest planet to the earth. It exerts more observable influence on us from day to day than any other planet. The effect is very personal, very intimate, and if we are not aware of how it works it can make us quite unstable in our ideas. And the annoying thing is that at these times we often see our own instability but can do nothing about it. A knowledge of what can be expected may help considerably. We can then be prepared to stand strong against the moon's negative influences and use its positive ones to help us to get ahead. Who has not heard of going with the tide?

Moon reflects, has no light of its own. It reflects the sun—the life giver—in the form of vital movement. Moon controls the tides, the blood rhythm, the movement of sap in trees and plants. Its nature is inconstancy and change so it signifies our moods, our superficial behavior—walking, talking and especially thinking. Being a true reflector of other forces, moon is cold, watery like the surface of a still lake, brilliant and scintillating at times, but easily ruffled and disturbed by the winds of change.

The moon takes 28½ days to circle the earth and the Zodiac. It spends just over 2¼ days in each sign. During that time it reflects the qualities, energies and characteristics of the sign and, to a degree, the planet which rules the sign. While the moon in its transit occupies a sign incompatible with our own birth sign, we can expect to feel a vague uneasiness, perhaps a touch of irritableness. We should not be discouraged nor let the feeling get us down, or, worse still, allow ourselves to take the discomfort out on others. Try to remember that the moon has to change signs within 55 hours and, provided you are not physically ill, your mood will probably change with it. It is amazing how frequently depression lifts with the shift in the moon's position. And, of course, when the moon is transiting a sign compatible or sympathetic to yours you will probably feel some sort of stimulation or just plain happy to be alive.

In the horoscope, the moon is such a powerful indicator that competent astrologers often use the sign it occupied at birth as the birth sign of the person. This is done particularly when the sun is on the cusp, or edge, of two signs. Most experienced astrologers, however, coordinate both sun and moon signs by reading and confirming from one to the other and secure a far more accurate and personalized analysis.

For these reasons, the moon tables which follow this section (see pages 28–35) are of great importance to the individual. They show the days and the exact times the moon will enter each sign of the Zodiac for the year. Remember, you have to adjust the indicated times to local time. The corrections, already calculated for most of the main cities, are at the beginning of the tables. What follows now is a guide to the influences that will be reflected to the earth by the moon while it transits each of the twelve signs. The influence is at its peak about 26 hours after the moon enters a sign.

MOON IN ARIES

This is a time for action, for reaching out beyond the usual self-imposed limitations and faint-hearted cautions. If you have plans in your head or on your desk, put them into practice. New ventures, applications, new jobs, new starts of any kind—all have a good chance of success. This is the period when original and dynamic impulses are being reflected onto the earth. The energies are extremely vital and favor the pursuit of pleasure and adventure in practically every form. Sick people should feel an improvement. Those who are well will probably find themselves exuding confidence and optimism. People fond of physical exercise should find their bodies growing with tone and well-being. Boldness, strength, determination should characterize most of your activities with a readiness to face up to old challenges. Yesterday's problems may seem petty and exaggerated—so deal with them. Strike out alone. Self-reliance will attract others to you. This is a good time for making friends. Business and marriage partners are more likely to be impressed with the man and woman of action. Opposition will be overcome or thrown aside with much less effort than usual. CAUTION: Be dominant but not domineering.

MOON IN TAURUS

The spontaneous, action-packed person of yesterday gives way to the cautious, diligent, hardworking "thinker." In this period ideas will probably be concentrated on ways of improving finances. A great deal of time may be spent figuring out and going over schemes and plans. It is the right time to be careful with detail. People will find themselves working longer than usual at their desks. Or devoting more time to serious thought about the future. A strong desire to put order into business and financial arrangements may cause extra work. Loved ones may complain of being neglected and may fail to appreciate that your efforts are for their ultimate benefit. Your desire for system may extend to criticism of arrangements in the home and lead to minor upsets. Health may be affected through overwork. Try to secure a reasonable amount of rest and relaxation, although the tendency will be to "keep going" despite good advice. Work done conscientiously in this period should result in a solid contribution to your future security. CAUTION: Try not to be as serious with people as the work you are engaged in.

MOON IN GEMINI

The humdrum of routine and too much work should suddenly end. You are likely to find yourself in an expansive, quicksilver world of change and self-expression. Urges to write, to paint, to experience the freedom of some sort of artistic outpouring, may be very strong. Take full advantage of them. You may find yourself finishing something you began and put aside long ago. Or embarking on something new which could easily be prompted by a chance meeting, a new acquaintance, or even an advertisement. There may be a yearning for a change of scenery, the feeling to visit another country (not too far away), or at least to get away for a few days. This may result in short, quick journeys. Or, if you are planning a single visit, there may be some unexpected changes or detours on the way. Familiar activities will seem to give little satisfaction unless they contain a fresh element of excitement or expectation. The inclination will be towards untried pursuits, particularly those that allow you to express your inner nature. The accent is on new faces, new places. CAUTION: Do not be too quick to commit yourself emotionally.

MOON IN CANCER

Feelings of uncertainty and vague insecurity are likely to cause problems while the moon is in Cancer. Thoughts may turn frequently to the warmth of the home and the comfort of loved ones. Nostalgic impulses could cause you to bring out old photographs and letters and reflect on the days when your life seemed to be much more rewarding and less demanding. The love and understanding of parents and family may be important, and, if it is not forthcoming you may have to fight against a bit of self-pity. The cordiality of friends and the thought of good times with them that are sure to be repeated will help to restore you to a happier frame of mind. The feeling to be alone may follow minor setbacks or rebuffs at this time, but solitude is unlikely to help. Better to get on the telephone or visit someone. This period often causes peculiar dreams and upsurges of imaginative thinking which can be very helpful to authors of occult and mystical works. Preoccupation with the more personal world of simple human needs should overshadow any material strivings. CAUTION: Do not spend too much time thinking—seek the company of loved ones or close friends.

MOON IN LEO

New horizons of exciting and rather extravagant activity open up. This is the time for exhilarating entertainment, glamorous and lavish parties, and expensive shopping sprees. Any merrymaking that relies upon your generosity as a host has every chance of being a spectacular success. You should find yourself right in the center of the fun, either as the life of the party or simply as a person whom happy people like to be with. Romance thrives in this heady atmosphere and friendships are likely to explode unexpectedly into serious attachments. Children and younger people should be attracted to you and you may find yourself organizing a picnic or a visit to a fun-fair, the cinema or the seaside. The sunny company and vitality of youthful companions should help you to find some unsuspected energy. In career, you could find an opening for promotion or advancement. This should be the time to make a direct approach. The period favors those engaged in original research. CAUTION: Bask in popularity but not in flattery.

MOON IN VIRGO

Off comes the party cap and out steps the busy, practical worker. He wants to get his personal affairs straight, to rearrange them, if necessary, for more efficiency, so he will have more time for more work. He clears up his correspondence, pays outstanding bills, makes numerous phone calls. He is likely to make inquiries, or sign up for some new insurance and put money into gilt-edged investment. Thoughts probably revolve around the need for future security—to tie up loose ends and clear the decks. There may be a tendency to be "finicky," to interfere in the routine of others, particularly friends and family members. The motive may be a genuine desire to help with suggestions for updating or streamlining their affairs, but these will probably not be welcomed. Sympathy may be felt for less fortunate sections of the community and a flurry of some sort of voluntary service is likely. This may be accompanied by strong feelings of responsibility on several fronts and health may suffer from extra efforts made. CAUTION: Everyone may not want your help or advice.

MOON IN LIBRA

These are days of harmony and agreement and you should find yourself at peace with most others. Relationships tend to be smooth and sweet-flowing. Friends may become closer and bonds deepen in mutual understanding. Hopes will be shared. Progress by cooperation could be the secret of success in every sphere. In business, established partnerships may flourish and new ones get off to a good start. Acquaintances could discover similar interests that lead to congenial discussions and rewarding exchanges of some sort. Love, as a unifying force, reaches its optimum. Marriage partners should find accord. Those who wed at this time face the prospect of a happy union. Cooperation and tolerance are felt to be stronger than dissension and impatience. The argumentative are not quite so loud in their bellowings, nor as inflexible in their attitudes. In the home, there should be a greater recognition of the other point of view and a readiness to put the wishes of the group before selfish insistence. This is a favorable time to join an art group. CAUTION: Do not be too independent—let others help you if they want to.

MOON IN SCORPIO

Driving impulses to make money and to economize are likely to cause upsets all round. No area of expenditure is likely to be spared the axe, including the household budget. This is a time when the desire to cut down on extravagance can become near fanatical. Care must be exercised to try to keep the aim in reasonable perspective. Others may not feel the same urgent need to save and may retaliate. There is a danger that possessions of sentimental value will be sold to realize cash for investment. Buying and selling of stock for quick profit is also likely. The attention may turn to having a good clean up round the home and at the office. Neglected jobs could suddenly be done with great bursts of energy. The desire for solitude may intervene. Self-searching thoughts could disturb. The sense of invisible and mysterious energies at work could cause some excitability. The reassurance of loves ones may help. CAUTION: Be kind to the people you love.

MOON IN SAGITTARIUS

These are days when you are likely to be stirred and elevated by discussions and reflections of a religious and philosophical nature. Ideas of far-away places may cause unusual response and excitement. A decision may be made to visit someone overseas, perhaps a person whose influence was important to your earlier character development. There could be a strong resolution to get away from present intellectual patterns, to learn new subjects and to meet more interesting people. The superficial may be rejected in all its forms. An impatience with old ideas and unimaginative contacts could lead to a change of companions and interests. There may be an upsurge of religious feeling and metaphysical inquiry. Even a new insight into the significance of astrology and other occult studies is likely under the curious stimulus of the moon in Sagittarius. Physically, you may express this need for fundamental change by spending more time outdoors: sports, gardening or going for long walks. CAUTION: Try to channel any restlessness into worthwhile study.

MOON IN CAPRICORN

Life in these hours may seem to pivot around the importance of gaining prestige and honor in the career, as well as maintaining a spotless reputation. Ambitious urges may be excessive and could be accompanied by quite acquisitive drives for money. Effort should be directed along strictly ethical lines where there is no possibility of reproach or scandal. All endeavors are likely to be characterized by great earnestness, and an air of authority and purpose which should impress those who are looking for leadership or reliability. The desire to conform to accepted standards may extend to sharp criticism of family members. Frivolity and unconventional actions are unlikely to amuse while the moon is in Capricorn. Moderation and seriousness are the orders of the day. Achievement and recognition in this period could come through community work or organizing for the benefit of some amateur group. CAUTION: Dignity and esteem are not always self-awarded.

MOON IN AQUARIUS

Moon in Aquarius is in the second last sign of the Zodiac where ideas can become disturbingly fine and subtle. The result is often a mental "no-man's land" where imagination cannot be trusted with the same certitude as other times. The dangers for the individual are the extremes of optimism and pessimism. Unless the imgination is held in check, situations are likely to be misread, and rosy conclusions drawn where they do not exist. Consequences for the unwary can be costly in career and business. Best to think twice and not speak or act until you think again. Pessimism can be a cruel self-inflicted penalty for delusion at this time. Between the two extremes are strange areas of self-deception which, for example, can make the selfish person think he is actually being generous. Eerie dreams which resemble the reality and even seem to continue into the waking state are also possible. CAUTION: Look for the fact and not just for the image in your mind.

MOON IN PISCES

Everything seems to come to the surface now. Memory may be crystal clear, throwing up long-forgotten information which could be valuable in the career or business. Flashes of clairvoyance and intuition are possible along with sudden realizations of one's own nature, which may be used for self-improvement. A talent, never before suspected, may be discovered. Qualities not evident before in friends and marriage partners are likely to be noticed. As this is a period in which the truth seems to emerge, the discovery of false characteristics is likely to lead to disenchantment or a shift in attachments. However, where qualities are realized it should lead to happiness and deeper feeling. Surprise solutions could bob up for old problems. There may be a public announcement of the solving of a crime or mystery. People with secrets may find someone has "guessed" correctly. The secrets of the soul or the inner self also tend to reveal themselves. Religious and philosophical groups may make some interesting discoveries. CAUTION: Not a time for activities that depend on secrecy.

MOON TABLES

TIME CORRECTIONS FOR GREENWICH MOON TABLES

London, Glasgow, Dublin, Dakar	Same time
Vienna, Prague, Rome, Kinshasa, Frankfurt, Stockholm, Brussels, Amsterdam, Warsaw, Zurich	Add 1 hour
Bucharest, Istanbul, Beirut, Cairo, Johannesburg, Athens, Cape Town, Helsinki, Tel Aviv	Add 2 hours
Dhahran, Baghdad, Moscow, Leningrad, Nairobi, Addis Ababa, Zanzibar	Add 3 hours
Delhi, Calcutta, Bombay, Colombo	Add 5½ hours
Rangoon	Add 6½ hours
Saigon, Bangkok, Chungking	Add 7 hours
Canton, Manila, Hong Kong, Shanghai, Peking	Add 8 hours
Tokyo, Pusan, Seoul, Vladivostok, Yokohama	Add 9 hours
Sydney, Melbourne, Guam, Port Moresby	Add 10 hours
Azores, Reykjavik	Deduct 1 hour
Rio de Janeiro, Montevideo, Buenos Aires, Sao Paulo, Recife	Deduct 3 hours
LaPaz, San Juan, Santiago, Bermuda, Caracas, Halifax	Deduct 4 hours
New York, Washington, Boston, Detroit, Lima, Havana, Miami, Bogota	Deduct 5 hours
Mexico, Chicago, New Orleans, Houston	Deduct 6 hours
San Francisco, Seattle, Los Angeles, Hollywood, Ketchikan, Juneau	Deduct 8 hours
Honolulu, Fairbanks, Anchorage, Papeete	Deduct 10 hours

1990 MOON TABLES—GREENWICH TIME

JANUARY		FEBRUARY		MARCH	
Day Moon Enters		**Day Moon Enters**		**Day Moon Enters**	
1. Pisces	6:07 am	1. Taurus	7:25 pm	1. Taurus	1:38 am
2. Pisces		2. Taurus		2. Taurus	
3. Aries	10:48 am	3. Gemini	10:21 pm	3. Gemini	3:53 am
4. Aries		4. Gemini		4. Gemini	
5. Taurus	1:51 pm	5. Gemini		5. Cancer	7:14 am
6. Taurus		6. Cancer	1:33 am	6. Cancer	
7. Gemini	4:00 pm	7. Cancer		7. Leo	0:44 pm
8. Gemini		8. Leo	5:58 am	8. Leo	
9. Cancer	5:54 pm	9. Leo		9. Virgo	7:43 pm
10. Cancer		10. Virgo	Noon	10. Virgo	
11. Leo	9:26 pm	11. Virgo		11. Virgo	
12. Leo		12. Libra	8:59 pm	12. Libra	5:08 am
13. Leo		13. Libra		13. Libra	
14. Virgo	2:47 am	14. Libra		14. Scorpio	4:04 pm
15. Virgo		15. Scorpio	8:20 am	15. Scorpio	
16. Libra	0:12 pm	16. Scorpio		16. Scorpio	
17. Libra		17. Sagitt.	9:05 pm	17. Sagitt.	4:57 am
18. Libra		18. Sagitt.		18. Sagitt.	
19. Scorpio	0:19 am	19. Sagitt.		19. Capric.	5:09 pm
20. Scorpio		20. Capric.	8:40 am	20. Capric.	
21. Sagitt.	1:00 pm	21. Capric.		21. Capric.	
22. Sagitt.		22. Aquar.	4:40 pm	22. Aquar.	2:12 am
23. Capric.	11:38 pm	23. Aquar.		23. Aquar.	
24. Capric.		24. Pisces	9:23 pm	24. Pisces	7:42 am
25. Capric.		25. Pisces		25. Pisces	
26. Aquar.	7:28 am	26. Aries	11:56 pm	26. Aries	9:52 am
27. Aquar.		27. Aries		27. Aries	
28. Pisces	0:42 pm	28. Aries		28. Taurus	10:03 am
29. Pisces				29. Taurus	
30. Aries	4:26 pm			30. Gemini	10:51 am
31. Aries				31. Gemini	

Summer time to be considered where applicable.

1990 MOON TABLES—GREENWICH TIME

APRIL Day Moon Enters		MAY Day Moon Enters		JUNE Day Moon Enters	
1. Cancer	1:03 pm	1. Leo	0:27 am	1. Libra	11:25 pm
2. Cancer		2. Leo		2. Libra	
3. Leo	6:11 pm	3. Virgo	7:08 am	3. Libra	
4. Leo		4. Virgo		4. Scorpio	11:37 am
5. Leo		5. Libra	5:24 pm	5. Scorpio	
6. Virgo	1:59 am	6. Libra		6. Scorpio	
7. Virgo		7. Libra		7. Sagitt.	0:19 am
8. Libra	11:47 am	8. Scorpio	5:33 am	8. Sagitt.	
9. Libra		9. Scorpio		9. Capric.	0:24 pm
10. Scorpio	11:18 pm	10. Sagitt.	6:04 pm	10. Capric.	
11. Scorpio		11. Sagitt.		11. Aquar.	11:09 pm
12. Scorpio		12. Sagitt.		12. Aquar.	
13. Sagitt.	Noon	13. Capric.	6:25 am	13. Aquar.	
14. Sagitt.		14. Capric.		14. Pisces	7:56 am
15. Sagitt.		15. Aquar.	5:44 pm	15. Pisces	
16. Capric.	0:25 am	16. Aquar.		16. Aries	2:04 pm
17. Capric.		17. Aquar.		17. Aries	
18. Aquar.	10:52 am	18. Pisces	1:42 am	18. Taurus	4:47 pm
19. Aquar.		19. Pisces		19. Taurus	
20. Pisces	5:43 pm	20. Aries	6:19 am	20. Gemini	5:32 pm
21. Pisces		21. Aries		21. Gemini	
22. Aries	8:20 pm	22. Taurus	7:27 am	22. Cancer	5:29 pm
23. Aries		23. Taurus		23. Cancer	
24. Taurus	8:46 pm	24. Gemini	6:57 am	24. Leo	6:39 pm
25. Taurus		25. Gemini		25. Leo	
26. Gemini	8:06 pm	26. Cancer	6:40 am	26. Virgo	10:39 pm
27. Gemini		27. Cancer		27. Virgo	
28. Cancer	8:58 pm	28. Leo	8:47 am	28. Virgo	
29. Cancer		29. Leo		29. Libra	6:38 am
30. Cancer		30. Virgo	2:02 pm	30. Libra	
		31. Virgo			

Summer time to be considered where applicable.

1990 MOON TABLES—GREENWICH TIME

JULY		AUGUST		SEPTEMBER	
Day Moon Enters		**Day Moon Enters**		**Day Moon Enters**	
1. Scorpio	5:54 pm	1. Sagitt.		1. Aquar.	8:35 pm
2. Scorpio		2. Sagitt.		2. Aquar.	
3. Scorpio		3. Capric.	2:17 am	3. Aquar.	
4. Sagitt.	7:02 am	4. Capric.		4. Pisces	3:53 am
5. Sagitt.		5. Aquar.	0:11 pm	5. Pisces	
6. Capric.	6:45 pm	6. Aquar.		6. Aries	8:04 am
7. Capric.		7. Pisces	7:35 pm	7. Aries	
8. Capric.		8. Pisces		8. Taurus	11:00 am
9. Aquar.	4:58 am	9. Pisces		9. Taurus	
10. Aquar.		10. Aries	0:47 am	10. Gemini	1:11 pm
11. Pisces	1:28 pm	11. Aries		11. Gemini	
12. Pisces		12. Taurus	4:52 am	12. Cancer	4:17 pm
13. Aries	7:17 pm	13. Taurus		13. Cancer	
14. Aries		14. Gemini	7:50 am	14. Leo	7:59 pm
15. Taurus	11:40 pm	15. Gemini		15. Leo	
16. Taurus		16. Cancer	10:29 am	16. Leo	
17. Taurus		17. Cancer		17. Virgo	1:15 am
18. Gemini	1:54 am	18. Leo	1:14 pm	18. Virgo	
19. Gemini		19. Leo		19. Libra	8:19 am
20. Cancer	3:32 am	20. Virgo	5:23 pm	20. Libra	
21. Cancer		21. Virgo		21. Scorpio	5:51 pm
22. Leo	4:54 am	22. Libra	0:M00	22. Scorpio	
23. Leo		23. Libra		23. Scorpio	
24. Virgo	8:22 am	24. Libra		24. Sagitt.	5:45 am
25. Virgo		25. Scorpio	9:30 am	25. Sagitt.	
26. Libra	2:54 pm	26. Scorpio		26. Capric.	6:33 pm
27. Libra		27. Sagitt.	9:53 pm	27. Capric.	
28. Libra		28. Sagitt.		28. Capric.	
29. Scorpio	1:42 am	29. Sagitt.		29. Aquar.	5:48 am
30. Scorpio		30. Capric.	10:48 am	30. Aquar.	
31. Sagitt.	2:13 pm	31. Capric.			

Summer time to be considered where applicable.

1990 MOON TABLES—GREENWICH TIME

OCTOBER Day Moon Enters		NOVEMBER Day Moon Enters		DECEMBER Day Moon Enters	
1. Pisces	1:45 pm	1. Aries		1. Gemini	4:35 pm
2. Pisces		2. Taurus	5:38 am	2. Gemini	
3. Aries	5:33 pm	3. Taurus		3. Cancer	4:10 pm
4. Aries		4. Gemini	5:44 am	4. Cancer	
5. Taurus	7:11 pm	5. Gemini		5. Leo	4:32 pm
6. Taurus		6. Cancer	5:41 am	6. Leo	
7. Gemini	8:20 pm	7. Cancer		7. Virgo	8:02 pm
8. Gemini		8. Leo	7:55 am	8. Virgo	
9. Cancer	9:48 pm	9. Leo		9. Virgo	
10. Cancer		10. Virgo	0:34 pm	10. Libra	3:03 am
11. Cancer		11. Virgo		11. Libra	
12. Leo	1:14 am	12. Libra	9:09 pm	12. Scorpio	1:48 pm
13. Leo		13. Libra		13. Scorpio	
14. Virgo	7:07 am	14. Libra		14. Scorpio	
15. Virgo		15. Scorpio	8:00 am	15. Sagitt.	2:09 am
16. Libra	3:05 pm	16. Scorpio		16. Sagitt.	
17. Libra		17. Sagitt.	7:41 pm	17. Capric.	2:48 pm
18. Libra		18. Sagitt.		18. Capric.	
19. Scorpio	1:09 am	19. Sagitt.		19. Capric.	
20. Scorpio		20. Capric.	8:20 am	20. Aquar.	2:44 am
21. Sagitt.	1:12 pm	21. Capric.		21. Aquar.	
22. Sagitt.		22. Aquar.	8:52 pm	22. Pisces	1:20 pm
23. Sagitt.		23. Aquar.		23. Pisces	
24. Capric.	1:45 am	24. Aquar.		24. Aries	9:19 pm
25. Capric.		25. Pisces	7:03 am	25. Aries	
26. Aquar.	1:56 pm	26. Pisces		26. Aries	
27. Aquar.		27. Aries	1:24 pm	27. Taurus	1:47 am
28. Pisces	10:59 pm	28. Aries		28. Taurus	
29. Pisces		29. Taurus	4:32 pm	29. Gemini	3:19 am
30. Pisces		30. Taurus		30. Gemini	
31. Aries	3:50 am			31. Cancer	2:54 am

Summer time to be considered where applicable.

1990 PHASES OF THE MOON—GREENWICH TIME

New Moon	First Quarter	Full Moon	Last Quarter
(1989)	Jan. 4	Jan. 11	Jan. 18
Jan. 26	Feb. 2	Feb. 9	Feb. 17
Feb. 25	Mar. 4	Mar. 12	Mar. 19
Mar. 26	Apr. 2	Apr. 10	Apr. 18
Apr. 25	May 1	May 9	May 17
May 24	May 31	June 8	June 16
June 22	June 29	July 8	July 15
July 22	July 29	Aug. 6	Aug. 13
Aug. 20	Aug. 28	Sep. 5	Sep. 11
Sep. 19	Sep. 27	Oct. 4	Oct. 11
Oct. 18	Oct. 26	Nov. 2	Nov. 9
Nov. 17	Nov. 25	Dec. 2	Dec. 9
Dec. 17	Dec. 25	Dec. 31	(1991)

Summer time to be considered where applicable.

1990 PLANTING GUIDE

	Aboveground Crops	Root Crops	Pruning	Weeds Pests
January	1-2-6-10-29	17-18-19-20-24-25	19-20	12-13-14-15-22-23
February	2-3-6-7-25-26	13-14-15-16-20-21	15-16	10-11-18-19-23
March	1-2-5-6-29	13-14-15-16-20-21-24-25	15-16-24-25	17-18-22-23
April	2-9-25-29-30	10-11-12-16-17-21	11-12-21	14-15-19-23
May	6-7-8-26-27	13-14-18-19-22-23	18-19	11-12-16-17-20-21
June	2-3-4-5-6-23-29-30	10-11-14-15-19	14-15	12-13-17-21
July	1-2-3-7-27-28-29-30	8-12-16-17-20-21	12-20-21	9-10-14-15-18-19
August	3-4-23-24-25-26-31	8-9-12-13-17	8-9-17	10-11-14-15-19
September	4-19-20-21-22-23-27-28	5-9-13	5-13	6-7-11-15-16-17-18
October	2-19-20-24-25-29-30	6-10-11-17	10-11	8-12-13-14-15
November	2-20-21-25-26-30	3-6-7-13-14-15-16	6-7-15-16	4-5-8-9-10-11
December	18-19-23-27-28	4-10-11-12-13-14	4-13-14	2-6-7-8-9-15-16

1990 FISHING GUIDE

	Good	Best
January	4-8-9-11-12-13-14-26	10-18
February	8-9-10-11-12-17	2-6-7-25
March	4-9-10-11-19-26	12-13-14-15
April	7-8-13-18	2-9-10-11-12-25
May	1-10-11-12-17-24-31	6-7-8-9
June	7-8-9-16-22	5-6-10-11-29
July	5-6-9-10-11-15-22	7-8-29
August	5-6-7-20-28	3-4-8-9-13
September	2-3-6-7-8-11	4-5-19-27
October	1-3-4-5-7-26-31	2-6-11-18-30
November	1-4-5-9-17-29	2-3-25-30
December	1-2-3-5-9-17-25-29-30	4-28-31

MOON'S INFLUENCE OVER DAILY AFFAIRS

The Moon makes a complete transit of the Zodiac every 27 days 7 hours and 43 minutes. In making this transit the Moon forms different aspects with the planets and consequently has favorable or unfavorable bearings on affairs and events for persons according to the sign of the Zodiac under which they were born. Whereas the Sun exclusively represents fire, the Moon rules water. The action of the Moon may be described as fluctuating, variable, absorbent and receptive.

When the Moon is in conjunction with the Sun it is called a New Moon; when the Moon and Sun are in opposition it is called a Full Moon. From New Moon to Full Moon, first and second quarter—which takes about two weeks—the Moon is increasing or waxing. From Full Moon to New Moon, third and fourth quarter, the Moon is decreasing or waning. The Moon Table indicates the New Moon and Full Moon and the quarters.

ACTIVITY	MOON IN
Business:	
buying and selling	Sagittarius, Aries, Gemini, Virgo
new, requiring public support	1st and 2nd quarter
meant to be kept quiet	3rd and 4th quarter
Investigation	3rd and 4th quarter
Signing documents	1st & 2nd quarter, Cancer, Scorpio, Pisces
Advertising	2nd quarter, Sagittarius
Journeys and trips	1st & 2nd quarter, Gemini, Virgo
Renting offices, etc.	Taurus, Leo, Scorpio, Aquarius
Painting of house/apartment	3rd & 4th quarter, Taurus, Scorpio, Aquarius
Decorating	Gemini, Libra, Aquarius
Buying clothes and accessories	Taurus, Virgo
Beauty salon or barber shop visit	1st & 2nd quarter, Taurus, Leo, Libra, Scorpio, Aquarius
Weddings	1st & 2nd quarter

MOON'S INFLUENCE OVER YOUR HEALTH

ARIES	Head, brain, face, upper jaw
TAURUS	Throat, neck, lower jaw
GEMINI	Hands, arms, lungs, shoulders, nervous system
CANCER	Esophagus, stomach, breasts, womb, liver
LEO	Heart, spine
VIRGO	Intestines, liver
LIBRA	Kidneys, lower back
SCORPIO	Sex and eliminative organs
SAGITTARIUS	Hips, thighs, liver
CAPRICORN	Skin, bones, teeth, knees
AQUARIUS	Circulatory system, lower legs
PISCES	Feet, tone of being

Try to avoid work being done on that part of the body when the Moon is in the sign governing that part.

MOON'S INFLUENCE OVER PLANTS

Centuries ago it was established that seeds planted when the Moon is in certain signs and phases called Fruitful will produce more growth than seeds planted when the Moon is in a Barren sign.

FRUITFUL SIGNS	BARREN SIGNS	DRY SIGNS
Taurus	Aries	Aries
Cancer	Gemini	Gemini
Libra	Leo	Sagittarius
Scorpio	Virgo	Aquarius
Capricorn	Sagittarius	
Pisces	Aquarius	

ACTIVITY	MOON IN
Mow lawn, trim plants	**Fruitful sign:** 1st & 2nd quarter
Plant flowers	**Fruitful sign:** 2nd quarter; best in Cancer and Libra
Prune	**Fruitful sign:** 3rd & 4th quarter
Destroy pests; spray	**Barren sign:** 4th quarter
Harvest potatoes, root crops	**Dry sign:** 3rd & 4th quarter; Taurus, Leo, and Aquarius

THE SIGNS: DOMINANT CHARACTERISTICS

March 21–April 20

The Positive Side of Aries

The Arien has many positive points to his character. People born under this first sign of the Zodiac are often quite strong and enthusiastic. On the whole, they are forward-looking people who are not easily discouraged by temporary setbacks. They know what they want out of life and they go out after it. Their personalities are strong. Others are usually quite impressed by the Arien's way of doing things. Quite often they are sources of inspiration for others traveling the same route. Aries men and women have a special zest for life that is often contagious; for others, they are often the example of how life should be lived.

The Aries person usually has a quick and active mind. He is imaginative and inventive. He enjoys keeping busy and active. He generally gets along well with all kinds of people. He is interested in mankind, as a whole. He likes to be challenged. Some would say he thrives on opposition, for it is when he is set against that he often does his best. Getting over or around obstacles is a challenge he generally enjoys. All in all, the Arien is quite positive and young-thinking. He likes to keep abreast of new things that are happening in the world. Ariens are often fond of speed. They like things to be done quickly and this sometimes aggravates their slower colleagues and associates.

The Aries man or woman always seems to remain young. Their whole approach to life is youthful and optimistic. They never say die, no matter what the odds. They may have an occasional setback, but it is not long before they are back on their feet again.

The Negative Side of Aries

Everybody has his less positive qualities—and Aries is no exception. Sometimes the Aries man or woman is not very tactful in communicating with others; in his hurry to get things done he is apt to

be a little callous or inconsiderate. Sensitive people are likely to find him somewhat sharp-tongued in some situations. Often in his eagerness to achieve his aims, he misses the mark altogether. At times the Arien is too impulsive. He can occasionally be stubborn and refuse to listen to reason. If things do not move quickly enough to suit the Aries man or woman, he or she is apt to become rather nervous or irritable. The uncultivated Arien is not unfamiliar with moments of doubt and fear. He is capable of being destructive if he does not get his way. He can overcome some of his emotional problems by steadily trying to express himself as he really is, but this requires effort.

April 21–May 20

The Positive Side of Taurus

The Taurus person is known for his ability to concentrate and for his tenacity. These are perhaps his strongest qualities. The Taurus man or woman generally has very little trouble in getting along with others; it's his nature to be helpful toward people in need. He can always be depended on by his friends, especially those in trouble.

The Taurean generally achieves what he wants through his ability to persevere. He never leaves anything unfinished but works on something until it has been completed. People can usually take him at his word; he is honest and forthright in most of his dealings. The Taurus person has a good chance to make a success of his life because of his many positive qualities. The Taurean who aims high seldom falls short of his mark. He learns well by experience. He is thorough and does not believe in short-cuts of any kind. The Taurean's thoroughness pays off in the end, for through his deliberateness he learns how to rely on himself and what he has learned. The Taurus person tries to get along with others, as a rule. He is not overly critical and likes people to be themselves. He is a tolerant person and enjoys peace and harmony—especially in his home life.

The Taurean is usually cautious in all that he does. He is not a person who believes in taking unnecessary risks. Before adopting any one line of action, he will weigh all of the pros and cons. The

Taurus person is steadfast. Once his mind is made up it seldom changes. The person born under this sign usually is a good family person—reliable and loving.

The Negative Side of Taurus

Sometimes the Taurus man or woman is a bit too stubborn. He won't listen to other points of view if his mind is set on something. To others, this can be quite annoying. The Taurean also does not like to be told what to do. He becomes rather angry if others think him not too bright. He does not like to be told he is wrong, even when he is. He dislikes being contradicted.

Some people who are born under this sign are very suspicious of others—even of those persons close to them. They find it difficult to trust people fully. They are often afraid of being deceived or taken advantage of. The Taurean often finds it difficult to forget or forgive. His love of material things sometimes makes him rather avaricious and petty.

May 21–June 20

The Positive Side of Gemini

The person born under this sign of the Heavenly Twins is usually quite bright and quick-witted. Some of them are capable of doing many different things. The Gemini person very often has many different interests. He keeps an open mind and is always anxious to learn new things.

The Geminian is often an analytical person. He is a person who enjoys making use of his intellect. He is governed more by his mind than by his emotions. He is a person who is not confined to one view; he can often understand both sides to a problem or question. He knows how to reason; how to make rapid decisions if need be.

He is an adaptable person and can make himself at home almost anywhere. There are all kinds of situations he can adapt to. He is a person who seldom doubts himself; he is sure of his talents and his

ability to think and reason. The Geminian is generally most satisfied when he is in a situation where he can make use of his intellect. Never short of imagination, he often has strong talents for invention. He is rather a modern person when it comes to life; the Geminian almost always moves along with the times—perhaps that is why he remains so youthful throughout most of his life.

Literature and art appeal to the person born under this sign. Creativity in almost any form will interest and intrigue the Gemini man or woman.

The Geminian is often quite charming. A good talker, he often is the center of attraction at any gathering. People find it easy to like a person born under this sign because he can appear easygoing and usually has a good sense of humor.

The Negative Side of Gemini

Sometimes the Gemini person tries to do too many things at one time—and as a result, winds up finishing nothing. Some Geminians are easily distracted and find it rather difficult to concentrate on one thing for too long a time. Sometimes they give in to trifling fancies and find it rather boring to become too serious about any one thing. Some of them are never dependable, no matter what they promise.

Although the Gemini man or woman often appears to be well-versed on many subjects, this is sometimes just a veneer. His knowledge may be only superficial, but because he speaks so well he gives people the impression of erudition. Some Geminians are sharp-tongued and inconsiderate; they think only of themselves and their own pleasure.

June 21–July 20

The Positive Side of Cancer

The Cancerians's most positive point is his understanding nature. On the whole, he is a loving and sympathetic person. He would never go out of his way to hurt anyone. The Cancer man or woman

is often very kind and tender; they give what they can to others. They hate to see others suffering and will do what they can to help someone in less fortunate circumstances than themselves. They are often very concerned about the world. Their interest in people generally goes beyond that of just their own families and close friends; they have a deep sense of brotherhood and respect humanitarian values. The Cancerian means what he says, as a rule; he is honest about his feelings.

The Cancer man or woman is a person who knows the art of patience. When something seems difficult, he is willing to wait until the situation becomes manageable again. He is a person who knows how to bide his time. The Cancerian knows how to concentrate on one thing at a time. When he has made his mind up he generally sticks with what he does, seeing it through to the end.

The Cancerian is a person who loves his home. He enjoys being surrounded by familiar things and the people he loves. Of all the signs, Cancer is the most maternal. Even the men born under this sign often have a motherly or protective quality about them. They like to take care of people in their family—to see that they are well loved and well provided for. They are usually loyal and faithful. Family ties mean a lot to the Cancer man or woman. Parents and in-laws are respected and loved. The Cancerian has a strong sense of tradition. He is very sensitive to the moods of others.

The Negative Side of Cancer

Sometimes the Cancerian finds it rather hard to face life. It becomes too much for him. He can be a little timid and retiring, when things don't go too well. When unfortunate things happen, he is apt to just shrug and say, "Whatever will be will be." He can be fatalistic to a fault. The uncultivated Cancerian is a bit lazy. He doesn't have very much ambition. Anything that seems a bit difficult he'll gladly leave to others. He may be lacking in initiative. Too sensitive, when he feels he's been injured, he'll crawl back into his shell and nurse his imaginary wounds. The Cancer woman often is given to crying when the smallest thing goes wrong.

Some Cancerians find it difficult to enjoy themselves in environments outside their homes. They make heavy demands on others, and need to be constantly reassured that they are loved.

July 21–August 21

The Positive Side of Leo

Often Leos make good leaders. They seem to be good organizers and administrators. Usually they are quite popular with others. Whatever group it is that he belongs to, the Leo man is almost sure to be or become the leader.

The Leo person is generous most of the time. It is his best characteristic. He or she likes to give gifts and presents. In making others happy, the Leo person becomes happy himself. He likes to splurge when spending money on others. In some instances it may seem that the Leo's generosity knows no boundaries. A hospitable person, the Leo man or woman is very fond of welcoming people to his house and entertaining them. He is never short of company.

The Leo person has plenty of energy and drive. He enjoys working toward some specific goal. When he applies himself correctly, he gets what he wants most often. The Leo person is almost never unsure of himself. He has plenty of confidence and aplomb. He is a person who is direct in almost everything he does. He has a quick mind and can make a decision in a very short time.

He usually sets a good example for others because of his ambitious manner and positive ways. He knows how to stick to something once he's started. Although the Leo person may be good at making a joke, he is not superficial or glib. He is a loving person, kind and thoughtful.

There is generally nothing small or petty about the Leo man or woman. He does what he can for those who are deserving. He is a person others can rely upon at all times. He means what he says. An honest person, generally speaking, he is a friend that others value.

The Negative Side of Leo

Leo, however, does have his faults. At times, he can be just a bit too arrogant. He thinks that no one deserves a leadership position except him. Only he is capable of doing things well. His opinion of himself is often much too high. Because of his conceit, he is sometimes rather unpopular with a good many people. Some Leos are too materialistic; they can only think in terms of money and profit.

Some Leos enjoy lording it over others—at home or at their place of business. What is more, they feel they have the right to. Egocentric to an impossible degree, this sort of Leo cares little about how others think or feel. He can be rude and cutting.

August 22–September 22

The Positive Side of Virgo

The person born under the sign of Virgo is generally a busy person. He knows how to arrange and organize things. He is a good planner. Above all, he is practical and is not afraid of hard work.

The person born under this sign, Virgo, knows how to attain what he desires. He sticks with something until it is finished. He never shirks his duties, and can always be depended upon. The Virgo person can be thoroughly trusted at all times.

The man or woman born under this sign tries to do everything to perfection. He doesn't believe in doing anything half-way. He always aims for the top. He is the sort of a person who is constantly striving to better himself—not because he wants more money or glory, but because it gives him a feeling of accomplishment.

The Virgo man or woman is a very observant person. He is sensitive to how others feel, and can see things below the surface of a situation. He usually puts this talent to constructive use.

It is not difficult for the Virgoan to be open and earnest. He believes in putting his cards on the table. He is never secretive or under-handed. He's as good as his word. The Virgo person is generally plain-spoken and down-to-earth. He has no trouble in expressing himself.

The Virgo person likes to keep up to date on new developments in his particular field. Well-informed, generally, he sometimes has a keen interest in the arts or literature. What he knows, he knows well. His ability to use his critical faculties is well-developed and sometimes startles others because of its accuracy.

The Virgoan adheres to a moderate way of life; he avoids excesses. He is a responsible person and enjoys being of service.

The Negative Side of Virgo

Sometimes a Virgo person is too critical. He thinks that only he can do something the way it should be done. Whatever anyone else does is inferior. He can be rather annoying in the way he quibbles over insignificant details. In telling others how things should be done, he can be rather tactless and mean.

Some Virgos seem rather emotionless and cool. They feel emo-

tional involvement is beneath them. They are sometimes too tidy, too neat. With money they can be rather miserly. Some try to force their opinions and ideas on others.

September 23–October 22

The Positive Side of Libra

Librans love harmony. It is one of their most outstanding character traits. They are interested in achieving balance; they admire beauty and grace in things as well as in people. Generally speaking, they are kind and considerate people. Librans are usually very sympathetic. They go out of their way not to hurt another person's feelings. They are outgoing and do what they can to help those in need.

People born under the sign of Libra almost always make good friends. They are loyal and amiable. They enjoy the company of others. Many of them are rather moderate in their views; they believe in keeping an open mind, however, and weighing both sides of an issue fairly before making a decision.

Alert and often intelligent, the Libran, always fair-minded, tries to put himself in the position of the other person. They are against injustice; quite often they take up for the underdog. In most of their social dealings, they try to be tactful and kind. They dislike discord and bickering, and most Libras strive for peace and harmony in all their relationships.

The Libra man or woman has a keen sense of beauty. They appreciate handsome furnishings and clothes. Many of them are artistically inclined. Their taste is usually impeccable. They know how to use color. Their homes are almost always attractively arranged and inviting. They enjoy entertaining people and see to it that their guests always feel at home and welcome.

The Libran gets along with almost everyone. He is well-liked and socially much in demand.

The Negative Side of Libra

Some people born under this sign tend to be rather insincere. So eager are they to achieve harmony in all relationships that they will even go so far as to lie. Many of them are escapists. They find facing

the truth an ordeal and prefer living in a world of make-believe.

In a serious argument, some Librans give in rather easily even when they know they are right. Arguing, even about something they believe in, is too unsettling for some of them.

Librans sometimes care too much for material things. They enjoy possessions and luxuries. Some are vain and tend to be jealous.

October 23–November 22

The Positive Side of Scorpio

The Scorpio man or woman generally knows what he or she wants out of life. He is a determined person. He sees something through to the end. The Scorpion is quite sincere, and seldom says anything he doesn't mean. When he sets a goal for himself he tries to go about achieving it in a very direct way.

The Scorpion is brave and courageous. They are not afraid of hard work. Obstacles do not frighten them. They forge ahead until they achieve what they set out for. The Scorpio man or woman has a strong will.

Although the Scorpion may seem rather fixed and determined, inside he is often quite tender and loving. He can care very much for others. He believes in sincerity in all relationships. His feelings about someone tend to last; they are profound and not superficial.

The Scorpio person is someone who adheres to his principles no matter what happens. He will not be deterred from a path he believes to be right.

Because of his many positive strengths, the Scorpion can often achieve happiness for himself and for those that he loves.

He is a constructive person by nature. He often has a deep understanding of people and of life, in general. He is perceptive and unafraid. Obstacles often seem to spur him on. He is a positive person who enjoys winning. He has many strengths and resources; challenge of any sort often brings out the best in him.

The Negative Side of Scorpio

The Scorpio person is sometimes hypersensitive. Often he imagines injury when there is none. He feels that others do not bother to

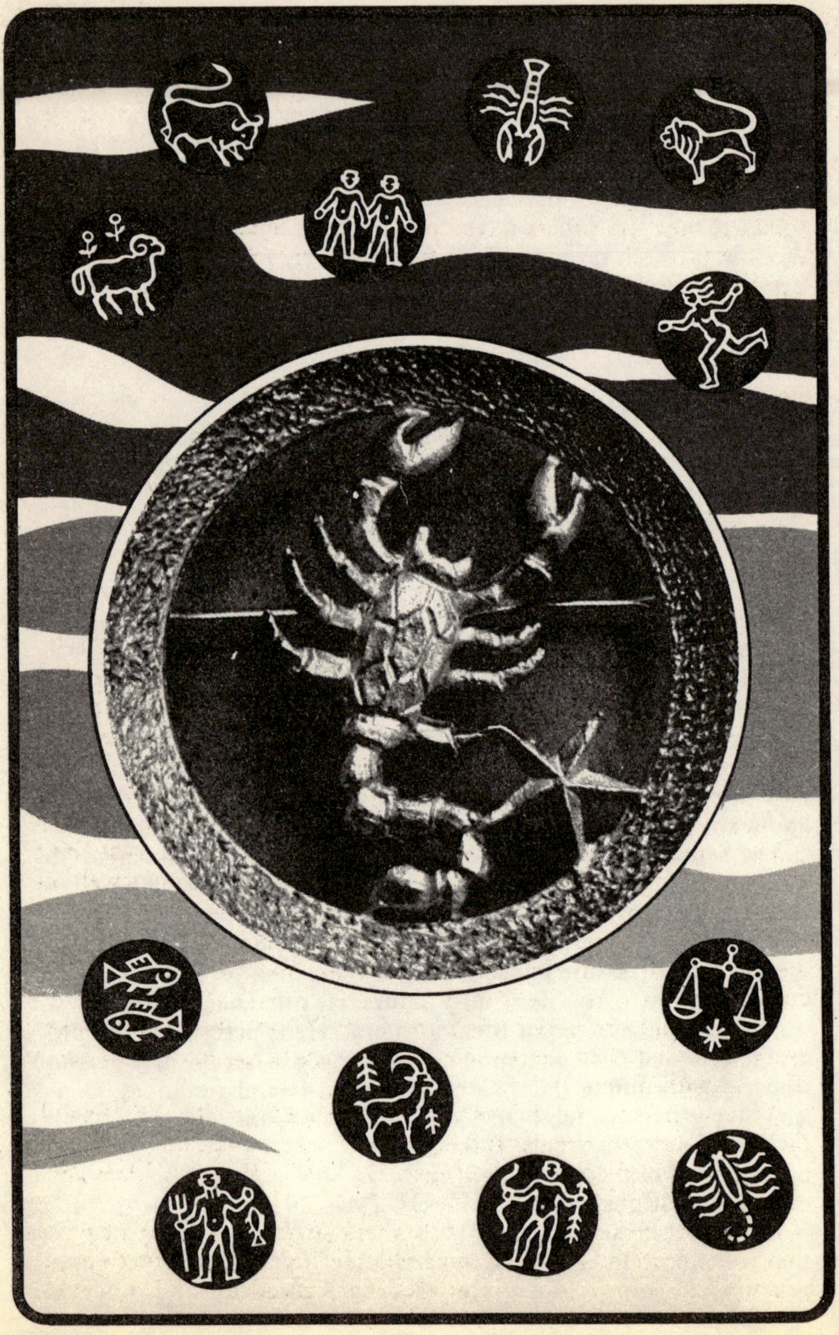

recognize him for his true worth. Sometimes he is given to excessive boasting in order to compensate for what he feels is neglect

The Scorpio person can be rather proud and arrogant. They can be rather sly when they put their minds to it and they enjoy outwitting persons or institutions noted for their cleverness.

Their tactics for getting what they want are sometimes devious and ruthless. They don't care too much about what others may think. If they feel others have done them an injustice, they will do their best to seek revenge. The Scorpion often has a sudden, violent temper; and this person's interest in sex is sometimes quite unbalanced or excessive.

November 23–December 20

The Positive Side of Sagittarius

People born under this sign are often honest and forthright. Their approach to life is earnest and open. The Sagittarian is often quite adult in his way of seeing things. They are broadminded and tolerant people. When dealing with others the person born under the sign of Sagittarius is almost always open and forthright. He doesn't believe in deceit or pretension. His standards are high. People who associate with the Sagittarian, generally admire and respect him.

The Sagittarian trusts others easily and expects them to trust him. He is never suspicious or envious and almost always thinks well of others. People always enjoy his company because he is so friendly and easy-going. The Sagittarius man or woman is often good-humored. He can always be depended upon by his friends, family, and co-workers.

The person born under this sign of the Zodiac likes a good joke every now and then; he is keen on fun and this makes him very popular with others.

A lively person, he enjoys sports and outdoor life. The Sagittarian is fond of animals. Intelligent and interesting, he can begin an animated conversation with ease. He likes exchanging ideas and discussing various views.

He is not selfish or proud. If someone proposes an idea or plan that is better than his, he will immediately adopt it. Imaginative yet practical, he knows how to put ideas into practice.

He enjoys sport and game, and it doesn't matter if he wins or loses. He is a forgiving person, and never sulks over something that has not worked out in his favor.

He is seldom critical, and is almost always generous.

The Negative Side of Sagittarius

Some Sagittarians are restless. They take foolish risks and seldom learn from the mistakes they make. They don't have heads for money and are often mismanaging their finances. Some of them devote much of their time to gambling.

Some are too outspoken and tactless, always putting their feet in their mouths. They hurt others carelessly by being honest at the wrong time. Sometimes they make promises which they don't keep. They don't stick close enough to their plans and go from one failure to another. They are undisciplined and waste a lot of energy.

December 21–January 19

The Positive Side of Capricorn

The person born under the sign of Capricorn is usually very stable and patient. He sticks to whatever tasks he has and sees them through. He can always be relied upon and he is not averse to work.

An honest person, the Capricornian is generally serious about whatever he does. He does not take his duties lightly. He is a practical person and believes in keeping his feet on the ground.

Quite often the person born under this sign is ambitious and knows how to get what he wants out of life. He forges ahead and never gives up his goal. When he is determined about something, he almost always wins. He is a good worker—a hard worker. Although things may not come easy to him, he will not complain, but continue working until his chores are finished.

He is usually good at business matters and knows the value of money. He is not a spendthrift and knows how to put something away for a rainy day; he dislikes waste and unnecessary loss.

The Capricornian knows how to make use of his self-control. He

can apply himself to almost anything once he puts his mind to it. His ability to concentrate sometimes astounds others. He is diligent and does well when involved in detail work.

The Capricorn man or woman is charitable, generally speaking, and will do what is possible to help others less fortunate. As a friend, he is loyal and trustworthy. He never shirks his duties or responsibilities. He is self-reliant and never expects too much of the other fellow. He does what he can on his own. If someone does him a good turn, then he will do his best to return the favor.

The Negative Side of Capricorn

Like everyone, the Capricornian, too, has his faults. At times, he can be over-critical of others. He expects others to live up to his own high standards. He thinks highly of himself and tends to look down on others.

His interest in material things may be exaggerated. The Capricorn man or woman thinks too much about getting on in the world and having something to show for it. He may even be a little greedy.

He sometimes thinks he knows what's best for everyone. He is too bossy. He is always trying to organize and correct others. He may be a little narrow in his tninking.

January 20–February 18

The Positive Side of Aquarius

The Aquarius man or woman is usually very honest and forthright. These are his two greatest qualities. His standards for himself are generally very high. He can always be relied upon by others. His word is his bond.

The Aquarian is perhaps the most tolerant of all the Zodiac personalities. He respects other people's beliefs and feels that everyone is entitled to his own approach to life.

He would never do anything to injure another's feelings. He is never unkind or cruel. Always considerate of others, the Aquarian is always willing to help a person in need. He feels a very strong tie between himself and all the other members of mankind.

The person born under this sign is almost always an individualist. He does not believe in teaming up with the masses, but prefers going his own way. His ideas about life and mankind are often quite advanced. There is a saying to the effect that the average Aquarian is fifty years ahead of his time.

He is broadminded. The problems of the world concern him greatly. He is interested in helping others no matter what part of the globe they live in. He is truly a humanitarian sort. He likes to be of service to others.

Giving, considerate, and without prejudice, Aquarians have no trouble getting along with others.

The Negative Side of Aquarius

The Aquarian may be too much of a dreamer. He makes plans but seldom carries them out. He is rather unrealistic. His imagination has a tendency to run away with him. Because many of his plans are impractical, he is always in some sort of a dither.

Others may not approve of him at all times because of his unconventional behavior. He may be a bit eccentric. Sometimes he is so busy with his own thoughts, that he loses touch with the realities of existence.

Some Aquarians feel they are more clever and intelligent than others. They seldom admit to their own faults, even when they are quite apparent. Some become rather fanatic in their views. Their criticism of others is sometimes destructive and negative.

February 19–March 20

The Positive Side of Pisces

The Piscean can often understand the problems of others quite easily. He has a sympathetic nature. Kindly, he is often dedicated in the way he goes about helping others. The sick and the troubled often turn to him for advice and assistance.

He is very broadminded and does not criticize others for their faults. He knows how to accept people for what they are. On the whole, he is a trustworthy and earnest person. He is loyal to his

friends and will do what he can to help them in time of need. Generous and good-natured, he is a lover of peace; he is often willing to help others solve their differences. People who have taken a wrong turn in life often interest him and he will do what he can to persuade them to rehabilitate themselves.

He has a strong intuitive sense and most of the time he knows how to make it work for him; the Piscean is unusually perceptive and often knows what is bothering someone before that person, himself, is aware of it. The Pisces man or woman is an idealistic person, basically, and is interested in making the world a better place in which to live. The Piscean believes that everyone should help each other. He is willing to do more than his share in order to achieve cooperation with others.

The person born under this sign often is talented in music or art. He is a receptive person; he is able to take the ups and downs of life with philosophic calm.

The Negative Side of Pisces

Some Pisceans are often depressed; their outlook on life is rather glum. They may feel that they have been given a bad deal in life and that others are always taking unfair advantage of them. The Piscean sometimes feel that the world is a cold and cruel place. He is easily discouraged. He may even withdraw from the harshness of reality into a secret shell of his own where he dreams and idles away a good deal of his time.

The Piscean can be rather lazy. He lets things happen without giving the least bit of resistance. He drifts along, whether on the high road or on the low. He is rather short on willpower.

Some Pisces people seek escape through drugs or alcohol. When temptation comes along they find it hard to resist. In matters of sex, they can be rather permissive.

THE SIGNS AND THEIR KEY WORDS

		POSITIVE	NEGATIVE
ARIES	self	courage, initiative, pioneer instinct	brash rudeness, selfish impetuosity
TAURUS	money	endurance, loyalty, wealth	obstinacy, gluttony
GEMINI	mind	versatility	capriciousness, unreliability
CANCER	family	sympathy, homing instinct	clannishness, childishness
LEO	children	love, authority, integrity	egotism, force
VIRGO	work	purity, industry, analysis	fault-finding, cynicism
LIBRA	marriage	harmony, justice	vacillation, superficiality
SCORPIO	sex	survival, regeneration	vengeance, discord
SAGITTARIUS	travel	optimism, higher learning	lawlessness
CAPRICORN	career	depth	narrowness, gloom
AQUARIUS	friends	human fellowship, genius	perverse unpredictability
PISCES	confinement	spiritual love, universality	diffusion, escapism

THE ELEMENTS AND QUALITIES OF THE SIGNS

ELEMENT	SIGN
FIRE	ARIES
	LEO
	SAGITTARIUS
EARTH	TAURUS
	VIRGO
	CAPRICORN
AIR	GEMINI
	LIBRA
	AQUARIUS
WATER	CANCER
	SCORPIO
	PISCES

QUALITY	SIGN
CARDINAL	ARIES
	LIBRA
	CANCER
	CAPRICORN
FIXED	TAURUS
	LEO
	SCORPIO
	AQUARIUS
MUTABLE	GEMINI
	VIRGO
	SAGITTARIUS
	PISCES

Every sign has both an element and a quality associated with it. The element indicates the basic makeup of the sign, and the quality describes the kind of activity associated with each.

Signs can be grouped together according to their *element* and *quality*. Signs of the same element share many basic traits in common. They tend to form stable configurations and ultimately harmonious relationships. Signs of the same quality are often less harmonious, but they share many dynamic potentials for growth as well as profound fulfillment.

THE FIRE SIGNS

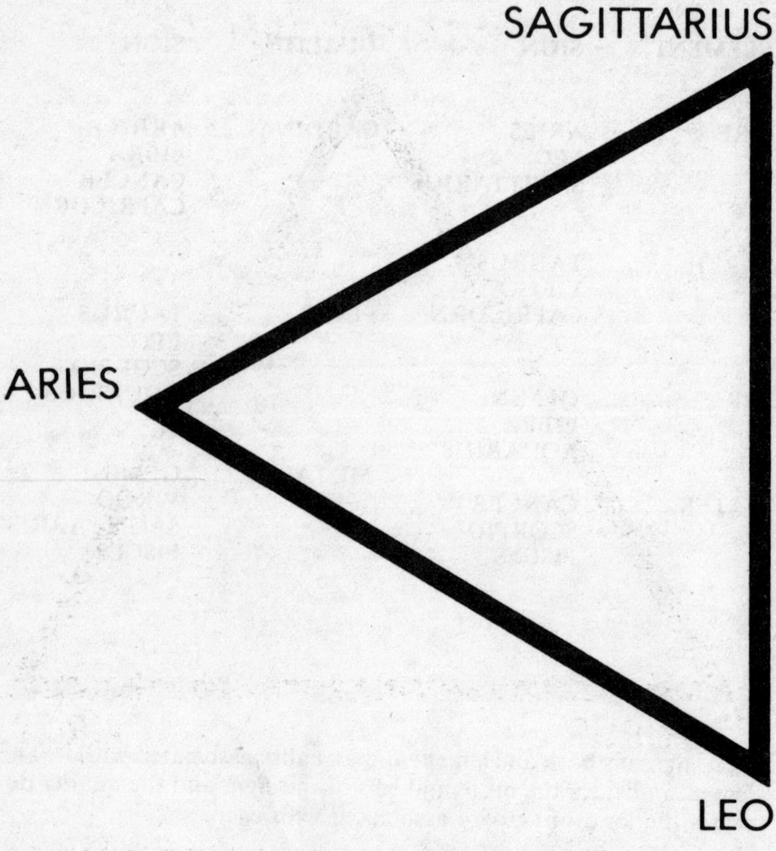

This is the fire group. On the whole these are emotional, volatile types, quick to anger, quick to forgive. They are adventurous, powerful people and act as a source of inspiration for everyone. They spark into action with immediate exuberant impulses. They are intelligent, self-involved, creative and idealistic. They all share a certain vibrancy and glow that outwardly reflects an inner flame and passion for living.

THE EARTH SIGNS

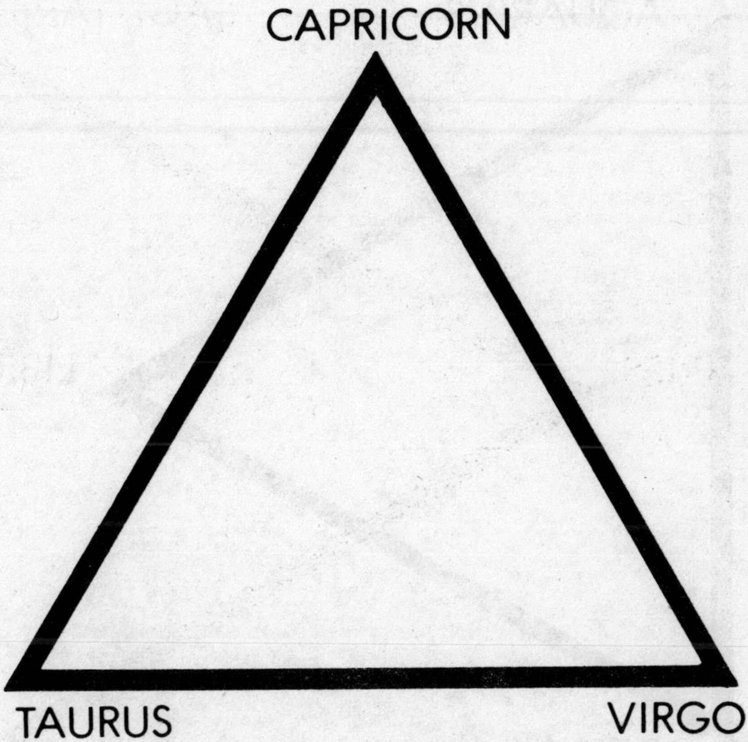

This is the earth group. They are in constant touch with the material world and tend to be conservative. Although they are all capable of spartan self-discipline, they are earthy, sensual people who are stimulated by the tangible, elegant and luxurious. The thread of their lives is always practical, but they do fantasize and are often attracted to dark, mysterious, emotional people. They are like great cliffs overhanging the sea, forever married to the ocean but always resisting erosion from the dark, emotional forces that thunder at their feet.

THE AIR SIGNS

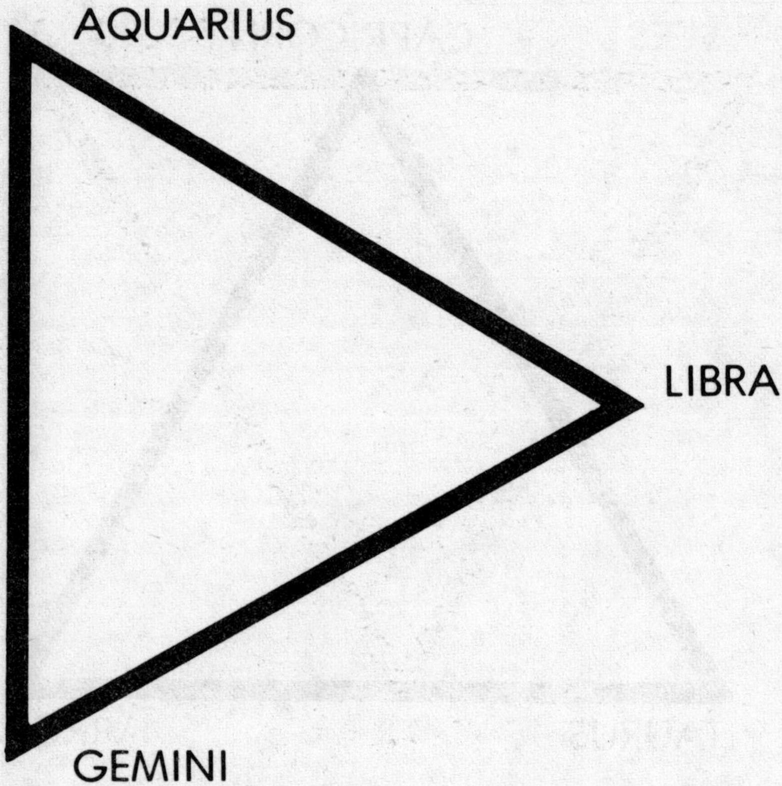

This is the air group. They are light, mental creatures desirous of contact, communication and relationship. They are involved with people and the forming of ties on many levels. Original thinkers, they are the bearers of human news. Their language is their sense of word, color, style and beauty. They provide an atmosphere suitable and pleasant for living. They add change and versatility to the scene, and it is through them that we can explore new territory of human intelligence and experience.

THE WATER SIGNS

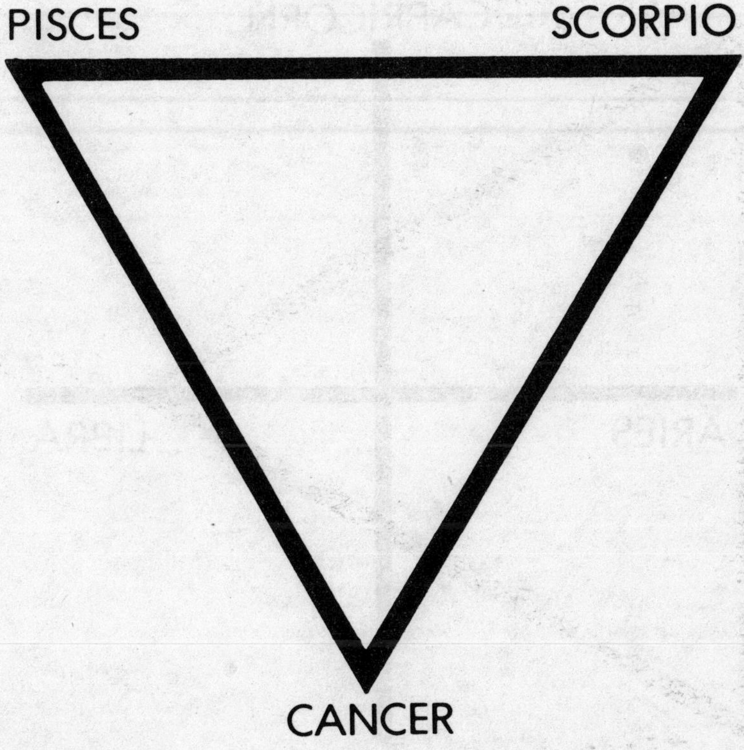

This is the water group. Through the water people, we are all joined together on emotional, non-verbal levels. They are silent, mysterious types whose magic hypnotizes even the most determined realist. They have uncanny perceptions about people and are as rich as the oceans when it comes to feeling, emotion or imagination. They are sensitive, mystical creatures with memories that go back beyond time. Through water, life is sustained. These people have the potential for the depths of darkness or the heights of mysticism and art.

THE CARDINAL SIGNS

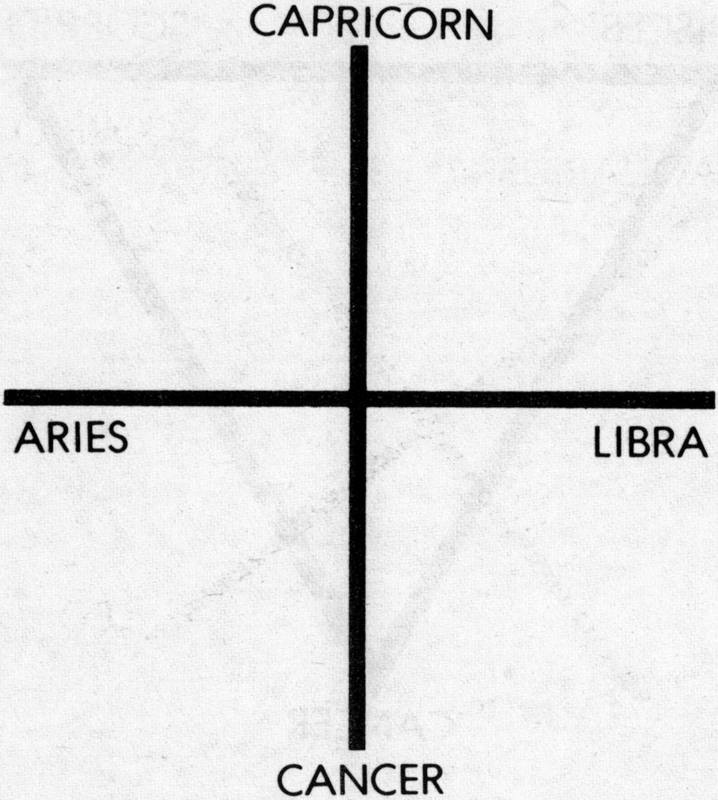

Put together, this is a clear-cut picture of dynamism, activity, tremendous stress and remarkable achievement. These people know the meaning of great change since their lives are often characterized by significant crises and major successes. This combination is like a simultaneous storm of summer, fall, winter and spring. The danger is chaotic diffusion of energy; the potential is irrepressible growth and victory.

THE FIXED SIGNS

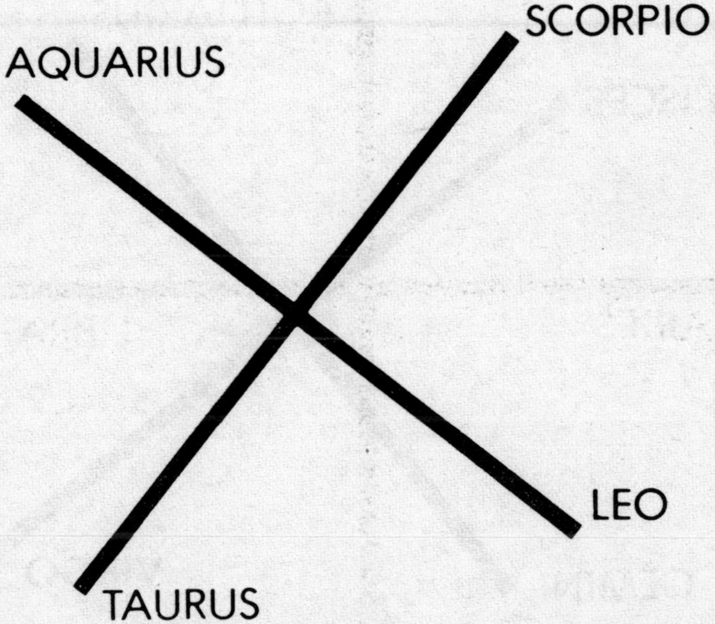

Fixed signs are always establishing themselves in a given place or area of experience. Like explorers who arrive and plant a flag, these people claim a position from which they do not enjoy being deposed. They are staunch, stalwart, upright, trusty, honorable people, although their obstinacy is well-known. Their contribution is fixity, and they are the angels who support our visible world.

THE MUTABLE SIGNS

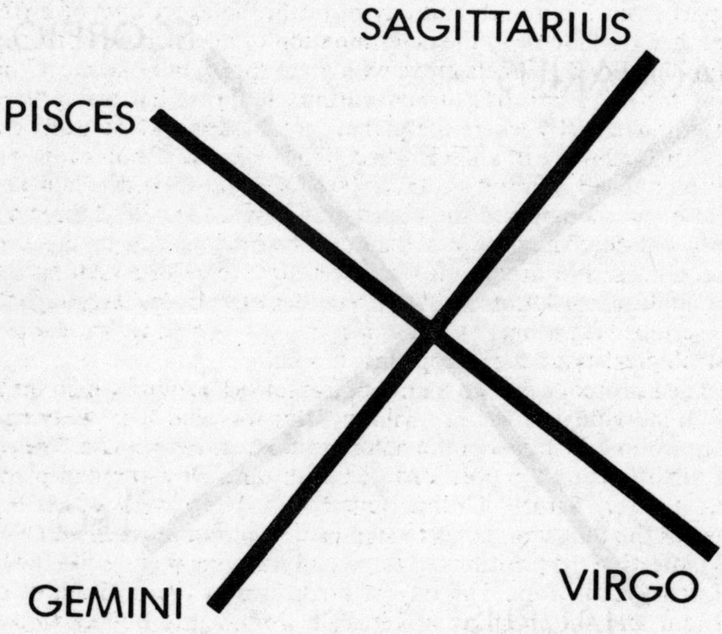

Mutable people are versatile, sensitive, intelligent, nervous and deeply curious about life. They are the translators of all energy. They often carry out or complete tasks initiated by others. Combinations of these signs have highly developed minds; they are imaginative and jumpy and think and talk a lot. At worst their lives are a Tower of Babel. At best they are adaptable and ready creatures who can assimilate one kind of experience and enjoy it while anticipating coming changes.

HOW TO APPROXIMATE YOUR RISING SIGN

Apart from the month and day of birth, the exact *time* of birth is another vital factor in the determination of an accurate horoscope. Not only do the planets move with great speed, but one must know how far the Earth has turned during the day. That way you can determine exactly where the planets are located with respect to the precise birthplace of an individual. This makes *your* horoscope *your* horoscope. In addition to these factors, another grid is laid upon that of the Zodiac and the planets: the houses. After all three have been considered, specific planetary relationships can be measured and analyzed in accordance with certain ordered procedures. It is the skillful translation of all this complex astrological language that a serious astrologer strives for in his attempt at coherent astrological synthesis. Keep this in mind.

The horoscope sets up a kind of framework around which the life of an individual grows like wild ivy, this way and that, weaving its way around the trellis of the natal positions of the planets. The year of birth tells us the positions of the distant, slow-moving planets like Jupiter, Saturn, Uranus and Pluto. The month of birth indicates the Sun sign, or birth sign as it is commonly called, as well as indicating the positions of the rapidly moving planets like Venus, Mercury and Mars. The day of birth locates the position of our Moon, and the moment of birth determines the houses through what is called the Ascendant, or Rising Sign.

As the Earth rotates on its axis once every 24 hours, each one of the twelve signs of the Zodiac appears to be "rising" on the horizon, with a new one appearing about every two hours. Actually it is the turning of the Earth that exposes each sign to view, but you will remember that in much of our astrological work we are discussing "apparent" motion. This *Rising Sign* marks the Ascendant and it colors the whole orientation of a horoscope. It indicates the sign governing the first house of the chart, and will thus determine which signs will govern all the other houses. The idea is a bit complicated at first, and we needn't dwell on complications in this introduction, but if you can imagine two color wheels with twelve divisions superimposed upon each other, one moving slowly and the other remaining still, you will have some idea of how the signs keep shifting the "color" of the houses as the Rising Sign continues to change every two hours.

The important point is that the birth chart, or horoscope, actually does define specific factors of a person's makeup. It contains a picture of being, much the way the nucleus of a tiny cell contains the potential for an entire elephant, or a packet of seeds contains a rosebush. If there were no order or continuity to the world, we could plant roses and get elephants. This same order that gives continuous flow to our lives often annoys people if it threatens to determine too much of their lives. We must grow from what we were planted, and there's no reason why we can't do that magnificently. It's all there in the horoscope. Where there is limitation, there is breakthrough; where there is crisis, there is transformation. Accurate analysis of a horoscope can help you find these points of breakthrough and transformation, and it requires knowledge of subtleties and distinctions that demand skillful judgment in order to solve even the simplest kind of personal question.

It is still quite possible, however, to draw some conclusions based upon the sign occupied by the Sun alone. In fact, if you're just being introduced to this vast subject, you're better off keeping it simple. Otherwise it seems like an impossible jumble, much like trying to read a novel in a foreign language without knowing the basic vocabulary. As with anything else, you can progress in your appreciation and understanding of astrology in direct proportion to your interest. To become really good at it requires study, experience, patience and above all—and maybe simplest of all—a fundamental understanding of what is actually going on right up there in the sky over your head. It is a vital living process you can observe, contemplate and ultimately understand. You can start by observing sunrise, or sunset, or even the full Moon.

In fact you can do a simple experiment after reading this introduction. You can erect a rough chart by following the simple procedure below:

1. Draw a circle with twelve equal segments.
2. Starting at what would be the nine o'clock position on a clock, number the segments, or houses, from 1 to 12 in a *counterclockwise direction.*
3. Label house number 1 in the following way: 4 A.M.-6 A.M.
4. In a counterclockwise direction, label the rest of the houses: 2 A.M.-4 A.M., MIDNIGHT-2 A.M., 10 P.M-MIDNIGHT, 8 P.M.-10 P.M., 6 P.M.-8 P.M., 4 P.M.-6 P.M., 2 P.M.-4 P.M., NOON-2 P.M., 10 A.M.-NOON, 8 A.M.-10 A.M., and6 A.M.-8 A.M.
5. Now find out what time you were born and place the sun in the appropriate house.

6. Label the edge of that house with your Sun sign. You now have a description of your basic character and your fundamental drives. You can also see in what areas of life on Earth you will be most likely to focus your constant energy and center your activity.

7. If you are really feeling ambitious, label the rest of the houses with the signs, starting with your Sun sign, in order, still in a *counterclockwise direction.* When you get to Pisces, start over with Aries and keep going until you reach the house behind the Sun.

8. Look to house number 1. The sign that you have now labeled and attached to house number 1 is your Rising sign. It will color your self-image, outlook, physical constitution, early life and whole orientation to life. Of course this is a mere approximation, since there are many complicated calculations that must be made with respect to adjustments for birth time, but if you read descriptions of the sign preceding and the sign following the one you have calculated in the above manner, you may be able to identify yourself better. In any case, when you get through labeling all the houses, your drawing should look something like this:

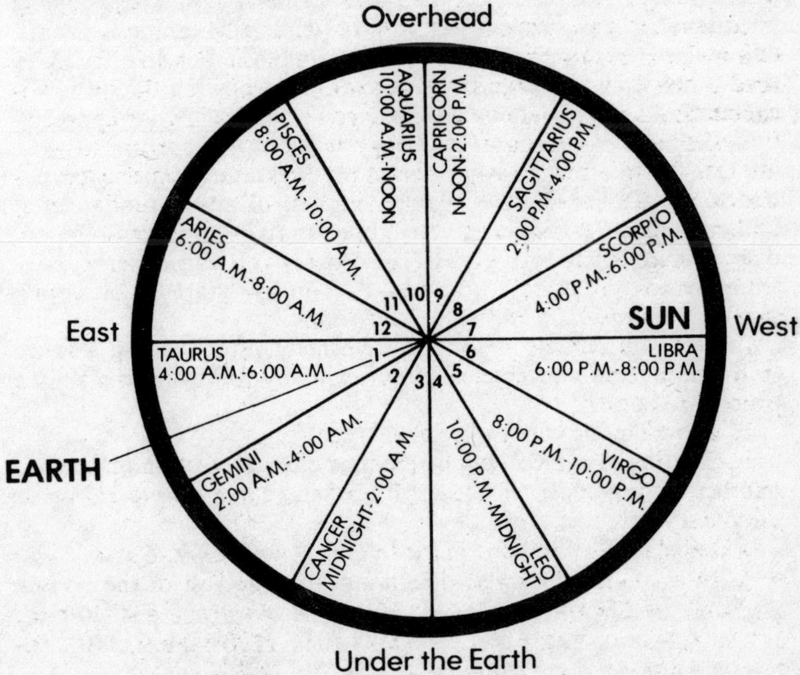

Basic chart illustrating the position of the Sun in Scorpio, with the Ascendant Taurus as the Rising Sign.'

This individual was born at 5:15 P.M. on October 31 in New York City. The Sun is in Scorpio and is found in the 7th house. The Rising sign, or the sign governing house number 1, is Taurus, so this person is a blend of Scorpio and Taurus.

Any further calculation would necessitate that you look in an ephemeris, or table of planetary motion, for the positions of the rest of the planets for your particular birth year. But we will take the time to define briefly all the known planets of our Solar System and the Sun to acquaint you with some more of the astrological vocabulary that you will be meeting again and again. (See page 21 for a full explanation of the Moon in all the Signs.)

THE PLANETS AND SIGNS THEY RULE

The signs of the Zodiac are linked to the planets in the following way. Each sign is governed or ruled by one or more planets. No matter where the planets are located in the sky at any given moment, they still rule their respective signs, and when they travel through the signs they rule, they have special dignity and their effects are stronger.

Following is a list of the planets and the signs they rule. After looking at the list, go back over the definitions of the planets and see if you can determine how the planet ruling *your* Sun sign has affected your life.

SIGNS	RULING PLANETS
Aries	Mars, Pluto
Taurus	Venus
Gemini	Mercury
Cancer	Moon
Leo	Sun
Virgo	Mercury
Libra	Venus
Scorpio	Mars, Pluto
Sagittarius	Jupiter
Capricorn	Saturn
Aquarius	Saturn, Uranus
Pisces	Jupiter, Neptune

THE PLANETS OF THE SOLAR SYSTEM

Here are the planets of the Solar System. They all travel around the Sun at different speeds and different distances. Taken with the Sun, they all distribute individual intelligence and ability throughout the entire chart.

The planets modify the influence of the Sun in a chart according to their own particular natures, strengths and positions. Their positions must be calculated for each year and day, and their function and expression in a horoscope will change as they move from one area of the Zodiac to another.

Following, you will find brief statements of their pure meanings.

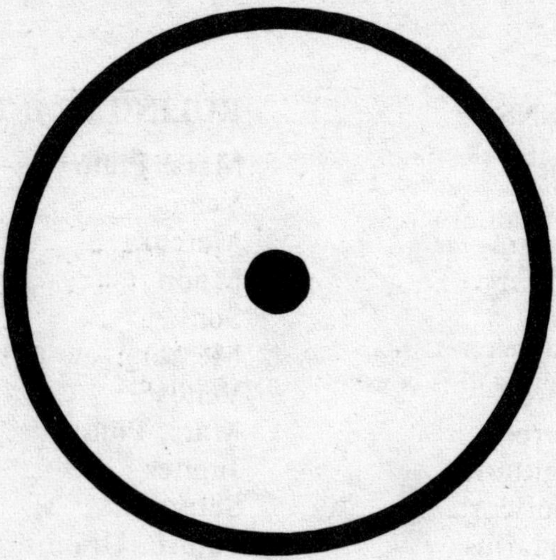

THE SUN

SUN

This is the center of existence. Around this flaming sphere all the planets revolve in endless orbits. Our star is constantly sending out its beams of light and energy without which no life on Earth would be possible. In astrology it symbolizes everything we are trying to become, the center around which all of our activity in life will always revolve. It is the symbol of our basic nature and describes the natural and constant thread that runs through everything that we do from birth to death on this planet.

To early astrologers, the sun seemed to be another planet because it crossed the heavens every day, just like the rest of the bodies in the sky.

It is the only star near enough to be seen well—it is, in fact, a dwarf star. Approximately 860,000 miles in diameter, it is about ten times as wide as the giant planet Jupiter. The next nearest star is nearly 300,000 times as far away, and if the Sun were located as far away as most of the bright stars, it would be too faint to be seen without a telescope.

Everything in the horoscope ultimately revolves around this singular body. Although other forces may be prominent in the charts of some individuals, still the Sun is the total nucleus of being and symbolizes the complete potential of every human being alive. It is vitality and the life force. Your whole essence comes from the position of the Sun.

You are always trying to express the Sun according to its position by house and sign. Possibility for all development is found in the Sun, and it marks the fundamental character of your personal radiations all around you.

It is the symbol of strength, vigor, wisdom, dignity, ardor and generosity, and the ability for a person to function as a mature individual. It is also a creative force in society. It is consciousness of the gift of life.

The underdeveloped solar nature is arrogant, pushy, undependable and proud, and is constantly using force.

MERCURY

Mercury is the planet closest to the Sun. It races around our star, gathering information and translating it to the rest of the system. Mercury represents your capacity to understand the desires of your own will and to translate those desires into action.

In other words it is the planet of Mind and the power of communication. Through Mercury we develop an ability to think, write, speak and observe—to become aware of the world around us. It colors our attitudes and vision of the world, as well as our capacity to communicate our inner responses to the outside world. Some people who have serious disabilities in their power of verbal communication have often wrongly been described as people lacking intelligence.

Although this planet (and its position in the horoscope) indicates your power to communicate your thoughts and perceptions to the world, intelligence is something deeper. Intelligence is distributed throughout all the planets. It is the relationship of the planets to each other that truly describes what we call intelligence. Mercury rules speaking, language, mathematics, draft and design, students, messengers, young people, offices, teachers and any pursuits where the mind of man has wings.

VENUS

Venus is beauty. It symbolizes the harmony and radiance of a rare and elusive quality: beauty itself. It is refinement and delicacy, softness and charm. In astrology it indicates grace, balance and the aesthetic sense. Where Venus is we see beauty, a gentle drawing in of energy and the need for satisfaction and completion. It is a special touch that finishes off rough edges. It is sensitivity, and affection, and it is always the place for that other elusive phenomenon: love. Venus describes our sense of what is beautiful and loving. Poorly developed, it is vulgar, tasteless and self-indulgent. But its ideal is the flame of spiritual love—Aphrodite, goddess of love, and the sweetness and power of personal beauty.

MARS

This is raw, crude energy. The planet next to Earth but outward from the Sun is a fiery red sphere that charges through the horoscope with force and fury. It represents the way you reach out for new adventure and new experience. It is energy and drive, initiative, courage and daring. The power to start something and see it through. It can be thoughtless, cruel and wild, angry and hostile, causing cuts, burns, scalds and wounds. It can stab its way through a chart, or it can be the symbol of healthy spirited adventure, well-channeled constructive power to begin and keep up the drive. If you have trouble starting things, if you lack the get-up-and-go to start the ball rolling, if you lack aggressiveness and self-confidence, chances are there's another planet influencing your Mars. Mars rules soldiers, butchers, surgeons, salesmen—any field that requires daring, bold skill, operational technique or self-promotion.

♃

JUPITER

This is the largest planet of the Solar System. Scientists have recently learned that Jupiter reflects more light than it receives from the Sun. In a sense it is like a star itself. In astrology it rules good luck and good cheer, health, wealth, optimism, happiness, success and joy. It is the symbol of opportunity and always opens the way for new possibilities in your life. It rules exuberance, enthusiasm, wisdom, knowledge, generosity and all forms of expansion in general. It rules actors, statesmen, clerics, professional people, religion, publishing and the distribution of many people over large areas.

Sometimes Jupiter makes you think you deserve everything, and you become sloppy, wasteful, careless and rude, prodigal and lawless, in the illusion that nothing can ever go wrong. Then there is the danger of over-confidence, exaggeration, undependability and over-indulgence.

Jupiter is the minimization of limitation and the emphasis on spirituality and potential. It is the thirst for knowledge and higher learning.

SATURN

Saturn circles our system in dark splendor with its mysterious rings, forcing us to be awakened to whatever we have neglected in the past. It will present real puzzles and problems to be solved, causing delays, obstacles and hindrances. By doing so, Saturn stirs our own sensitivity to those areas where we are laziest.

Here we must patiently develop *method,* and only through painstaking effort can our ends be achieved. It brings order to a horoscope and imposes reason just where we are feeling least reasonable. By creating limitations and boundary, Saturn shows the consequences of being human and demands that we accept the changing cycles inevitable in human life. Saturn rules time, old age and sobriety. It can bring depression, gloom, jealousy and greed, or serious acceptance of responsibilities out of which success will develop. With Saturn there is nothing to do but face facts. It rules laborers, stones, granite, rocks and crystals of all kinds.

The Outer Planets

The following three are the outer planets. They liberate human beings from cultural conditioning, and in that sense are the law breakers. In early times it was thought that Saturn was the last planet of the system—the outer limit beyond which we could never go. The discovery of the next three planets ushered in new phases of human history, revolution and technology.

URANUS

Uranus rules unexpected change, upheaval, revolution. It is the symbol of total independence and asserts the freedom of an individual from all restriction and restraint. It is a breakthrough planet and indicates talent, originality and genius in a horoscope. It usually causes last-minute reversals and changes of plan, unwanted separations, accidents, catastrophes and eccentric behavior. It can add irrational rebelliousness and perverse bohemianism to a personality or a streak of unaffected brilliance in science and art. It rules technology, aviation and all forms of electrical and electronic advancement. It governs great leaps forward and topsy-turvy situations, and *always* turns things around at the last minute. Its effects are difficult to ever really predict, since it rules sudden last-minute decisions and events that come like lightning out of the blue.

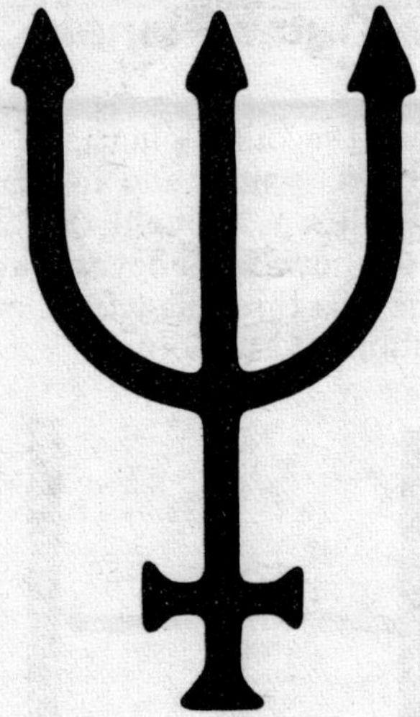

NEPTUNE

Neptune dissolves existing reality the way the sea erodes the cliffs beside it. Its effects are subtle like the ringing of a buoy's bell in the fog. It suggests a reality higher than definition can usually describe. It awakens a sense of higher responsibility often causing guilt, worry, anxieties or delusions. Neptune is associated with all forms of escape and can make things seem a certain way so convincingly that you are absolutely sure of something that eventually turns out to be quite different.

It is the planet of illusion and therefore governs the invisible realms that lie beyond our ordinary minds, beyond our simple factual ability to prove what is "real." Treachery, deceit, disillusionment and disappointment are linked to Neptune. It describes a vague reality that promises eternity and the divine, yet in a manner so complex that we cannot really fathom it at all. At its worst Neptune is a cheap intoxicant; at its best it is the poetry, music and inspiration of the higher planes of spiritual love. It has dominion over movies, photographs and much of the arts.

PLUTO

Pluto lies at the outpost of our system and therefore rules finality in a horoscope—the final closing of chapters in your life, the passing of major milestones and points of development from which there is no return. It is a final wipeout, a closeout, an evacuation. It is a distant, subtle but powerful catalyst in all transformations that occur. It creates, destroys, then recreates. Sometimes Pluto starts its influence with a minor event or insignificant incident that might even go unnoticed. Slowly but surely, little by little, everything changes, until at last there has been a total transformation in the area of your life where Pluto has been operating. It rules mass thinking and the trends that society first rejects, then adopts and finally outgrows.

Pluto rules the dead and the underworld—all the powerful forces of creation and destruction that go on all the time beneath, around and above us. It can bring a lust for power with strong obsessions.

It is the planet that rules the metamorphoses of the caterpillar into a butterfly, for it symbolizes the capacity to change totally and forever a person's life style, way of thought and behavior.

FAMOUS PERSONALITIES

ARIES: Hans Christian Andersen, Pearl Bailey, Marlon Brando, Wernher Von Braun, Charlie Chaplin, Joan Crawford, Da Vinci, Bette Davis, Doris Day, W. C. Fields, Alec Guinness, Adolf Hitler, William Holden, Thomas Jefferson, Nikita Khrushchev, Elton John, Arturo Toscanini, J. P. Morgan, Paul Robeson, Gloria Steinem, Lowell Thomas, Vincent van Gogh, Tennessee Williams

TAURUS: Fred Astaire, Charlote Brontë, Carol Burnett, Irving Berlin, Bing Crosby, Salvador Dali, Tchaikovsky, Queen Elizabeth II, Duke Ellington, Ella Fitzgerald, Henry Fonda, Sigmund Freud, Orson Welles, Joe Louis, Lenin, Karl Marx, Golda Meir, Eva Peron, Bertrand Russell, Shakespeare, Kate Smith, Benjamin Spock, Barbra Streisand, Shirley Temple, Harry Truman

GEMINI: Mikhail Baryshnikov, Boy George, Igor Stravinsky, Carlos Chavez, Walt Whitman, Bob Dylan, Ralph Waldo Emerson, Judy Garland, Paul Gauguin, Allen Ginsberg, Benny Goodman, Bob Hope, Burl Ives, John F. Kennedy, Peggy Lee, Marilyn Monroe, Joe Namath, Cole Porter, Laurence Olivier, Harriet Beecher Stowe, Queen Victoria, John Wayne, Frank Lloyd Wright

CANCER: "Dear Abby," David Brinkley, Yul Brynner, Pearl Buck, Marc Chagall, Jack Dempsey, Mildred (Babe) Zaharias, Mary Baker Eddy, Henry VIII, John Glenn, Ernest Hemingway, Lena Horne, Oscar Hammerstein, Helen Keller, Ann Landers, George Orwell, Nancy Reagan, Rembrandt, Richard Rodgers, Ginger Rogers, Rubens, Jean-Paul Sartre, O. J. Simpson

LEO: Neil Armstrong, Russell Baker, James Baldwin, Emily Brontë, Wilt Chamberlain, Julia Child, Cecil B. De Mille, Ogden Nash, Amelia Earhart, Edna Ferber, Arthur Goldberg, Dag Hammarskjöld, Alfred Hitchcock, Mick Jagger, George Meany, George Bernard Shaw, Napoleon, Jacqueline Onassis, Henry Ford, Francis Scott Key, Andy Warhol, Mae West, Orville Wright

VIRGO: Ingrid Bergman, Warren Burger, Maurice Chevalier, Agatha Christie, Sean Connery, Lafayette, Peter Falk, Greta Garbo, Althea Gibson, Arthur Godfrey, Goethe, Buddy Hackett, Michael Jackson, Lyndon Johnson, D. H. Lawrence, Sophia Loren, Grandma Moses, Arnold Palmer, Queen Elizabeth I, Walter Reuther, Peter Sellers, Lily Tomlin, George Wallace

LIBRA: Brigitte Bardot, Art Buchwald, Truman Capote, Dwight D. Eisenhower, William Faulkner, F. Scott Fitzgerald, Gandhi, George Gershwin, Micky Mantle, Helen Hayes, Vladimir Horowitz, Doris Lessing, Martina Navratalova, Eugene O'Neill, Luciano Pavarotti, Emily Post, Eleanor Roosevelt, Bruce Springsteen, Margaret Thatcher, Gore Vidal, Barbara Walters, Oscar Wilde

SCORPIO: Vivien Leigh, Richard Burton, Art Carney, Johnny Carson, Billy Graham, Grace Kelly, Walter Cronkite, Marie Curie, Charles de Gaulle, Linda Evans, Indira Gandhi, Theodore Roosevelt, Rock Hudson, Katherine Hepburn, Robert F. Kennedy, Billie Jean King, Martin Luther, Georgia O'Keeffe, Pablo Picasso, Jonas Salk, Alan Shepard, Robert Louis Stevenson

SAGITTARIUS: Jane Austen, Louisa May Alcott, Woody Allen, Beethoven, Willy Brandt, Mary Martin, William F. Buckley, Maria Callas, Winston Churchill, Noel Coward, Emily Dickinson, Walt Disney, Benjamin Disraeli, James Doolittle, Kirk Douglas, Chet Huntley, Jane Fonda, Chris Evert Lloyd, Margaret Mead, Charles Schulz, John Milton, Frank Sinatra, Steven Spielberg

CAPRICORN: Muhammad Ali, Isaac Asimov, Pablo Casals, Dizzy Dean, Marlene Dietrich, James Farmer, Ava Gardner, Barry Goldwater, Cary Grant, J. Edgar Hoover, Howard Hughes, Joan of Arc, Gypsy Rose Lee, Martin Luther King, Jr., Rudyard Kipling, Mao Tse-tung, Richard Nixon, Gamal Nasser, Louis Pasteur, Albert Schweitzer, Stalin, Benjamin Franklin, Elvis Presley

AQUARIUS: Marian Anderson, Susan B. Anthony, Jack Benny, Charles Darwin, Charles Dickens, Thomas Edison, John Barrymore, Clark Gable, Jascha Heifetz, Abraham Lincoln, John McEnroe, Yehudi Menuhin, Mozart, Jack Nicklaus, Ronald Reagan, Jackie Robinson, Norman Rockwell, Franklin D. Roosevelt, Gertrude Stein, Charles Lindbergh, Margaret Truman

PISCES: Edward Albee, Harry Belafonte, Alexander Graham Bell, Frank Borman, Chopin, Adelle Davis, Albert Einstein, Jackie Gleason, Winslow Homer, Edward M. Kennedy, Victor Hugo, Mike Mansfield, Michelangelo, Edna St. Vincent Millay, Liza Minelli, John Steinbeck, Linus Pauling, Ravel, Diana Ross, William Shirer, Elizabeth Taylor, George Washington

VIRGO

CHARACTER ANALYSIS

People born under the sign of Virgo are generally practical. They believe in doing things thoroughly; there is nothing slipshod or haphazard about the way they do things. They are precise and methodical. The man or woman born under this sixth sign of the Zodiac respects common sense and tries to be rational in his or her approach to tasks or problems.

The Virginian—as people under this sign are sometimes called—has excellent critical abilities; he knows how to analyze things. He is seldom fooled by superficialities.

The Virgo knows how to break things down to the minutest detail; he prefers to work on things piece by piece. Inwardly, he is afraid of being overwhelmed by things that seem larger than life. For this reason, one often finds the Virgo occupied with details. His powers of concentration are greatest when he can concentrate on small, manageable things.

The Virgo person believes in doing things correctly; he's thorough and precise. He's seldom carried away by fantasy; he believes in keeping his feet firmly on the ground. People who seem a bit flighty or impractical sometimes irritate him.

The Virgo knows how to criticize others. It is very easy for him to point out another's weaknesses or faults; he is seldom wrong. However, the Virgo is sometimes a bit sharp in making criticisms and often offends a good friend or acquaintance. At times, he is not very tactful and this can lead to considerable social discord. Quite often, the person born under this sign does not feel that he has done anything wrong by telling another of his faults. The cultivated Virgo, however, knows how to apply criticism tactfully. He is considerate of another's feelings.

The Virgo person believes in applying himself in a positive

manner to whatever task is set before him. He is a person full of purpose and goodwill. He is generally intelligent in his approach to work. He is seldom given to impulse, but works along steadily and constructively. Anything that isn't practical or scientific arouses his distrust. He is not very impressed by artistic or imaginative approaches to work. The Virgo person is usually intelligent, but frequently he does not like to be bothered with deep study. He likes his colleagues to be as well informed as he is, if not more. He has a deep respect for culture and intellect.

Usually, the Virgo takes in stride whatever comes into his life. Basically, he is an uncomplicated person, who views things clearly and sharply. He has a way of getting right down to the meat of the matter. Generally a serious-minded person, he believes in being reliable. He is not one who will take great risks in life as he has no interest in playing the hero or the idealist. The Virgo believes in doing what he can, but without flourishes.

Quite often he is a quiet, modest person. He believes that appearance is important and thus does his best to look well-groomed. He feels that being neat is important and dislikes untidiness in anything.

The Virgo man or woman likes to deal with life on a practical level and very seldom has the urge to look into the mystical side of existence.

Some Virgos are very talented in artistic matters. Others are great readers. They have a deep appreciation for the uncomplicated things of life.

On the whole, the Virgo person is even tempered. He does not allow himself to become angry easily. He knows how to take the bitter with the sweet. But if someone does him a wrong turn, he is not likely to forget it. His good nature is not to be abused.

Health

Many persons born under this sign are amazingly healthy. They frequently live to see a ripe old age. This longevity is generally due to the fact that people born under this sign take all things in moderation. The Virgo is not the type of person who burns the candle at both ends. He acknowledges his limits; he avoids excesses.

Frequently Virgos are small and neat featured. Virgo women are sometimes quite attractive in a sort of dry way. Both men and women of this sign have a youthful appearance throughout life. When young, Virgos are generally very active. However, as they reach middle age and beyond they have a tendency to put on a bit of weight.

The Virgo person usually enjoys good health, although some have a tendency to be overly concerned about it. They imgaine ailments they do not really have. Still, they do manage to stay fit. Other Virgos see themselves as being rather strong and resourceful, even when they are ill; for that reason they seldom feel moved to feel sorry for another ailing Virgo. Actually, serious illnesses frighten the Virgo; he will do all he can to remain in good health.

The medicine cabinet of someone born under this sign is often filled with all sorts of pills, tablets, and ointments; most of them will never be used.

As a rule, the Virgo watches his diet. He stays away from foods that won't agree with him. He keeps a balanced diet and is moderate in his drinking habits. The Virgo person needs plenty of exercise to keep his body fit. Most Virgos do not have a particular liking for strenuous movement; however, the wise Virgo sees to it that his body gets a workout daily. Another thing that the person under this sign needs is rest; he should get at least eight hours sleep per day.

On the whole, the Virgo is a sensitive person. His nerves may be easily affected if he finds himself in a disagreeable situation. The stomach is another area of concern. When a Virgo becomes sick, this area is usually affected. Digestion complaints are not rare among persons born under this sign. Regular meals are important for the Virgo. Quick snacks and the like may play havoc with his digestive system. In spite of this particular weakness, the Virgo manages to lead a normal, healthy life. He should try to avoid becoming too concerned with his ups and downs; many of his illnesses may turn out to be imaginary.

Occupation

Virgos delight in keeping busy. They are not afraid of hard work. By nature, they are ambitious people and are happiest when they are putting their talents and abilities to good use. They can best be described as goal-directed; they never lose sight of their objective once committed. They are very thorough in whatever they undertake. Even routine work is something that they can do without finding fault. In fact, work that is scheduled—or that follows a definite pattern—is well suited to their steady natures. Virgos will put aside other things, if necessary, in order to attain a goal. They prefer to work under peaceful conditions, and will seldom do anything to irritate their superiors.

They learn well and are not afraid to undertake any kind of work—even the most menial—if it is necessary. Sometimes, however, they neglect their own conditions because they are so involved in their work. For this reason, Virgos occasionally fall ill or become a bit nervous. Any kind of work that allows them to make use of their talent for criticism will please them.

Virgo men and women usually shine as bookkeepers, accountants, teachers, and pharmacists. The cultivated Virgo person often turns to the world of science where he is likely to do well. Some great writers and poets have been born under this sixth sign of the Zodiac.

It is very important that the Virgo has the kind of work that is suited to his personality. It may take a while before he actually finds his niche in life, and he may have to struggle at times in order to make ends meet. But, because he is not afraid of work, he manages to come out on top.

The Virgo person is a perfectionist. He is always looking for ways to improve his work scheme or technique. He is never satisfied until things are working smoothly. He will even do more than his share in order to secure regularity and precision in a job he is doing. It is not unusual for the average Virgo to have various ideas about how to better the job he is doing, how to streamline things. He is an extremely resourceful person as far as energy is concerned. In most cases, he can work longer than others, without letting it show. Because the Virgo is so concerned with detail, he may seem a trifle slow to his co-workers.

The enterprising Virgo can go far in business if his partner is somewhat adventurous and enthusiastic—qualities which tend to balance those of the Virgo person. At times, the Virgo can be quite a worrier; battling problems large and small may prevent him from making the headway he feels is necessary in his work. A partner who knows how to cut the work and worries in half by taking advantage of shortcuts is someone the average Virgo businessman could learn to value. People enjoy working with Virgo men and women, generally, because they are so reliable and honest. They usually set a good example for others on the job.

If he is not careful, the ambitious Virgo can become the type of person who thinks about nothing else but his job. He is not afraid of taking on more than the average man; but sometimes he makes the mistake of expecting the same of others. This attitude can lead to conflict and unpleasantness. Generally, he does achieve what he sets out for, because he knows how to apply himself. He is seldom the envy of others because he is not the type of person who is easily noticed or recognized.

The Virgo is a quiet person. He enjoys working in peaceful and harmonious surroundings. Conflict at work is bound to upset him and affect his nerves. He works well under people. He is not against taking orders from those who prove themselves his superiors. Virgo women make excellent secretaries. On the whole, the man or woman born under this sign, does not like to be delegated with the full responsibility of a task or project; he or she would rather have a supporting or a subordinate role.

Virgo men frequently excel in a trade. They often make good metalsmiths and carpenters, or they like to take up wood carving or sheetmetal work as a hobby.

The Virgo person is one who is very concerned about security. Now and again he may have cause to worry about his financial position. On the whole, he is conscious of the value of money. He is a person who will never risk his securities by going out on a limb. He knows how to put money away for a rainy day. Many times he will scout about for new ways of increasing his savings. Bettering his financial situation is something that constantly concerns him. When he does invest, it usually turns out to his advantage. He generally makes sure that the investment he makes is a sure thing. He does not believe in gambling or taking big risks.

Sometimes the Virgo, because of his keen interest in money and profit, is the victim of a fraud. Dishonest people may try to take advantage of his interest in monetary gain. The well-off Virgo is extremely generous and enjoys looking after the needs of others. He sees to it that those he cares for live in comfort.

Not all Virgos are fortunate enough to become extremely wealthy, but all of them must work hard for what they achieve.

Home and Family

People born under this sign are generally homebodies. They like to spend as much time as possible surrounded by the things and the people they enjoy. They make excellent hosts and enjoy entertaining guests and visitors. It is important to the Virgo that the people around him be happy and content. He enjoys himself most in the company of others if their behavior is "correct," that is, if they are respectful of others and their property. He does not like people to take advantage of his hospitality and abuse what he considers to be a privilege. On the whole, he is easygoing; the demands he may make of his guests and family are usually reasonable.

A harmonious atmosphere at home is important to the person born under this sign. So long as this can be guaranteed, the Virgo person remains in good humor. He is the type of person who is likely to have a number of insurance policies on his home, family, and possessions. He believes that you can never be safe enough.

In spite of his love of home, the Virgo is likely to have a keen interest in travel. If he cannot make changes in his environment, then he is bound to make them in his home. The Virgo woman enjoys making changes in her house; she never tires of rearranging things. Generally speaking, she has a good sense of beauty and harmony. She knows how to make a room inviting and comfortable. Change is always of interest to the person born under this sign. He likes to read of faraway places, even if he never gets a chance to visit them. A new job or a new home address from time to time can brighten his spirits immeasurably.

The Virgo woman is as neat as a pin. Usually she is an excellent cook, and takes care that her kitchen never gets out of order or becomes untidy even while she is working in it. She believes that everything has its proper place and should be kept there. Because she is so careful with her possessions, they often appear brand new.

Others may feel that the Virgo man or woman, because of his or her cool, calm ways, is not especially cut out to be a good parent. But the opposite is true: Virgo people know how to bring up their offspring correctly. They generally pass on their positive qualities to their children without any trouble. They teach them that honesty and diligence are important; they instill them with an appreciation for common sense in all matters.

Although the Virgo father or mother may deeply love their children, they have a tendency to be rather strict. They are deeply concerned that their children turn out well. Sometimes they expect too much of them. Some of them are rather old-fashioned and believe that a child belongs in a child's place. They expect this not only of their own offspring but also of other people's children.

Social Relationships

The Virgo man or woman is particular about the friends he makes. He is fond of people who have a particular direction in life. He is inclined to avoid drifters or irresolute people. Those who have made their mark win his admiration. The Virgo likes intelligent people—those who are somewhat cultured in their interests. As a good friend, the Virgo person is invaluable; there is nothing he would not do to help someone in need. He stands by his friends even in their most difficult moments. The only demand he makes is that his interest in another's affairs be valued. He does not like to feel that his help is not appreciated. It is important to him that he be thanked for even the slightest favor.

Quite often people born under this sign are rather timid or at least retiring; they have to be drawn out by others. After the Virgo gets to know someone well, however, he blooms. In spite of his initial shyness, he does not enjoy being alone. He likes company; he likes to be reassured by the people around him. He prefers intelligent, informed people as companions. He is the type of person who can overlook negative qualities in a particular person if he feels that that person is basically sincere in his behavior toward others. The Virgo person needs friends. In his solitude, the average Virgo is apt to feel stranded or deserted. He enjoys having someone around who will make a fuss over him, no matter how small.

The Virgo person is a perfectionist; sometimes he criticizes others too strongly for their faults and as a result, he may not have as many friends as he would like.

VIRGO

LOVE AND MARRIAGE

In love matters, the person born under this sign is not inclined to be overly romantic. To his partner, he may seem rather reserved and inhibited. His practical nature prevails even in affairs of the heart. He is the person least likely to be swept off his feet when in love. Chances are he may flirt a bit in the beginning of a relationship, but soon thereafter he settles down to the serious side of love. His standards are very high and it may be some time before he finds someone who can measure up to them. As a consequence, the Virgo person frequently marries rather late in life.

It is important for the Virgo man or woman to find the right person because he is easily influenced by someone he loves. On the other hand, the Virgo has a protective side to his nature; when in love he will try to shield the object of his affection from the unpleasant things in life.

The person born under the sign of Virgo may be disappointed in love more than once. People whom he sets great store in may prove to be unsuitable. Sometimes it is the Virgo's own fault. He may be too critical of small weaknesses that his partner or lover has.

Some Virgos are rather prim and proper when it comes to romance. They would prefer to think that it was not absolutely necessary and that intellect is everything. It may take some doing to get such a Virgo to change this attitude. At any rate, he is not fond of being demonstrative as far as affection goes. He does not like to make a show of his love in front of others. If the Virgo's lover is too demanding or forceful in the relationship, he may feel inclined to break off the affair. The Virgo person appreciates gentleness and consideration in his love life. On the whole, he is not easy to approach. The person who finds him or her interesting will have to be very tactful and patient when trying to convince the Virgo of his love.

In married life, the person born under the sign of Virgo is apt to be very practical. He is interested in preserving the happiness he has found and will do everything in his power to keep the relationship alive. It is quite important that the Virgo man or woman marry someone with a similar outlook. Someone quite opposite may misinterpret his calm and cool manner as being unfeeling. The Virgo person makes a faithful mate. He can always be depended upon. He knows how to keep things in the home running smoothly. He will do what he can to preserve harmony as he dislikes discord and unpleasantness. A cooperative person, the Virgo is willing to make concessions if they seem necessary. In short, the Virgo person can make a success of marriage if he has had the good fortune to choose the right person.

Romance and the Virgo Woman

The Virgo woman is often a serious person. She knows what she wants out of life and what to expect from people. She is discriminating in her choice of men. It may take considerable time before she will admit to herself that she is in love. She is not afraid to wait in matters of romance; it is important to her that she select the right person. She may be more easily attracted to an intelligent man than to a handsome one. She values intellect more than physical attributes.

It is important for the Virgo woman to trust someone before she falls in love with him. She is apt to allow a relationship to develop into a love affair after she has gotten to know the man well on strictly a companionship basis.

The Virgo woman generally makes a good wife. She knows how to keep household matters in shipshape. She likes looking after people she loves. She is efficient and industrious. There is almost nothing she will not do for the man she loves. She is capable of deep affection and love, but must be allowed to express herself in her own way.

Some Virgo women have the opinion that sex is not altogether proper. A gentle and considerate man can persuade such a woman to give up her old-fashioned ideas.

As a mother, she is ideal. She trains her offspring well, teaches them to be polite and well-mannered. Sometimes she may be a bit too strict. However, she always has their best interests at heart.

Romance and the Virgo Man

The Virgo man, practical and analytical as he is in most matters, is rather cautious when it comes to love and romance. He is not what one would call romantic. He may be rather shy on the whole. It may be up to the female to begin the relationship. He may prefer not to begin a romance until he has known the girl as a companion first. He is particular. If the girl makes one false move, he is likely to dissolve the relationship. An understanding and patient woman, however, can help him to be a little more realistic and open in his approach to love.

He enjoys family life and does everything he can to keep his wife and children happy and secure. He may want to have a hand in running the household because he feels he is more efficient than his mate. He is a calm, steady, and faithful person.

As a father he could be a bit of a fuss. He may not know how to communicate with his children effectively in some matters. However, he is loving and responsible. He does what he can to see that they have a proper upbringing.

Woman—Man

VIRGO WOMAN
ARIES MAN

Although it's possible that you could find happiness with a man born under the sign of the Ram, it's uncertain as to how long that happiness would last.

An Arien who has made his mark in the world and is somewhat steadfast in his outlooks and attitudes could be quite a catch for you. On the other hand, men under this sign are often swift-footed and quick-minded; their industrious mannerisms may fail to impress you, especially if you feel that much of their get-up-and-go often leads nowhere.

When it comes to a fine romance, you want someone with a nice, broad shoulder to lean on. You are likely to find a relationship with someone who doesn't stay put for too long somewhat upsetting.

The Arien may have a little trouble in understanding you, too—at least, in the beginning of the relationship. He may find you a bit too shy and moody. An Arien tends to speak his mind; he's liable to criticize you at the drop of a hat.

You may find a man born under this sign too demanding. He may give you the impression that he expects you to be at his constant beck and call. You have a lot of patience at your disposal and he may try every last bit of it. He may not be as thorough as you in everything he does. In order to achieve success or a goal quickly, he is liable to overlook small but important details, and regret the oversight when it is far too late.

Being married to an Arien does not mean that you'll have a secure and safe life as far as finances are concerned. Not all Ariens are rash with cash, but they lack the sound head you perhaps have for putting away something for that inevitable rainy day. He'll do his best, however, to see that you're adequately provided for, even though his efforts may leave something to be desired as far as you're concerned.

With an Aries man for a mate, you'll find yourself constantly among people. An Arien generally has many friends—and you may not heartily approve of them all. People born under the sign of the Ram are often more interested in "interesting" people than they are in influential ones. Although there may be a family squabble from time to time, you are stable enough to take it in your stride.

Aries men love children. They make wonderful fathers. Kids take to them like ducks to water. Their quick minds and behavior appeal to the young.

VIRGO WOMAN
TAURUS MAN

Some Taurus men are strong and silent. They do all they can to protect and provide for the women they love. In general, the Taurus man will never let you down. He's steady, sturdy, and reliable. He's pretty honest and practical, too. He says what he means and means what he says. He never indulges in deceit and will always put his cards on the table.

The Taurean is a very affectionate man. Being loved, appreciated and understood are very important for his well-being. Like you, he is also looking for peace and security in his life. If you both work toward these goals together, you'll find that they are easily attained.

If you should marry a Taurus man, you can be sure that the wolf will never darken your door. He is a notoriously good provider and will do everything he can to make his family comfortable and happy.

He'll appreciate the way you have of making a home warm and inviting. Slippers and pipe, and the evening papers are essential ingredients in making your Taurus husband happy at the end of the workday. Although he may be a big lug of a guy, you'll find that he's fond of gentleness and soft things. If you puff up his pillow and tuck him in at night, he won't complain.

You probably will like his friends. The Taurean tends to seek out those who are successful or prominent. You admire people, too, who work hard and achieve their goals.

The Taurus man doesn't care too much for change. He's a stay-at-home of the first order. Chances are that the house you move into after you're married will be the house you'll live in for the rest of your life.

You'll find that the man born under this sign is easy to get along with. It's unlikely that you'll have many quarrels or arguments.

Although he'll be gentle and tender with you, your Taurus man is far from being a sensitive type. He's a man's man. More than likely, he loves such sports as fishing and football. He can be earthy as well as down to earth.

Taureans love their children very much but do everything they can not to spoil them. They believe in children staying in their places. They make excellent disciplinarians. Your children will be polite and respectful.

VIRGO WOMAN GEMINI MAN

The Gemini man is a good catch. Many a woman has set her cap for him and failed to bag him. Generally, Gemini men are intelligent, witty, and outgoing. Many of them tend to be versatile.

On the other hand, some of them seem to lack that sort of common sense that you set so much store in. Their tendency to start a half-dozen projects, then toss them up in the air out of boredom may do nothing more than exasperate you.

One thing that causes a Twin's mind and affection to wander is a bore, and it is unlikely that an active woman like you would ever allow herself to be accused of being one. The Gemini man who has caught your heart will admire you for your ideas and intellect, perhaps even more than for your homemaking talents and good looks.

A strong-willed woman could easily fill the role of rudder for her Gemini's ship-without-a-sail. The intelligent Gemini is often aware of his shortcomings and doesn't mind if someone with better bearings gives him a shove in the right direction—when it's needed. The average Gemini doesn't have serious ego-hangups and will even accept a well-deserved chewing out from his mate or girl friend gracefully.

A successful and serious-minded Gemini could make you a very happy woman, perhaps, if you gave him half a chance. Although he may give you the impression that he has a hole in his head, the Gemini man generally has a good head on his shoulders. Some Geminis, who have learned the art of being steadfast, have risen to great heights in their professions: President Kennedy, Thomas Mann, and William Butler Yeats.

Once you convince yourself that not all people born under the sign of the Twins are witless grasshoppers, you won't mind dating a few to test your newborn conviction. If you do wind up walking down the aisle with one, accept the fact that married life with him will mean your taking the bitter with the sweet.

Life with a Gemini man can be more fun than a barrel of clowns. You'll never be allowed to experience a dull moment. Don't leave money matters to him or you'll both wind up behind the eight ball.

Gemini men are always attractive to the opposite sex. You'll perhaps have to allow him an occasional harmless flirt; it will seldom amount to more than that if you're his proper mate.

The Gemini father is a pushover for children. See that you keep the young ones in line otherwise they'll be running the house.

VIRGO WOMAN
CANCER MAN

The man born under the sign of Cancer may very well be the man after your own heart. Generally, Cancerians are steady people. They are interested in security and practicality. Despite their seemingly grouchy exterior at times, men born under the sign of the Crab are rather sensitive and kind individuals. They are almost always hard workers and are very interested in making successes of themselves economically as well as socially. You'll find that their conservative outlook on many things often agrees with yours. They will be men on whom you can depend come rain or come shine. They will never shirk their responsibilities as providers; they will always see that their family never wants.

Your patience will come in handy if you decide it's a Cancerian you want for a mate. He isn't the type that rushes headlong into romance. He wants to be sure about love as you do. If, after the first couple of months of dating, he suggests that you take a walk with him down lovers' lane, don't jump to the conclusion that he's about to make his "great play." Chances are he'll only hold your hand and seriously observe the stars. Don't let his coolness fool you, though. Beneath his starched reserve lies a very warm heart. He's just not interested in showing off as far as affection is concerned. Don't think his interest is wandering if he doesn't kiss you goodnight at the front door; that just isn't his style. For him, affection should only be displayed for two sets of eyes—yours and his. He's passionate only in private.

He will never step out of line. He's too much of a gentleman for that. When you're alone with him and there's no chance of being disturbed or spied upon, he'll pull out an engagement ring (that used to belong to his grandmother) and slip it on your trembling finger.

Speaking of relatives, you'll have to get used to the fact that the Cancerian is overly fond of his mother. When he says his mother's the most wonderful woman in the world, you'd better agree with him, that is, if you want to become his wife.

He'll always be a faithful husband; a Cancerian never pussyfoots around after he has taken that marriage vow. He doesn't take marriage responsibilities lightly. He'll see that everything in the house runs smoothly and that bills are paid promptly. He's liable to take out all kinds of insurance policies on his family and property. He'll arrange it so that when retirement time rolls around, you'll both be very well off.

Men under this sign make patient and understanding fathers.

VIRGO WOMAN
LEO MAN

To know a man born under the sign of the Lion is not necessarily to love him, even though the temptation may be great. When he fixes most girls with his leonine double-whammy, it causes their hearts to pitter-patter and their minds to cloud over.

You are a little too sensible to allow yourself to be bowled over by a regal strut and a roar. Still, there's no denying that Leo has a way with women, even sensible women like yourself. Once he's swept a girl off her feet, it may be hard for her to scramble upright again. Still, you are no pushover for romantic charm, expecially if you feel it's all show.

He'll wine you and dine you in the fanciest places. He'll croon to you under the moon and shower you with diamonds if he can get a hold of them. Still, it would be wise to find out just how long that shower is going to last before consenting to be his wife.

Lions in love are hard to ignore, let alone brush off. Your no's will have a way of nudging him on until he feels he has you completely under his spell. Once mesmerized by this romantic powerhouse, you will probably find yourself doing things of which you never dreamed. Leos can be vain pussycats when involved romantically. They like to be cuddled, curried, and tickled under the chin. This may not be your cup of tea exactly. Still when you're romantically dealing with a man born under the sign of Leo, you'll find yourself doing all kinds of things to make him purr.

Although he may be big and magnanimous while trying to win

you, he'll let out a bloodcurdling roar if he thinks he's not getting the tender love and care he feels is his due. If you keep him well supplied with affection, you can be sure his eyes will never look for someone else and his heart will never wander.

A Leo man often tends to be authoritarian; he can be depended upon to lord it over others in one way or another. If he is the top banana at his firm, he'll most likely do everything he can to stay on top. If he's not number one, he's probably working on it and will be sitting on the throne before long.

You'll have more security than you can use if he is in a position to support you in the manner to which he feels you should be accustomed. He is inclined to be too lavish, though—at least, by your standards.

You'll always have plenty of friends when you have a Leo for a mate. He's a natural-born friend-maker and entertainer. He loves to let his hair down at parties.

As fathers, Leos tend to spoil their children.

VIRGO WOMAN
VIRGO MAN

The Virgo man is all business or so he may seem to you. He is usually very cool, calm, and collected. He's perhaps too much of a fussbudget to arouse deep romantic interests in a woman like you. Torrid romancing to him is just so much sentimental mush. He can do without it and can make that quite evident in short order. He's keen on chastity and, if necessary, he can lead a sedentary, sexless life without caring very much about the fun others think he's missing. In short, you are liable to find him a first-class dud. He doesn't have much of an imagination; flights of fancy don't interest him. He is always correct and likes to be handled properly. Almost everything about him is orderly. "There's a place for everything . . ." is likely to be an adage he'll fall upon quite regularly.

He does have an honest-to-goodness heart, believe it or not. The woman who finds herself strangely attracted to his cool, feet-flat-on-the-ground ways, will discover that his is a constant heart, not one that goes in for flings or sordid affairs. A practical man, even in matters of the heart, he wants to know just what kind of person you are before he takes a chance on you.

The impulsive girl had better not make the mistake of kissing her Virgo friend on the street, even if it's only a peck on the cheek. He's not at all demonstrative and hates public displays of affection. Love, according to him, should be kept within the confines of one's home—with the curtains drawn. Once he believes that you are on the level with him as far as your love is concerned, you'll see how fast he can lose his cool. Virgos are considerate, gentle lovers. He'll spend a long time, though, getting to know you. He'll like you before he loves you.

A romance with a Virgo man can be a sometime or, rather, a one-time thing. If the bottom ever falls out, don't bother reaching for the adhesive tape. Nine times out of ten he won't care about patching up. He's a once-burnt-twice-shy guy. When he crosses your telephone number out of his address book, he's crossing you out of his life for good.

Neat as a pin, he's thumbs-down on what he considers "sloppy" housekeeping. An ashtray with just one stubbed out cigarette in it can annoy him even if it's only two seconds old. Glassware should always sparkle and shine if you want to keep him happy. If you marry him, keep your sunny-side up.

Your children should be kept as spotless as your house. Kids with dirty faces and hands displease him. Train them to be kind and courteous.

VIRGO WOMAN
LIBRA MAN

Men born under the sign of Libra are frequently too wrapped up in their own private dreams to be really interesting as far as love and romance are concerned. Many times, the Libra man is a difficult person to bring back down to earth; it is hard for him to face reality. Although he may be very cautious about weighing both sides of an argument, he may never really come to a reasonable decision about anything. Decision-making is something that often makes the Libra man uncomfortable; he'd rather leave that job to someone else. Don't ask him why, he probably doesn't know himself.

Qualities such as permanence and constancy are important to you in a love relationship. The Libra man may be an enigma to you. One moment he comes on hard and strong with declarations of his love; the next moment you find he's left you like yesterday's mashed potatoes. It does no good to wonder what went wrong. Chances are it was nothing on which you can put your finger. It's just one of Libra's strange ways.

He is not exactly what you would term an ambitious person; you are perhaps looking for a mate or friend with more drive and fidelity. You are the type of person who is interested in making some headway in the areas that interest you; the Libran is often contented to drift along. He does have drive, however, but it's not the long-range kind. It's not that he's shiftless or lazy; he's interested in material things and he appreciates luxuries, but he may not be willing to work hard enough to obtain them. Beauty and harmony interest him. He'll dedicate a lot of time to arranging things so that they are aesthetically pleasing. It would be difficult to call the Libra man practical; nine times out of ten, he isn't.

If you do begin a relationship with a man born under this sign, you will have to coax him now and again to face various situations in a realistic manner. You'll have your hands full, that's for sure. But if you love him, you'll undoubtedly do your best to understand him, no matter how difficult this may be.

If you become involved with a Libra man, either temporarily or permanently, you'd better take over the task of managing his money. Often he has little understanding of financial matters; he tends to spend without thinking, following his whims.

VIRGO WOMAN
SCORPIO MAN

Some people have a hard time understanding the man born under the sign of Scorpio; few, however, are able to resist his fiery charm. When angered, he can act like an overturned wasp's nest; his sting can leave an almost permanent mark. If you find yourself interested in the Scorpio man, you'd better learn how to keep on his good side.

The Scorpio man can be rather blunt when he chooses; at times, he may seem hardhearted. He can be touchy every now and then and this sensitiveness may get on your nerves after a while. When you feel as though ycu can't take it anymore, you'd better tiptoe away from the scene rather than chance an explosive confrontation. He's capable of giving you a sounding-out that will make you pack your bags and go back to Mother—for good.

If he finds fault with you, he'll let you know. He's liable to misinterpret your patience and think it a sign of indifference. But, you are the type of woman who can adapt to almost any sort of relationship or circumstance if you put your heart and mind to it.

Scorpio men are all very perceptive and intelligent. In some respects, they know how to use their brains more effectively than most. They believe in winning, in whatever they do; second-place holds no interest for them. In business, they usually achieve the position they want through a combination of drive and intellect.

Your interest in homelife probably won't be shared by him. No matter how comfortable you've managed to make the house, it will have very little influence on him with regard to making him aware of his family responsibilities. He does not like to be tied down, generally, and would rather be out on the battlefield of life, belting away at what he feels to be a just and worthy cause. Don't try to keep the homefires burning too brightly while you wait for him to come home from work—you may just run out of firewood.

The Scorpio man is passionate in all things, including love. Most women are easily attracted to him and you are perhaps no exception. Those who allow themselves to be swept off their feet by a Scorpio man, find out shortly thereafter that they're dealing with a carton of romantic fireworks. The Scorpio man is passionate with a capital P, make no mistake about that. Some women may find that he's just too love-happy, but that's their problem.

Scorpio men are straight to the point. They can be as sharp as a razor blade and just as cutting to anyone who crosses them.

Scorpio fathers like large families, generally.

VIRGO WOMAN SAGITTARIUS MAN

The woman who has set her cap for a man born under the sign of Sagittarius may have to use a great deal of strategy before she can get him to drop down on bended knee. Although some Sagittarians may be marriage-shy, they're not ones to skitter away from romance. A high-spirited woman may find a relationship with a Sagittarian, whether a fling or "the real thing," a very enjoyable experience.

As a rule, Sagittarians are bright, happy, and healthy people. They have a strong sense of fair play. Often they're a source of inspiration to others. They're full of ideas and drive.

You'll be taken by the Sagittarian's infectious grin and his lighthearted friendly nature. If you do wind up being the woman in his life, you'll find that he will treat you more like a buddy than the love of his life. It's his way.

You'll admire his broadmindedness in most matters, including that of the heart. If, while dating you, he claims that he still wants to play the field, he'll expect you to enjoy the same liberty. Once he's promised to love, honor, and obey, however, he does just that.

A woman who has a keen imagination and a great love of freedom will not be disappointed if she does marry a Sagittarian. The Sagittarius man is often quick-witted, and has a genuine interest in equality.

If he does insist on a night out with the boys once a week, he won't scowl if you decide to let him shift for himself in the kitchen once a week while you pursue some of your own interests. He believes in fairness.

The Sagittarian is not much of a homebody. Many times he's occupied with faraway places either in his dreams or in reality. He enjoys—just as you do—being on the go. Humdrum routine, especially at home, bores him. At the drop of a hat, he may ask you to whip off your apron and dine out for a change. He likes surprising people. He'll take great pride in showing you off to his friends. He'll always be a considerate mate; he will never embarrass or disappoint you intentionally. He's very tolerant when it comes to friends; you'll probably spend a lot of time entertaining people.

Sagittarians become interested in their children when they have passed through the baby stage.

VIRGO WOMAN
CAPRICORN MAN

The Capricorn man is frequently not the romantic lover that attracts most women. Still, with his reserve and calm, he is capable of giving his heart completely once he has found the right girl. The Capricorn man is thorough and deliberate in all that he does; he is slow and sure.

He doesn't believe in flirting and would never lead a heart on a merry chase just for the game of it. If you win his trust, he'll give you his heart on a platter. Many times, it is the woman who has to take the lead when romance is in the air. As long as he knows you're making the advances in earnest, he won't mind—in fact, he'll probably be grateful. Don't start thinking he's a cold fish; he isn't. While some Capricorns are indeed very capable of expressing passion, others often have difficulty in trying to display affection. He should have no trouble in this area, however, once he has found a patient and understanding girl.

The Capricorn man is very interested in getting ahead. He's quite ambitious and usually knows how to apply himself well to whatever task he undertakes. He certainly isn't a spendthrift. Like you, he knows how to handle money with extreme care. You, with your knack for putting away pennies for that rainy day, should have no difficulty understanding his way with money. The Capricorn man thinks in terms of future security. He wants to make sure that he and his wife have something to fall back on when they reach retirement age. There's nothing wrong with that; in fact, it's a plus quality.

The Capricorn man will want you to handle household matters efficiently. Most Capricorn-oriented women will have no trouble doing so. If he should check up on you from time to time, don't let it irritate you. Once you assure him that you can handle everything to his liking, he'll leave you alone.

Although he's a hard man to catch when it comes to marriage, once he's made that serious step, he's inclined to become possessive. The Capricorn man needs to know that he has the support of his wife in whatever he does, every step of the way.

The Capricorn man wants to be liked. He may seem dull to some, but underneath his reserve there is sometimes an adventurous streak that has never had a chance to express itself. He may be a real daredevil in his heart of hearts. The right woman, the affectionate, adoring woman can bring out that hidden zest in his nature.

He makes a loving, dutiful father, even though he may not understand his children completely.

VIRGO WOMAN
AQUARIUS MAN

You are liable to find the Aquarius man the most broadminded man you have ever met; on the other hand, you are also liable to find him the most impractical. Many times, he's more of a dreamer than a doer. If you don't mind putting up with a man whose heart and mind are as wide as the Missouri but whose head is almost always in the clouds, then start dating that Aquarian who has somehow captured your fancy. Maybe you, with your good sense, can bring him back down to earth when he gets too starry-eyed.

He's no dumbbell, make no mistake about that. He can be busy making some very complicated and idealistic plans when he's got that out-to-lunch look in his eyes. But more than likely, he'll never execute them. After he's shared one or two of his progressive ideas with you, you are liable to ask yourself, "Who is this nut?" But don't go jumping to conclusions. There's a saying that Aquarians are a half-century ahead of everybody else in the thinking department.

If you decide to answer "Yes" to his "Will you marry me?" you'll find out how right his zany whims are on or about your 50th anniversary. Maybe the waiting will be worth it. Could be that you have an Einstein on your hands and heart.

Life with an Aquarian won't be one of total despair if you can learn to temper his airiness with your down-to-earth practicality. He won't gripe if you do. The Aquarian always maintains an open mind; he'll entertain the ideas and opinions of everybody. But he may not agree with all of them.

Don't go tearing your hair out when you find that it's almost impossible to hold a normal conversation with your Aquarius friend at times. He's capable of answering your how-are-you-feeling with a rundown on the price of Arizona sugar beets. Always try to keep in mind that he means well.

His broadmindedness doesn't stop when it comes to you and

your personal freedom. You won't have to give up any of your hobbies or projects after you're married; he'll encourage you to continue them.

He'll be a kind and generous husband. He'll never quibble over petty things. Keep track of the money you both spend. He can't. Money burns a hole in his pocket.

At times, you may feel like calling it quits. Chances are, though, that you'll always give him another chance.

He's a good family man. He understands and loves children.

VIRGO WOMAN PISCES MAN

The man born under Pisces is quite a dreamer. Sometimes he's so wrapped up in his dreams that he's difficult to reach. To the average, active woman, he may seem a little sluggish.

He's easygoing most of the time. He seems to take things in his stride. He'll entertain all kinds of views and opinions from just about everyone, nodding or smiling vaguely, giving the impression that he's with them one hundred percent while that may not be the case at all. His attitude may be "why bother" when he's confronted with someone who is wrong but thinks he's right. The Pisces man will seldom speak his mind if he thinks he'll be rigidly opposed.

The Pisces man is oversensitive at times; he's afraid of getting his feelings hurt. He'll sometimes imagine a personal affront when none's been made. More than likely, you'll find this complex of his maddening; at times you may feel like giving him a swift kick where it hurts the most. It won't do any good, though.

One thing you'll admire about this man is his concern for people who are sickly or troubled. He'll make his shoulder available to anyone in the mood for a good cry. He can listen to one hard-luck story after another without seeming to tire. When his advice is asked, he can be depended upon to offer some wise counsel. He often knows what is bugging someone before that person is aware of it himself. Still, at the end of the day, this man will want some peace and quiet. If you've got a problem when he comes home, don't unload it in his lap. If you do, you are liable to find him short-tempered. He's a good listener but he can only take so much.

Pisceans are not aimless although they may seem so at times. The positive sort of Pisces man is often successful in his profession and is likely to become rich and influential. Material gain, however, is never a direct goal for a man born under this sign.

The weaker Pisces is usually content to stay on the level where he finds himself.

Because of their seemingly laissez-faire manner, people under this sign are immensely popular with children. For tots they play the double role of confidant and playmate. It will never enter their mind to discipline a child, no matter how spoiled or incorrigible that child becomes.

Man—Woman

VIRGO MAN
ARIES WOMAN

The Aries woman may be a little too bossy and busy for you. Generally speaking, the Arien is an ambitious creature. She can become a little impatient with people who are more thorough and deliberate than she is, especially if she feels they're taking too much time. The Aries woman is a fast worker. Sometimes she's so fast she forgets to look where she's going. When she stumbles or falls, it would be nice if you were there to catch her. But the Arien is a proud woman; she doesn't like to be told "I told you so" when she errs. Tongue lashings can turn her into a block of ice. Don't begin to think that the Aries woman frequently gets tripped up in her plans. Many times she is capable of taking aim and hitting the bull's-eye. You'll be flabbergasted by her accuracy as well as by her ambition. On the other hand, you're apt to spot a flaw in your Arien's plans before she does.

You are perhaps somewhat slower than the Arien in attaining your goals. Still, you are not inclined to make mistakes along the way; you're almost always well prepared.

The Aries woman is rather sensitive at times. She likes to be handled with gentleness and respect. Let her know that you love her for her brains as well as for her good looks. Never give her cause to become jealous. When your Aries date sees green, you'd better forget about sharing a rosy future together. Handle her with tender love and care and she's yours.

The Aries woman can be giving if she feels her partner is deserving. She is no iceberg; she responds to the proper masculine flame. She needs a man she can admire and of whom she can feel proud. She can cause you plenty of heartache if you've made up your mind about her but she hasn't made up hers about you. The

Aries woman is very demanding at times. Some tend to be high-strung; they can be difficult if they feel their independence is being hampered.

The cultivated Aries woman makes a wonderful homemaker and hostess. You'll find she's very clever in decorating and using color. Your house will be tastefully furnished; she'll make sure that it radiates harmony. The Aries wife knows how to make guests feel at home.

Although the Aries woman may not be keen on burdensome responsibilities, she is fond of children and the joy they bring.

VIRGO MAN
TAURUS WOMAN

A Taurus woman could perhaps understand you better than most women. She is very considerate and loving. She is thorough and methodical in whatever she does. She is anxious to avoid mistakes.

Home is very important to the Taurus woman. She is an excellent homemaker. Although your home may not be a palace, it will become, under her care, a comfortable and happy abode. She'll love it when friends drop by for the evening. She is a good cook and enjoys feeding people well.

The Taurus woman is serious about love and affection. When she has taken a tumble for someone, she'll stay by him forever, if possible. She will try to be practical in romance, to some extent. When she decides she wants a certain man, she keeps after him until he's won her. Generally, the Taurus woman is a passionate lover, even though she may appear otherwise at first glance. She is on the lookout for someone who can return her affection fully. Taureans are sometimes given to fits of jealousy and possessiveness. They expect fair play in the area of marriage; when it doesn't come about, they can be bitingly sarcastic and mean.

The Taurus woman is usually an easygoing person, who is fond of keeping peace. She won't argue unless she must. She'll do her best to keep your love relationship on an even keel.

Marriage is generally a one-time thing for Taureans. Once they've taken the serious step, they seldom try to back out of it. They are fond of love and warmth and with the right man, they become ideal wives.

The Taurus woman will respect you for your steady ways; she'll have confidence in your common sense. Taurus women seldom put up with nonsense from their children. It is not that they are strict, but rather that they are concerned. They like their children to be well behaved and dutiful. Nothing pleases a Taurus mother more than a compliment from a neighbor or teacher about her child's behavior. Although some children may inwardly resent the iron hand of a Taurus mother, in later life they are often thankful that they were brought up in such an orderly and conscientious way.

VIRGO MAN
GEMINI WOMAN

You may find a romance with a woman born under the sign of the Twins a many-splendored thing. She will provide the intellectual companionship you often look for in a friend or mate. A Gemini girl friend can appreciate your aims and desires because she travels pretty much the same road as you do intellectually, that is, at least part of the way. She may share your interests but she will lack your tenacity.

She suffers from itchy feet. She can be here, there, all over the place. Her eagerness to move about may make you dizzy; still, you'll enjoy and appreciate her liveliness and mental agility.

The Gemini woman often has a sparkling personality; you'll be attracted to her warmth and grace. While she's on your arm you'll probably notice that many male eyes are drawn to her. She may even return a gaze or two, but don't let that worry you. All women born under this sign have nothing against a harmless flirt once in a while. But if she feels she is already spoken for, she will never let it get out of hand.

Although she may not be as handy as you'd like in the kitchen, you'll never go without a filling and tasty meal. The Gemini girl is always in a rush; she won't feel she's cheating by breaking out the instant mashed potatoes or the frozen peas. She may not be a good cook but she is clever; with a dash of this and a suggestion of that, she can make an uninteresting TV dinner taste like something out of a Jim Beard cookbook. Then, again, maybe you've struck it rich and have a Gemini girl friend who finds complicated recipes a challenge to her intellect. If so, you'll find every meal a tantalizing and mouthwatering surprise.

When you're beating your brains out over the Sunday crossword puzzle and find yourself stuck, just ask your Gemini woman; she'll give you all the right answers without batting an eyelash.

Just like you, she loves all kinds of people. You may even find that you're a bit more discriminating than she. Often all that a Geminian requires is that her friends be interesting and stay interesting. But one thing she's not able to abide is a dullard.

Leave the party-organizing to your Gemini sweetheart or mate and you'll never have a chance to know what a dull moment is. She'll bring out the swinger in you if you give her half the chance.

A Gemini mother enjoys her children. Like them, she's often restless, adventurous, and easily bored.

VIRGO MAN
CANCER WOMAN

The girl born under Cancer needs to be protected from the cold, cruel world. She'll love you for your masculine yet gentle manner; you make her feel safe and secure. You don't have to pull any he-man or heroic stunts to win her heart; that's not what interests her. She's more likely to be impressed by your sure, steady ways—that way you have of putting your arm around her and making her feel she's the only girl in the world. When she's feeling glum and tears begin to well up in her eyes, you have that knack of saying just the right thing—you know how to calm her fears, no matter how silly some of them may seem

The girl born under this sign is inclined to have her ups and downs. You have that talent for smoothing out the ruffles in her sea of life. She'll probably worship the ground you walk on or put you on a very high pedestal. Don't disappoint her if you can help it; she'll never disappoint you. The Cancer woman will take great pleasure in devoting the rest of her natural life to you. She'll darn your socks, mend your overalls, scrub floors, wash windows, shop, cook, and do just about anything in order to please you and let you know that she loves you. Sounds like that legendary good old-fashioned girl, doesn't it? Contrary to popular belief, there are still a good number of them around, and many of them are Cancerians.

Of all the signs of the Zodiac, the women under the Cancer sign are the most maternal. In caring for and bringing up children, they know just how to combine the right amount of tenderness with the proper dash of discipline. A child couldn't ask for a better mother. Cancer women are sympathetic, affectionate, and patient with their children.

While we're on the subject of motherhood, there's one thing you should be warned about: never be unkind to your mother-in-law. It will be the only golden rule your Cancerian wife will probably expect you to follow. No mother-in-law jokes in the presence of your Mrs., please. They'll go over like a lead balloon. Mother is something pretty special for her. She may be the crankiest, nosiest old bat this side of the Great Divide, but she's your wife's mother. You'd better treat her like she's one of the landed gentry. Sometimes this may be difficult to swallow, but if you want to keep your home together and your wife happy, learn to grin and bear it.

Treat your Cancer wife like a queen and she'll treat you royally.

VIRGO MAN
LEO WOMAN

The Leo woman can make most men roar like lions. If any woman in the Zodiac has that indefinable something that can make men lose their heads and find their hearts, it's the Leo woman.

She's got more than a fair share of charm and glamour and she knows how to make the most of her assets, especially when she's in the company of the opposite sex. Jealous men are apt to lose their cool or their sanity when trying to woo a woman born under the sign of the Lion. She likes to kick up her heels quite often and doesn't care who knows it. She frequently makes heads turn and tongues wag. You don't necessarily have to believe any of what you hear—it's probably jealous gossip or wishful thinking. Needless to say, other women in her vicinity turn green with envy and will try anything short of shoving her into the nearest lake in order to put her out of the running.

Although this vamp makes the blood rush to your head and makes you momentarily forget all the things you thought were important and necessary in your life, you may feel differently when you come back down to earth and the stars are out of your eyes. You may feel that she isn't the type of girl you planned to bring home to Mother. Not that your mother might disapprove of your choice, but *you* might after the shoes and rice are a thing of the past. Although the Leo woman may do her best to be a good wife for you, chances are she'll fall short of your idea of what a good wife should be like.

If you're planning on not going as far as the altar with the Leo woman you'd better be financially equipped for some very expensive dating. Be prepared to shower her with expensive gifts and to take her dining and dancing to the smartest spots in town. Promise her the moon if you're in a position to go that far. Luxury and glamour are two things that are bound to lower a Leo's resistance. She's got expensive tastes and you'll have to cater to them if you expect to get to first base with this femme.

If you've got an important business deal to clinch and you have doubts as to whether you can swing it or not, bring your Leo woman along to the business luncheon. More than likely, with her on your arm, you'll be able to win any business battle with both hands tied. She won't have to say or do anything, just be there at your side. The grouchiest oil magnate can be transformed into a gushing, obedient schoolboy if there's a charming Leo woman in the room.

Leo mothers are blind to the faults of their children. They

make very loving and affectionate mothers and tend to spoil their offspring.

VIRGO MAN
VIRGO WOMAN

The Virgo woman may be a little too difficult for you to understand at first. Her waters run deep. Even when you think you know her, don't take any bets on it. She's capable of keeping things hidden in the deep recesses of her womanly soul—things she'll only release when she's sure that you're the man she wants. But it may take her some time to come around to this decision. Virgo girls are finicky about almost everything. Many of them have the idea that the only people who can do things correctly are Virgos.

Nothing offends a Virgo woman more than slovenly dress, sloppy character, or a careless display of affection. Make sure your tie is not crooked and your shoes sport a bright shine before you go calling on this lady. Keep your off-color jokes for the locker-room; she'll have none of that. Take her arm when crossing the street, but don't rush the romance. Trying to corner her in the back of a cab may be one way of striking out. Never criticize the way she looks. In fact, the best policy is to agree with her as much as possible. Still, there's just so much a man can take; all those dos and don'ts you have to observe if you want to get to first base with a Virgo may be just a little too much to ask of you. After a few dates, you may decide that she just isn't worth all that trouble. However, the Virgo woman is usually mysterious enough to keep her men running back for more. Chances are you'll be intrigued by her airs and graces.

If lovemaking means a great deal to you, you'll be disappointed at first in the cool ways of your Virgo woman. However, under her glacial facade there lies a hot cauldron of seething excitement. If you're patient and artful in your romantic approach, you'll find that all that caution was well worth the trouble. When Virgos love, it's all or nothing as far as they're concerned.

One thing a Virgo woman can't stand in love is hypocrisy. She doesn't care what the neighbors say, if her heart tells her "Go ahead." She is very concerned with human truths—if her heart stumbles upon another fancy, she is liable to be true to that new heartthrob and leave you standing in the rain.

She's honest to her heart and will be as true to you as you are with her, generally. Do her wrong once, however, and it's farewell.

She's both strict and tender with children. As a mother she'll try to bring out the best in her children.

VIRGO MAN
LIBRA WOMAN

The song goes: it's a woman's prerogative to change her mind. The lyricist must have had the Libra woman in his thoughts when he jotted this ditty out. Her changeability, in spite of its undeniable charm (sometimes) could actually drive even a man of your patience up the wall. She's capable of smothering you with love and kisses one day and on the next avoid you like the plague. If you think you're a man of steel nerves then perhaps you can tolerate these sudden changes without suffering too much. However, if you admit that you're only a mere mortal who can take so much, then you'd better fasten your attention on a girl who's somewhat more constant.

But don't get the wrong idea: a love affair with a Libran can have a lot of plusses to it. The Libra woman is soft, very feminine, and warm. She doesn't have to vamp all over the place in order to gain a man's attention. Her delicate presence is enough to warm the cockles of any man's heart. One smile and you're like a piece of putty in the palm of her hand.

She can be fluffy and affectionate, which you like in a girl. On the other hand, her indecision about which dress to wear, what to cook for dinner, or whether to redo the rumpus room or not could make you tear your hair out. What will perhaps be more exasperating is her flat denial to the accusation that she cannot make even the simplest decision. The trouble is that she wants to be fair or just in all matters; she'll spend hours weighing pros and cons. Don't make her rush into a decision; that will only irritate her.

The Libra woman likes to be surrounded by beautiful things. Money is no object when beauty is concerned. There will always be plenty of flowers in the house. She'll know how to arrange them tastefully, too. Women under this sign are fond of beautiful clothes and furnishings. They will run up bills without batting an eyelash, if given the chance.

Once she's involved with you, the Libra woman will do everything in her power to make you happy. She'll wait on you hand and foot when you're sick and bring you breakfast in bed Sundays. She'll be very thoughtful and devoted. If anyone dares suggest you're not the grandest man in the world, your Libra wife will give that person a good sounding-out.

The Libra woman works wonders with children. Gentle persuasion and affection are all she uses in bringing them up. It works.

VIRGO MAN
SCORPIO WOMAN

When the Scorpio woman chooses to be sweet, she's apt to give the impression that butter wouldn't melt in her mouth but, of course, it would. When her temper flies, so will everything else that isn't bolted down. She can be as hot as a *tamale* or as cool as a cucumber when she wants. Whatever mood she's in, you can be sure it's for real. She doesn't believe in poses or hypocrisy.

The Scorpio woman is often seductive and sultry. Her femme fatale charm can pierce through the hardest of hearts. The Scorpio woman can be a whirlwind of passion. Life with a girl born under this sign will not be all smiles and smooth sailing. If you think you can handle a woman who can purr like a pussycat when handled correctly but spits bullets once her fur is ruffled, then try your luck. Your stable and steady nature will probably have a calming effect on her. You're the kind of man she can trust and rely on. But never cross her, even on the smallest thing; if you do, you'd better tell Fido to make room for you in the doghouse.

Generally, the Scorpio woman will keep family battles within the walls of your home. When company visits, she can be depended upon to give the impression that married life with you is one big joy-ride. It's just her way of expressing her loyalty to you—at least, in front of others. The Scorpio woman will certainly see that others have a high opinion of you both. She'll support you in whatever it is you want to do. Although she's an individualist, after she has married, she'll put her own interests aside for those of the man she loves. With a woman like this behind you, you can't help but go far. She'll never try to take over your role as boss of the family and she'll give you all the support you need in order to fulfill that role. She won't complain if the going gets rough, for she is a courageous woman. She's as anxious as you to find that place in the sun for you both. She is as determined a person as you are.

Although the Scorpio woman may love her children, she may not be very affectionate toward them. She'll make a devoted mother, though and will encourage them to develop their talents. She'll teach the children to be courageous and steadfast.

VIRGO MAN
SAGITTARIUS WOMAN

You'll most likely never meet a more good-natured girl than the one under the sign of Sagittarius. Generally, she is full of bounce and good cheer. Her sunny disposition seems almost permanent and can be relied upon even on the rainiest of days.

The woman born under this sign is rarely malicious. The Sagittarian is often a little short on tact and says literally anything that comes into her pretty head, regardless of the occasion. Sometimes the words that tumble out of her mouth are downright cutting and cruel, but no matter what she says, she means well. Unfortunately, the Sagittarius woman is capable of losing some of her friends—and perhaps even some of yours—through such carelessness.

On the other hand, you are liable to appreciate her honesty and good intentions. To you, qualities of this sort play an important part in life. With a little patience and practice, you can probably help cure your Sagittarian of her loose tongue; in most cases, she'll give in to your better judgement and try to follow your advice to the letter.

Chances are, she'll be the outdoors type of girl friend. Long hikes, fishing trips, and white-water canoeing will probably appeal to her. She's a busy person, who sets great store in mobility. She won't sit still for one minute if it's not necessary.

She is great company most of the time, and even if your buddies drop by for poker and beer, she won't have any trouble fitting in.

On the whole, she is a very kind and sympathetic woman. If she feels she's made a mistake, she'll be the first to call your attention to it. She's not afraid to own up to her own faults and shortcomings.

You might lose your patience with her once or twice. After she's seen how upset her shortsightedness or tendency to blabbermouth has made you, she'll do her best to please you.

The Sagittarius woman is not the kind who will pry into your business affairs. But she'll always be there, ready to offer advice if you need it.

The Sagittarius woman is seldom suspicious. Your word will almost always be good enough for her.

She is a wonderful and loving friend to her children.

VIRGO MAN
CAPRICORN WOMAN

The Capricorn may not be the most romantic woman of the Zodiac, but she's certainly not frigid when she meets the right man. She believes in true love; she doesn't appreciate getting involved in flings. To her, they're just a waste of time. She's looking for a man who means "business"—in life as well as in love. Although she can be very affectionate with her boyfriend or mate, she tends to let her head govern her heart. That is not to say she is a cool, calculating cucumber. On the contrary, she just feels she can be more honest about love if she consults her brains first.

The Capricorn woman is faithful, dependable, and systematic in just about everything she undertakes. She is very concerned with security and makes sure that every penny she spends is spent wisely. She is very economical about using her time, too. She does not believe in whittling away her energy on a scheme that is bound not to pay off.

Ambitious herself, she is often attracted to the ambitious man—one who is interested in getting somewhere in life. If a man of this sort wins her heart, she'll stick by him and do all she can to help him get to the top.

The Capricorn woman is almost always diplomatic. She makes an excellent hostess. She can be very influential when your business acquaintances come to dinner.

The Capricorn woman is likely to be very concerned, if not extremely proud, of her family tree. Relatives are very important to her, particularly if they're socially prominent. Never say a cross word about her family members. She is likely to punish you by not talking to you for days.

As a rule, she's thorough in whatever she does. The Capricorn woman is well mannered and gracious, no matter what her background.

If you should marry a woman born under this sign, you need never worry about her going on a wild shopping spree. She understands the value of money better than most women. If you turn over your pay check to her at the end of the week, you can be sure that a good hunk of it will wind up in the bank.

The Capricorn mother is loving and correct.

VIRGO MAN
AQUARIUS WOMAN

If you find that you've fallen head over heels for a woman born under the sign of the Water Bearer, you'd better fasten your safety belt. It may take you quite a while to actually discover what this girl is like; even then, you may have nothing to go on but a series of vague hunches. The Aquarian is like a rainbow, full of bright and shining hues; she's like no other girl you've ever known. There is something elusive about her.

The Aquarius woman can be pretty odd and eccentric at times. Some say this is the source of her mysterious charm. You are liable to think she's just a plain screwball; you may be 50 percent right. The Aquarius woman often has her head full of dreams. By nature, she is often unconventional; she has her own thoughts about how the world should be run. Sometimes her ideas may seem weird, but chances are they're just a little too progressive. There is a saying that goes, "The way the Aquarian thinks, so will the world in 50 years."

She'll probably be the most tolerant and open-minded woman

you've ever encountered.

If you find that she's too much mystery and charm for you to handle, tell her so and say that you think it would be best to call it quits. She'll probably give you a peck on the cheek and say, "Okay, but let's still be friends." The Aquarius woman is like that. Perhaps you'll both find it easier to get along in a friendship than in a romance.

The Aquarius woman is not a jealous person and, while you're romancing her, she won't expect you to be, either. You'll find her a free spirit most of the time. Just when you think you know her inside-out, you'll discover that you don't really know her at all.

She's a very sympathetic and warm person; she is often helpful to those in need of assistance and advice.

She'll seldom be suspicious even when she has every right to be. If the man she loves makes a little slip, she's inclined to forgive and forget it.

She makes a fine mother. Her positive and big-hearted qualities are easily transmitted to her offspring.

VIRGO MAN
PISCES WOMAN

Many a man dreams of a Piscean kind of a girl. She's soft, cuddly and very domestic. She'll let you be the brains of the family; she's content to just lean on your shoulder and let you be the master of the household.

She can be very ladylike and proper. Your business associates and friends will be dazzled by her warmth and femininity. Although she's a charmer, there is a lot more to her than just a pretty exterior. There is a brain ticking away behind that soft, womanly facade. But you may never become aware of it unless you're married to her.

If she feels you're botching up your married life through careless behavior or if she feels you could be earning more money than you do, she'll tell you so. But any wife would, really.

If anyone dares to say one uncomplimentary word about you in her presence, she is liable to break into tears. The Pisces woman is usually a very sensitive being. Her reaction to adversity, frustration, or anger is just a plain, good, old-fashioned cry.

She'll have an extra-special dinner prepared for you when you make a new conquest in your profession. Don't bother to go into details, though, at the dinner table; she doesn't have much of a head for business matters.

She can do wonders with a house. She is very fond of soft and beautiful things. There will always be plenty of fresh-cut flowers around the house. She'll see that you always have plenty of socks and underwear in that top drawer of your dresser.

Treat her with tenderness and your relationship will be an enjoyable one. She will probably appreciate a box of chocolates. A bunch of beautiful flowers will never fail to make her eyes light up. See that you never forget her birthday or your anniversary. These things are very important to her. If you let them slip your mind, you'll send her into a crying fit that could last a considerable length of time. If you are patient and kind, you can keep a Pisces woman happy for a lifetime. She, however, is not without her faults. Her "sensitivity" may get on your nerves after a while; you may find her lacking in imagination and zest; you may even feel that she uses her tears as a method of getting her own way.

She makes a strong, self-sacrificing mother.

VIRGO

YEARLY FORECAST: 1990

Forecast for 1990 Concerning Business and Financial Matters, Job Prospects, Travel, Health, Romance and Marriage for Those Born with the Sun in the Zodiacal Sign of Virgo. August 22–September 22

You can use all the discrimination and versatility of your ruling planet, Mercury, to promote your interests and talents this year. Seldom will you have opportunities like these offered in 1990 to push yourself to the limit in order to develop your social or public life. A diversity of creative talent can be used and promoted to win you recognition from your contemporaries. You will not wish to be tied down to mundane or routine involvement, but will look for greater issues and wider areas of life in which to develop. As a result your love life and social participation can be more than usually interesting. You may traverse unknown territory for part of the year and gain wider understanding. Career or business prospects can be dependent on the way you develop your creative acumen. Many things you have dreamed of may be realized in concrete form during the year. Your practical mind will keep you attuned to opportunities for increasing earnings and promoting means to secure material security. Much may depend on your intuition and sense of timing. Speculation can pay, once you have established guidelines and are sure of your facts. You are naturally particular about the way you use or make money, so will be able to judge the right time to save and the right time to spend. Be discriminating and look out for those who will try to mislead. Travel should give you a lot of pleasure. As you are never one to relish loneliness, enjoy the company of friends to the full. Get around in a wider circle than up to now and see the sights. Health should be good. There may be some need to take care of others. As you have a talent for this, it will not be a hardship. The health of younger members of the family may be cause for concern, but you have the ability to cope. You may take on too much yourself in some way and this is probably your only potential failing or weakness. So, as long as you act positively and don't feel sorry for yourself you have little to fear. Your life could have changes, and major decisions could be made. Old ideas can go out of the window. Once something is started and making progress, you will not want to fall back into old habits and routines. Look for a strengthening of your resolve to make your mark in the way you know best. Don't be afraid to blow your trumpet and let all see the stuff of what you are made.

Business success can depend to some extent on good publicity and sound public relations. Be discriminating in the way you advertise. But make your point. Time and space can be vital. You have room for the traditional, that which gets to the heart of a subject. There is also scope for material that is entirely novel in this generation. Up till about August 17, be aware that finances should be boosted or developed. This may mean spending, but it is essential to take opportunities that will bring in a greater return. Judgment is necessary. In a year of financial expansion, you will appreciate the need to temper speculation with timing. There may be many possibilities. It will be up to you to sort out those which will pay off. Risks can be too much at times. From August 18 onward to the end of the year, you may be able to take a more detached view and be less conspicuous. Private advice will be helpful. Between January 20 and February 17, it could be wise to increase your staff complement. See that their interests are well protected. You do not want a discontented work force when more production can be expected. Consider ways and means of expanding or sharing the load between February 18 and March 19. This is a good time to consider partnership or joint trading. Get legalities sorted out between April 20 and May 30. Positive action may arouse opposition but can also settle issues. Cooperation of friendly people can open up doors to you between June 21 and July 22. This could be a time, also, when you see the full fruits of your labors in trying to boost profits. Two periods can give you financial or territorial headaches. From March 20 to April 19, and again from May 21 to July 11, you may be pressed about mergers or involvement with larger concerns. Consider taxation consequences and other possible repercussions before making any move. You may be better as a big fish in a small pool than the other way around.

Traditional methods of handling finances may or may not pay off. You should be open to suggestion and give yourself plenty of room to maneuver. Firm decisions may have to be made. Some will wish to be responsible for their own material needs and will make determined efforts to promote their particular talents. Initiative will be rewarded if initial bearings are right and assessments can be proved sound. There can be many a slip between cup and lip. Only by having a go will some be able to gauge the speed of the current. It should be a good year for you who are taking examinations or studying to improve your earning prospects. Tax matters could cause problems in late March and in the first three weeks of April. During the period June to about July 11, you should be careful how far you push in order to make a profit. It may be a success or you could find that outgoings are greater than returns. Young single folk can survive more easily than those who are married and carry family responsibilities. Bank loans should be avoided. You should not lack optimism nor the spirit of adventure; but you must see that your books balance on the right side at the end of the day. Children's expenses can rise. There could be weddings and other social events that must be catered for. Life will not be dull, that's certain. Make the most of your chances and you cannot go far wrong. From August 18 you should be in a position to take life more easily. You may make gains from private or from inside information.

Your desire to enjoy life will keep you fit and in a positive frame of mind. No doubt some will go at it too hard in an effort to make the most of time available. Be careful, as only you can, not to take things too strenuously. Enjoy what you are doing. Once the enjoyment disappears it is time to make a change. You know this simple rule. Active sports or work you enjoy are fine. Traveling when you should be resting is not good for you. From August 18 you will probably want to slow down. If you are doing your usual stint of looking after someone else who is under the weather, a break that will keep you in the background will be welcome. If you have pushed yourself too far, you will need a bit of peace and quiet for yourself. Whatever way it affects you, be philosophical and positive. There's no point in being a martyr. The health of young folk may be worrying, or it could bring out the best in you. The first three weeks of the year, between January 29 and March 10, and the last ten days of December, are possible periods when your attention can be drawn to this particular situation. If there is any long-term condition here, look for opportunities to relieve tension by giving children or yourself a change of air and scenery. Young people always appreciate a change, none more than those who may be obliged to stay cooped up indoors for any length of time.

Major travel can best be undertaken between April 20 and May 20. There should be opportunity to combine work with pleasure. You may wish to develop your love life through travel or may find it a good way to entertain those you love. You are not one for traveling alone.

Work is always something you consider to be important. This year you can be looking further afield for development of your talents. Keeping up your naturally efficient service comes with the package. An early initiative between January 20 and February 17 can start the year on the right foot. Self-employment can appeal to you more than usual this year. Extra effort can lead to recognition between March 11 and April 19. Your services could be needed more than ever after August 18. But you may have some reason to keep your activities under the counter or behind the scenes. Those in the nursing profession should find reward and opportunity in the second half of the year.

Your friends could get a pleasant surprise this year at the way you come out of your shell. A new spirit of adventure can color your love life. This is not time to play second fiddle or to be out of the action. Social activities can bring a sparkle to your eye. If you are on the lookout for a partner, what better way to first cast your net? Practicalities may encourage you to be less choosy. In no way should you lower standards, but you can attract a larger selection group. So life can be very interesting. For you who have marriage on the agenda, the period between April 6 and May 3 could fill the bill. This can be a time when happily married folks can reaffirm their mutual feelings in a practical way as any good Virgo will know. Life can be exciting. From February 1 to March 10 you can take chances more often than usual. Something started then may not be put to rights till the end of December. Variety in your love life will bring ups and downs. There are bound to be disappointments and possibly some heartache. But you will know there is a much wider world in which you can play and your eyes can be opened. Do not take the pain of disappointment too hard. Neither should you cheat or you will find you are being cheated, and that will hurt too. It may be that after August 18 you are ready to relax and take things more easily. By then you will appreciate that privacy is much more important in personal love affairs. So you can have your fling along with the best, but know instinctively how far you should go. Go out of your way to enjoy your year. Do not be afraid and be loving to those who merit your blessings: you have much to give and much to collect.

DAILY FORECAST

January–December 1990

JANUARY

1. MONDAY. Fair. Readers who have been doing a lot of gadding about over the festive season should try now to spend more time in the company of other members of the family. In any case, you are likely to be feeling the strain and you should now be doing what you can to gather your strength. There is quite a lot that you will be wanting to achieve in connection with your career. You should therefore do all in your power to ensure that you are adequately prepared. This is a happy day for the Virgo in love. Romance would appear to be in the cards. Some of you may even be naming a wedding day. Your opposite number may have a special surprise for you.

2. TUESDAY. Deceptive. Be careful in whom you put your trust. This is not a good period to go jumping into new business deals that are highly speculative feetfirst. Friends and associates may be trying to get you to invest in schemes where there is an element of risk. You must be guided by your own intuition. The only sort of people you should be listening to now are relatives who are older and more experienced than you are. This is the right day for placing advertisements in newspapers if you have any special purchases that you wish to make. Business partnership enterprises can be especially successful. But influential people may make promises to you that they will not be able to keep.

3. WEDNESDAY. Uncertain. People may be trying to impress you with wild stories of their successes that are simply not true. Do not try to rival friends who say that they have made gains through speculation. Stick doggedly to routine jobs that you know will yield gains over a long period of time. You need only to prove to influential people if you wish to gain promotion that you have staying power and plenty of grit and determination. Loans that you were hoping would come from professional people may not be forthcoming. Bankers and insurance companies may let you down. Any money that you are holding on behalf of others should not be used for speculation or any other risky venture.

4. THURSDAY. Tricky. Perhaps you have not been getting enough sleep lately. Many of you may still be recovering from the recent round of partying and celebrating in general. Count the cost of Christmas. There seems to be every reason why you should now be making certain important cutbacks. Play your hand very close when it comes to dealing with your career. You must not allow competitors to expose your weak spots. When you see the chance to make a gain at your place of employment you should do all that you can to bring yourself to the attention of superiors. Go along more with the wishes of others. If people are not in the mood for talking, do not keep on chattering constantly.

5. FRIDAY. Changeable. You may be feeling a little disappointed at this time. You have not been able to make the gains that you were hoping to thus far in this new decade. However, you must not become disenchanted with the 1990's so soon. Remember that the year is only five days old. There are still quite a few tasks that you have to complete in connection with the year that has just ended. It could be some time before you can make the exciting new starts that you had planned. This looks like a promising day in the personal area of your life. Someone who you have been secretly carrying a torch for may now show that he or she has more than a passing interest in you. Travel is starred whether it be for business or pleasure.

6. SATURDAY. Mixed. A good deal of paperwork will probably have to be carried out. Quite a lot of your time today is likely to be taken up with odd jobs. These may perhaps stop you from obtaining all of the pleasure and entertainment that you had been hoping for. More self-discipline will have to be exercised. Younger readers, and Virgo-born people who are taking courses after leaving school or college, will find that professors and teachers will be particularly helpful. You should not try to go it alone when experienced people will be only too keen to assist you in any way that they can. When it comes to evening time, it is inadvisable to leave loved ones alone.

7. SUNDAY. Rewarding. This will be just the kind of a day that you need. You will be able to get on with chores in and around the house. They have been nagging away at the back of your mind during the past weeks. Pay up on all outstanding bills connected with Christmas and the New Year. You will feel far more comfortable if you can get a picture of your financial situation in its totality. This is a day for mulling over your plans for the future. Secret thoughts can be made more practical. You may well have a chance to put them into practice later in the week. Listen to what loved ones have to say as they may be able to give you some good advice in connection with your career.

8. MONDAY. Uncertain. It may be somewhat difficult to motivate yourself this first workday. Try to bring more flair and originality to your work. This piece of advice will be especially relevant to those who are involved in any jobs connected with the arts and show business. You may be well aware that some of your efforts have been getting rather stale and lacking in luster of late. You may also have some trouble in keeping a hold on your temper. There may be some people out to frustrate Virgos' ambitions deliberately. In all professional matters it is important not to tread on other people's toes. Make sure that you are covered by adequate insurance where it counts.

9. TUESDAY. Useful. It is not going to be at all easy to knuckle down to routine matters today. But it is essential that you do so. Influential people will be expecting quite a lot from you today. There will not be much opportunity to earn bonus payments, either. But Virgos who are self-employed will have better opportunities to increase business profits. Meetings with influential people will go off quite well for you. However, you must beware of trying to push your luck too far if you are hoping to arrange for a loan. At home, you may have to give youngsters more individual attention. This will be true especially if you feel that their performance at school has been dropping off. Take time to listen to their problems and to share their hopes.

10. WEDNESDAY. Difficult. Get more fresh air and exercise. You may not be feeling one hundred percent physically fit. Perhaps some of you have put on quite a bit of weight over the recent festive season. It would not do you any harm, probably a lot of good to exercise a little more self-discipline generally. Hopes for the future can be dashed. It may well be that you have been expecting too much of superiors. A new job that you were hoping to land may be given to someone else. In fact, this person may well be promoted over you. Perhaps this is a good time to look for another job. Influential people are not likely to grant favors. But the evening will be a pleasant time for socializing with friends.

11. THURSDAY. Difficult. This will be an unsettled sort of a day. News that you were hoping to come through, either by the mail or telephone, is not likely to arrive on time. Loved ones' preferences will be difficult to pin down. Plans for changes in the home that you were hoping to make are going to have to be left up in the air. You must try to discipline your thinking and not become overly reliant on others. There will be times when you find it difficult to concentrate on routine work. Your own worrying and fretting could be your greatest drawback. Try to get some exercise and fresh air. It may be necessary to pay a visit to your doctor because of minor ailments.

12. FRIDAY. Disquieting. Today will be very similar to yesterday. So far, this week has been something of a disappointment to you. You do not appear to have been able to get many of the plans that you were hoping to launch in 1990 off the ground yet. The decade has not begun as successfully as you would have hoped. Virgos can easily go astray and forget what their true aims and aspirations actually are. Energy and thought must be concentrated on what can do you the most good from the work point of view. Time should not be frittered away. Steer clear of the company of people who are aimless and do not have enthusiasm for getting on in the world. There may be problems with youngsters.

13. SATURDAY. Demanding. You should not overspend today. You may not be as well off as you would like to think. Remember the bills connected with Christmas and the New Year that you still have to pay. You could be tempted to splurge on so-called bargains that are being advertised in the January sales. First you should ask yourself if you really do need the various things that are being reduced. Loved ones will not give you the sort of sound advice that you have come to expect from them. Your mate or partner may want you to dip into funds that have been earmarked to pay regular bills. If the reason for this is spending the money for pleasure and entertainment, refuse.

14. SUNDAY. Happy. Many of you will be relieved to realize that this day of rest has dawned again. You will be grateful for the opportunity to draw a deep breath and go back to sleep. It looks as though Virgos will be doing quite a lot of replanning for their careers. This is the result of what has taken place in the past week. You will certainly feel a lot better if you can change your routine in any way. This is an easier day for exercising self-discipline. Start diets and keep-fit courses. Now is the time to explore new avenues and to venture into the unknown. Discussions with strangers that you meet while traveling could be especially stimulating. You resent giving up, no matter what.

15. MONDAY. Productive. Try to put more effort into your regular job. People at your place of employment will be impressed if you show added enthusiasm. There must be ways that you can find to brighten up jobs that have become dull and routine. Think of different work patterns and finds ways to speed up chores. Loved ones will be helpful. There will not be as many interruptions to cope with for Virgos who are attempting to operate from their home base. Taking on additional responsibilities will have long-term advantages for you. Those of you who have recently left school may find that they can get involved in some charity work. This could prove to be a useful stopgap until something more worthwhile can be found.

16. TUESDAY. Satisfactory. Virgos could well be highly rated for their stability and efficiency today. You should be going all out to impress influential people now. You will have the chance to put yourself in line for some sort of promotion. This will not only increase your income but also your status. The health of loved ones which may have been giving you some cause for concern is more likely to improve. There will not be as many problems of a personal nature to contend with. This will mean that you can channel your concentration much more positively. But be wary of allowing yourself to be proposed as a member of a club or society. This could be far more expensive than you might imagine.

17. WEDNESDAY. Disconcerting. Perseverance when dealing with creative or artistic jobs is likely to be rewarded. You should be able to make good progress with anything that gives you an outlet for your natural talents. Influential people will be impressed by your imaginative qualities. Virgo readers who are able to operate from their home base are likely to be more successful today than they had imagined. But Virgos must be careful not to slip when it comes to being practical and realistic. Do not allow yourself to be carried away on the wave of another's enthusiasm. You may be feeling more emotional under the surface than you would care to admit. Try to pinpoint the reasons.

18. THURSDAY. Mixed. This is not a day for taking gambles. Do not risk investment in any project where the stakes are high or the possibility of loss is great. Hang on to your savings. You are likely to have to use the money that you have on reserve sooner than you think. Do not look to rich friends or relatives to advance you any loans. This is a period when you are likely to find that you have to stand very much on your own two feet. It will be easier than usual to become friendly with influential people at your place of employment. This will make it considerably easier to concentrate on your regular job. The evening will be favorable for meeting people with whom you would like to become involved.

19. FRIDAY. Rewarding. There will be no doubt about it. This will be one of the best days that you have experienced so far this month and this year. You will be able to regain control over work situations that you may have felt were slipping from your grasp. Now is the time to take the initiative and do your utmost to get your original ideas accepted by those in authority. Draw your natural talents to the attention of your boss. Try to get out and about more. You will be able to score some success with people at a distance. This will be especially true if you are trying to win orders from them. Virgos should attempt to collect any unusual tidbits of information that might come in useful to them at a later date.

20. SATURDAY. Sensitive. Much of this day is likely to be spent tidying up the loose ends of your work and business affairs. You certainly do not want to have any of these hanging over your head when the time comes to take your weekend break. This is an excellent period for coming to grips with accounts and for paying regular bills. Even if you are left a bit short of ready cash, it is the best way for keeping solvent. Go over the books. Discuss with loved ones ways in which additional savings can be made. Neighbors may be trying to stir up trouble. Do not get involved in gossip. Keep your nose out of others' affairs in the locality in which you live. The evening will be a favorable period for entertaining influential people.

21. SUNDAY. Happy. Keep your composure and you should have no problems. Do not allow youngsters to rattle you into losing your temper with their way-out and fanciful ideas. Be confident that what you have learned through your own experience is right for you. The husbands and wives of Virgo folk may be unpredictable. This should not affect you adversely unless you try to correct them or react emotionally. You will probably feel most comfortable at home. There are plenty of little jobs in and around the home that you usually enjoy attending to. Take this golden opportunity to do exactly as you like. Read, or watch TV, or take the children on a special trip such as a Zoo or museum.

22. MONDAY. Quiet. A peaceful beginning to the work week would appear to be in store for you. You should be able to move easily into top gear. What will please you most about the conditions this Monday is the fact that you will be able to work at a pace that suits you. It's far better than having to dance to the tune that other people are trying to call. It is good for tying up the loose ends of work and business. You will be pleased to get rid of jobs that have been hanging over your head all too long. Influential people will show greater understanding for what you are trying to achieve. If you manage to bring outstanding work loads to a close today, employers can be especially pleased.

23. TUESDAY. Confusing. What will worry you most about today is a matter connected with a member of your family. It seems that news you receive about a relative who lives at a distance will give you cause for some concern. There does not seem to be very much that you can do to assist in any way at this point. Still, it is matters such as these that will affect your concentration at your work place. Influential people may notice the fact that your job performance is not up to your usual high standards. Do not overreach yourself though. It would be best to stick to the kind of work that is well within your capacity. Children should be treated with more discipline if they remain disobedient.

24. WEDNESDAY. Mixed. Try to engage in some new interest that will include your mate. Loved ones may have been feeling a little left out of your life recently. Make sure that you do all that you can to strengthen the ties of affection between you and your opposite number. This can be a day of rapid ups and downs. But Virgo people should aim for the middle path and not allow themselves to become too elated or too depressed. Romantic partners may insist on trying something out of the ordinary. You will have to go along with them for the sake of a quiet life. Spare time is favorable for creative or artistic work. If you have talent, don't let it slide. Widen your scope at every chance.

25. THURSDAY. Successful. This will probably be the best day of the week, if not the year thus far. You will have more energy and driving force on tap. Loved ones will be eager for you to advance in your career. You will not feel so restricted or tied down to home and family affairs. Loved ones will be more willing to take responsibilities for their own actions. This will come as something of a huge relief to you. Older relatives will come forward with advice that should be heeded. It is a day when the Virgo-born person can afford to spend some of his or her money on a little gift for a loved one or sweetheart. This is a good time for implementing pleasure or entertainment plans for later on.

26. FRIDAY. Lucky. Follow through on your own ideas as well as others' today. Your fertile imagination should be working overtime. But there is no point in being mentally creative if you do not put your ideas into action once they are workable. Virgo people who deal with the public should enjoy more success than usual. Communication of all kinds will be especially important. Advertising, newspapers, broadcasting and the like should have great significance. You will be able to perform at your very best at your place of employment. This may mean that you will be putting yourself in line for promotion in the not-too-distant future. New diets could become health aids, provided they are based on sound, nutritional values.

27. SATURDAY. Difficult. There is likely to be a last-minute change of plans which will upset your apple cart. You and your mate or partner are not likely to see eye-to-eye on many matters. This is a period when you will have to try much harder than usual not to lose your temper. Take things easy. It is important that you do not overdo mentally or physically. It looks as if there could be an end to a romantic relationship. An affair with someone who you have been going out with for quite awhile may be terminated this weekend. You may feel that you have lost your direction a little bit for the moment. Feelings of resentment may be in the air. If you have them, try to concentrate on something important.

28. SUNDAY. Rewarding. A more optimistic mood is likely to prevail today. Family affairs, on the whole, will go in a direction that pleases you a great deal more. Some useful information may come from people behind the scenes. There could be a way by which you can advance considerably in your career plans, even though this is a Sunday. People whom you meet during a social functions may be able to supply you with information that you would not be able to come by otherwise. A constructive balance can be achieved between business and marital partnerships. Virgos will delight in performing humanitarian or compassionate actions. They benefit equally with those they try to help.

29. MONDAY. Lucky. Short trips may be numerous and will prove to be more effective than the telephone. If you want any special favors granted by influential people, it would be best to deal with them face-to-face. You will have more driving force at your disposal than usual. You will also be in a more constructive and positive frame of mind. Discretion will be invaluable in dealing with matters of a sensitive legal nature. You may be able to work out a deal with someone behind the scenes that will save you the expense of going to a court of law. Favor compromise solutions wherever possible. This is an auspicious day for marital affairs. The confidence of your beloved will be more easily won today.

30. TUESDAY. Difficult. The chances are that this will be a rather unsettled day from the domestic point of view. It would seem that there are likely to be fights over the breakfast table. Try to avoid head-on collisions with other members of the family. Such rifts will not be easy to heal. They could also have the effect of damaging your work performance. Mixing business with pleasure will not be a good idea. Do not allow friends to interfere with the way you handle your job. Influential people will be critical of your work performance if you veer away from the guidelines laid down for you. Bills may have to be paid which you thought you had settled in full. There could be some discrepancies in your accounts.

31. WEDNESDAY. Disconcerting. This month comes to an end with your feeling rather unsure of yourself. You may consider that you have not achieved all that you could have during the first month of the year. But perhaps, on reflection, you will see that you were probably aiming too high from the start. Friends will be quick to anger today. It would be a wise policy for you to keep off subjects on which you know, from past experience, you hold widely differing views. Misunderstandings can easily arise in romance and any attempts at smoothing over differences could actually make matters worse. Pleasure plans for this evening may have to be written off.

FEBRUARY

1. THURSDAY. Successful. It will be easier now for you to attend to jobs that you may have been putting off during the first month of the year. There will not be so many interruptions to contend with for Virgo readers who are attempting to operate from their home base. But it will be helpful if you make an early start. Do not linger over that early morning cup of tea or coffee. Business dealings with people at a distance will be lucrative. This is a good day for travel for those of you with a mind to improve your overall prospects. Today would be favorable for putting more exertion into creative and artistic projects. The longer the time lapse between work on these, the harder it will be to return.

2. FRIDAY. Sensitive. Virgo people must follow their own plans and stick to their own ideas, whatever the opposition. After all, if you do not believe in yourself, who is going to believe in you? Perseverance will bring you much nearer to your goals. Do not take no for an answer. This is a period when you should simply keep plugging away. A more subtle and indirect approach will be beneficial for Virgos who are dealing with publishers and other kinds of people in the literary world. Distant government officials may be obstructive. The media can be hostile to those of you who, because of the nature of your work, are in the public eye. It all depends, of course, on just how much influence you have.

3. SATURDAY. Confusing. A rather unsettled ending to the week would appear to be in store for you. There will be interruptions to your plans at home. This will also be true for Virgos who are attending their regular place of employment. They are trying to wind up outstanding jobs and will be delayed. Youngsters will be difficult to handle. It will not be easy for you to keep control of your temper. But you should make an extra effort to rise above petty emotional differences. It is important that you try harder to keep things in perspective. Do not do anything that would put you on the wrong side of the law. Make every effort to keep your accounts in order. It could only save you time later.

4. SUNDAY. Excellent. Business can be mixed with pleasure in a most satisfactory way today. Minor problems can be straightened out. You will have more control over your career. This is a good day for arranging to see influential people under informal conditions. You will find it easier to put your point of view across in a calm and orderly fashion. In all matters, personal work and service will be invaluable. Your mate or partner should not be neglected, either. Do what you can to patch up little differences in the home by suggesting a special treat. This could range from having dinner out to some kind of entertainment. Today is favorable for the single Virgo who is keen to further his or her plans.

5. MONDAY. Good. This will be an important beginning to the working week. Make sure that you start out today as you mean to finish at your place of employment. Work out a plan of campaign that will be easier for you to stick to. Loved ones will be more understanding and will show greater sympathy for what your are attempting to achieve. Your mate or partner may be willing to take over certain duties within the home. That would leave you more time to attend to outside matters. Virgos may find that they benefit, in an indirect way, from other people's good luck. New career opportunities can be especially lucrative. Business profits can be boosted in an unexpected and beneficial way.

6. TUESDAY. Frustrating. This will be a rather unsettled day from a domestic point of view. The health of elders may impose some restrictions on your personal pleasure. Your mate may have some rather peculiar ideas that you will find hard to understand. It will contribute to your peace of mind to let others go their own way. Any zeal to reform people or to show them the way according to your beliefs should be stifled. Just as you like to be a free agent, so will others today. Do not tire yourself out by living on the edge of your nerves. Rest and quiet will be essential for a few hours if you are feeling jittery or strained. Find companions who share your interests tonight. Avoid the argumentative types.

7. WEDNESDAY. Demanding. This could be another day when you may find that you are having to concern yourself with the affairs of others. They will embroil you rather more than you really like. Virgo people will feel frustrated. They are not able to get on with matters that would help them to advance their own career interests. There may also be problems of a romantic nature that make you feel rather emotional. Virgos are unlikely to be able to make the progress that they had counted on. People's suspicions may be unfounded, but will nevertheless tend to slow down the proceedings even further. Friendship and romance will simply not mix very well. Gambling should be avoided.

8. THURSDAY. Easygoing. This will be just the sort of a day that your mind and body require. You will have a chance to slow down the tempo of your life. The pace will be one that you find reasonably able to cope with. The chances are you have been attempting to cram too much into your schedule this week. All in all, this will be a fairly undemanding kind of a day. Virgos must resist the temptation to invent problems when there are really none! Today is good for working for other people. You should be able to win the support of superiors. It might even be possible to get the O.K. from superiors to launch new projects that are very close to your heart next week.

9. FRIDAY. Disturbing. There are likely to be financial problems brewing that you find extremely difficult to cope with. Loved ones will be extravagant and this is more than likely to add to your worries. This is a day when you will have to be looking at your spending policy and attempting to find ways in which cuts can be made. Virgo people may find that they have taken on rather more than they have bargained for. Terms of agreement will have to be spelled out in full. Attempts at putting your hands on confidential information could lead to trouble with the authorities. Do not do anything that could put you on the wrong side of the law. Children should be kept away from dangerous tools and machinery.

10. SATURDAY. Happy. The week ends on an upward swing for you. You will suddenly find that you have the energy and the know-how to cope with certain problems that have been weighing you down all week. Loved ones will be more understanding today than has been the case recently. There are likely to be new avenues opening up for you that will enable you to cope with problems in the home. Virgos' ability to turn complex situations to their own advantage will stand them in good stead. You may find that you are able to handle difficult matters without so much as blinking an eye. The evening will be a good period for socializing and also for romance.

11. SUNDAY. Enjoyable. This will be a day full of surprises, but do not worry. Most of them will be pleasant ones. It looks as if you will be renewing an acquaintance with someone whom you have not seen for quite some time. A friend who has been out of your life in recent years is likely to come back into it with pleasant consequences. Do not limit yourself in any direction. You have had a pretty topsy-turvy sort of a week and this is the day when you should be getting out and about and having fun. But Virgo people are right to be more cautious as far as work and business are concerned. There will be a good chance for attending to little repair jobs, in and around the home, that require attention.

12. MONDAY. Uncertain. Perhaps this will not be quite the promising start to the work week that you had been hoping for. Still and all, you will be able to make good, if fairly limited, progress. People at your place of employment will be pleasant enough. But it may not be possible to get anything that requires team effort off the ground. In matters of speculation, the stakes will be high, probably far too high. Do not invest your hard-earned savings in the fanciful schemes of others, however persuasively they are proposed to you. Group and club events will be far too expensive for you to organize. Quick thinking on the part of Virgo employees can win them bonuses. Today would be favorable for attending to medical checkups.

13. TUESDAY. Demanding. This will not be a very exciting day. You will be hampered by difficult conditions at home. Loved ones will be hard to get along with. There will be particular problems for the Virgo parent. You may have to be stricter with youngsters than you like and this will cause upheavals. You may also have some difficulty in controlling your temper. At your place of employment you are likely to find it difficult to concentrate. This, of course, could lead you into open conflict with your boss. Employers will be expecting more of you. You must do better at keeping your work neat and tidy. Departing from the stipulations and guidelines laid down for you will certainly cause trouble.

14. WEDNESDAY. Sensitive. Do not try to dictate to other people how they should live their lives. People will be finding you far too dogmatic. You must take more of a live-and-let-live attitude. This is not a particularly favorable day for either borrowing or lending money. Emergencies may arise in connection with children. This could mean that you have to take time off from work in order to get home to attend to domestic problems. Experience may be an insufficient guideline for handling financial matters. You need to handle your savings with a good deal more caution. But romance looks more promising. Virgos who are dating tonight should be well pleased at the way things go.

15. THURSDAY. Sensitive. This will be another day very similar to yesterday. You may be getting just a little frustrated this week so far. You have not been able to make the progress with new projects that you were hoping to. One of the problems that your are likely to encounter is raising capital for projects that need more money. You are not able, of course, to put money into them personally. Influential people who may have said they would support you may now renege on their promises at the last moment. Concentration may not be as good as usual. You will find it difficult to deal with accounts. Virgo people may find that they go in for a good deal of clock watching at the office or store.

16. FRIDAY. Mixed. This would be a good day for giving loved ones a special treat or surprise. Your mate or partner will warm to you if you show that you really do have his or her interests at heart. You do not need to spend a great deal of money on pleasure and entertainment. But it is important that you do more in conjunction with other members of the family. It may be possible to wind up a job that you had been thinking you would have to leave until after the weekend. Virgos may perceive subtleties that no one else has noticed. People can be persuaded to follow any lead that you give. But you should remember that they must be led and not pushed and this will be a long-term process.

17. SATURDAY. Tricky. Leave yourself more time to wind up jobs than you may have earmarked. This is not a day for rushing any work that needs attention to detail. You are well known for this latter quality, so you do not want to do anything to spoil your reputation with your employers. Members of your family will be making more demands on you than ever. It may not be possible to get away with friends on your own unless you are prepared to face the consequences with your mate or partner. It may even be necessary to put in some overtime. Neighbors may appeal to the law if you are mixed up in any kind of dispute with them. It's a favorable time for drawing up long-term agreements with agencies.

18. SUNDAY. Good. It will be just the sort of a day that the doctor ordered! You will be feeling in a much more confident and optimistic mood. It may be possible to find solutions to problems that have been bothering you for some time. This is a favorable day for home entertaining, especially if you can mix business with pleasure. Loved ones will help you if you are attempting to do yourself some good in your career by asking superiors over. This would be a good day for working in and around the home. With time and effort, you can make it a more attractive and comfortable place in which to live. You will get a great deal of pleasure from puttering around and dealing with odd jobs.

19. MONDAY. Happy. There should be welcome change of pace today. You will be pleased to come to grips with new jobs that represent any kind of a challenge to you. But less effort will be required to produce outstanding results. Influential people will be giving you more of an opportunity to show off your natural talents in a favorable light. There will be no need to rush or hurry. In fact, the best results will be obtained if Virgos carry on their activities at a pace that suits them. Creative work is starred and can be turned into major sources of income. Your mind will be as active as ever and the chances are there will be much mental work to be done. Evening will find you keen to pursue hobbies for spare time.

20. TUESDAY. Sensitive. You are in the midst of a period when health may dominate situations. It may be necessary to call in on your doctor for a checkup. Do not ever ignore minor ailments. The best way to counteract them is to nip them in the bud. Legal decisions that are made today will tend to favor the Virgo person. You should be pleased if any court cases in which you are involved are heard today. If children or older relatives seem to be in the need of medical attention, make sure that they get it. People in positions of authority can help in your efforts to turn creative enterprises into major sources of income. Such people can be treated more as equals than superiors in this sort of situation.

21. WEDNESDAY. Mixed. You really must make more of an effort to come to grips with jobs that you may have been putting off for some considerable time. You will find that there are many people who will be willing to give you a helping hand if you do not try to do it alone. Remember that no man or woman is an island unto themselves. This is a day for sharing, both materially and emotionally. At your place of employment, however, you must be careful when dealing with influential people. There is a greater risk than ever that Virgos will try to push their luck too far. Children may ask their Virgo parents for explanations. These should be given without any beating about the bush, insofar as is possible.

22. THURSDAY. Manageable. Those of you attending social functions may easily find yourselves involved in a clandestine affair. Or you could be making arrangements you do not want the world to know about. In business, secrecy is apt to further your chances for success. Beware of associates who are loud-mouthed or indiscreet as a result of too much liquor. Do not be drawn into their conversations. Influential people are apt to show Virgo folk special favors. There should be at least one opportunity for you to make new friends today. This is a favorable day, too, for coming to grips with all routine matters in and around the home. These may have been delayed for one reason or another.

23. FRIDAY. Uncertain. Keep your wits about you. Be first. If you are quick enough off the mark you may be able to make such progress that it could lead to promotion and a salary increase. Of course these advantages are not likely to become available to you right away. Employment activities should be given more of your time. Do not allow your personal desires to get in the way of your career. Influential people will only be willing to give you a helping hand if they can see that you are really determined to get to the top of the tree. Go over your bank accounts. Make sure that any money that you have on deposit is earning the best possible interest for you. But although Virgos can be accurate when it comes to details, they may be off the track with their overall appraisals.

24. SATURDAY. Rewarding. A pleasant and even stirring end to the working week is all but assured. You seem to be in the kind of a mood in which you can make important gains. You can even get through a greater work load than usual. Your mate or partner will be more amenable than heretofore to your ideas for change and progress. This is a favorable day for family shopping expeditions. There may be articles that you have been wanting to get for the home that you can pick up at rock bottom prices. Go to markets and attend auctions as these are the places where you are the most likely to find the bargains. This is a good day for launching business partnership ventures and getting publicity for them.

25. SUNDAY. Excellent. Coupled with what took place yesterday, this is likely to be a first-class weekend. In fact, this will probably be the best weekend period that you have experienced so far this year. Loved ones will be easy to see eye-to-eye with. You may be able to have some of your more important changes that you have been wanting to put into practice for some time accepted by other members of the family. Partners may also be able to provide valuable introductions to people in positions of power and authority. Some Virgos may have been unhappy with present employment conditions. They may now be able to effect the changes that they have been wanting to make for some time. Today would be good for seeking new diversions and entertainment.

26. MONDAY. Mixed. Do not beat about the bush. Start this working week as you mean to finish it. You will find that there is plenty of incentive for you to come to grips with work. You should be making more of an effort now to replace money that you spent as long ago as Christmas and the New Year. Remember all of the heavier winter bills that are now and soon will be coming in. This is not a day when you can afford to give way to extravagant impulses. But it is a pleasant day for romance. You may be able to strengthen long-term relationships that have been getting a bit mundane. Some of you may be able to fix up second honeymoons.

27. TUESDAY. Uncertain. Aim at branching out into new fields of endeavor, but take loved ones with you if you possibly can. The understanding and affectionate helpfulness of family members is likely to be a boon. You will have a better chance of getting through odd jobs connected with home and family affairs if you do all that you can to promote teamwork. Benefits and gains of a material nature are apt to come your way through strangers. These will probably become your friends in time. By joining a lively group of people with interests similar to your own it will do you a world of good. But appeals for tax exemptions are likely to be turned down.

28. WEDNESDAY. Difficult. Domestic problems that crop up are not likely to be easy to solve. Matters connected with legacies or inheritances may involve considerable embarrassment. You will not be able to reach any agreement with older relatives who have some kind of an emotional hold over you. It is also possible that Virgos will be prevented from having free access to their own or their partners' assets. Investments may not be providing the economic security that they were intended to secure. At your place of employment you will be bored with talk. You are ill at ease with such a waste of time and will want to get on with some action. You may be hiding something from yourself at this point. The sooner you face up to it, the better off you will be.

MARCH

1. THURSDAY. Successful. You will now be turning your attention to planning some of the things that you want to achieve in the coming Spring weeks. You probably feel that there is much that you have not achieved as yet this year. Such feelings of frustration will serve to push you into action. You may realize that you have been a little negative thus far this year. So you will be anxious to put the record straight. Loved ones will be helpful and will show more understanding for what you are trying to achieve. This will be particularly helpful and will provide more incentive. Unconventional methods will be successful in the handling of business and professional affairs. But don't carry these too far.

2. FRIDAY. Fair. Do what you can to broaden your horizons. Sometimes you reveal a somewhat one-track mind. Unfortunately, this can limit you and put the damper on many of the prize talents that you possess. The future should be looking more secure now. It might be a good idea to take it upon yourself to find a second job that would enable you to supplement your income. Remember the big bills that are always associated with this time of the year. Youngsters should be encouraged to take more initiative. Offspring may need a little pushing to make more of their natural talents. They will welcome your interest and thank you for the help. Favorable for making a move in new romantic attractions.

3. SATURDAY. Disconcerting. You will have rather more work to deal with than you like. There will be matters connected with your regular job that will really demand your attention. You may suddenly realize that you need more money to keep afloat. Actors and other members of artistic professions will have studies to carry on. These will probably require them to cut themselves off from friends for a time. Virgo people must not waste time and opportunities by splitting hairs. Do not allow yourself to get sidetracked by getting involved in petty arguments with your mate or partner. You may be feeling that you are not getting the recognition from loved ones that is due to you.

4. SUNDAY. Enjoyable. This will be a specially happy and joyful day of rest. You will find that it is extremely pleasant to do your own thing. There may be unusual and out-of-the-way opportunities available for enjoying yourself. Friends may be on the phone to you with plans for going out. These will enable you to let your hair down and forget about your work-a-day problems. You will enjoy a change of scenery and environment. Today would also be good for furthering secret business negotiations under social conditions. Making a greater effort to get on more intimate terms with influential people could have favorable results. Children will thrive on understanding, sympathy and encouragement.

5. MONDAY. Uncertain. Perhaps it will be a little difficult today for you to get back into the routine. There may be demands on you at home that will prevent your getting to work on time. Try to let superiors know in advance by telephoning them if you are going to be late. There could also be delays on public transportation systems as well as on the roads. Do more to promote team effort, once you do get to the office or store. There are many jobs that you can handle much better by joining forces with others. This could be a favorable time for signing legal documents or partnership agreements. Do what you can to make the future look more secure for you and yours.

6. TUESDAY. Sensitive. The advice of friends may be valuable. There appear to be certain personal problems that are bottled up inside of you. These would definitely be helped with a little sympathy and understanding on the part of others. Business financial procedures are best kept as they are. Do not borrow from money that you may have earmarked to pay regular bills. Casual acquaintances can turn into close friends. People with whom you have only been on nodding terms will surprise you. Current contracts that you would very much like to be rid of will unfortunately be binding. You must not do anything to upset influential people who have been helpful to you in the past.

7. WEDNESDAY. Demanding. Don't be such a worrier. Do not try to straighten out problems that have not even developed yet. This would be a useful day for doing more work in the background. You may find it a little hard to get on with others. Attempts at self-expression are not likely to live up to your expectations. Loved ones may not be feeling in the best of spirits. Your mate or partner could put a bit of a damper on home life. The more time that you are able to spend on your own the better it is likely to suit you. Reassuring members of your family that they are cared for and badly needed will take quite a lot of your time. But you know that it will have been worth every minute.

8. THURSDAY. Useful. It looks as though you will be back on the right track once again. There is not likely to be anything to stop you from doing the things that you want to do. Try to reach a better understanding with the people you have to work alongside. You can do a lot to improve the atmosphere at the office or store. Suspicions that you have been harboring about a loved one are quite likely to turn out to be entirely unfounded. Virgo people should not voice their opinions prematurely. Driving will require far more care than usual. Do not take any silly risks if you are behind the wheel. Do not speed or go through red lights even if you are late for important appointments.

9. FRIDAY. Happy. This will be one of the best days of the year you have experienced so far, if not the best. You will be able to pull many things together. You had not been able to do so because of other demands. This is a particularly good day for Virgos who are trying to break into the world of entertainment. This will be especially true of the jazz world. The time is good for combining with others to write songs or create anything else of an artistic nature. This is a time when secret hopes and wishes can be fulfilled. Going out with romantic partners this evening will be exciting. You and your beloved may decide that the time has come to get engaged or to name that all-important day.

10. SATURDAY. Uncertain. Virgo people can afford to take a chance today without serious risk. A calculated one is likely to pay off. You may receive a tip to bet on a horse, but do not put your life's savings on it. If the horse is not first past the finishing post you would be a big loser. It appears as though long shots have a better chance of bringing you in extra money. The voice of your own conscience is likely to be right. The advice of other people is as likely to be wrong as it is right. This is especially true in all matters connected with your career. People may forget to pass messages on to you. Evening is a time for going out, but not for spending too much money.

11. SUNDAY. Manageable. This is not a day for crossing swords with people in authority. Keep your nose clean. Do not do anything that could put you on the wrong side of the law. Try to spend more time at home. There are people there who need both your time and assistance. Try to make it up to loved ones if you have been neglecting them somewhat in the week just come to a close. Superiors should not be challenged. You may be feeling a little depressed about the situation at your place of employment. Do not bring such issues up with the boss, however, until you have the chance to discuss the matter with him or her at the office or factory. Perseverance in all matters will be rewarded.

12. MONDAY. Changeable. Make sure that you get to work on time. This will be one of those days when you cannot afford to be late. Schedules may have been altered. You could find that you have to go into action quicker than you would have imagined. Routine occupational activities will turn out to be more lucrative than you might have thought possible. Those of you who work in direct contact with the public should experiment more and maintain a friendly manner. A little more charm can work wonders for you today. Today will also be favorable for deepening romantic involvements. Overspending on unnecessary luxuries should be avoided if you are keeping within your budget.

13. TUESDAY. Useful. Financial matters are likely to take up a great deal of your time today. At the end of the day, though, you will be sure to feel that it was not time wasted. Come to grips with accounting jobs that you have been putting off. Make sure that you use your spare time in a meaningful way. Virgo people may be trying to get back money that is owed to them. They could have trouble, however, in tracking down those people who owe them. You will doubtless feel quite annoyed about this. You gave a helping hand to someone who is not now willing to repay you within the time limit that you had both agreed upon.

14. WEDNESDAY. Mixed. Relatives can be especially generous. This is a happy day for Virgos who are getting married or are strengthening romantic involvements in other ways. Good news can be received through the mail. You may get a check for some work that you completed some time ago. You should certainly be feeling a lot more confident about the future from the romantic point of view. The time is favorable for travel for pleasure, provided that work and health permit. Speeding can be more hazardous than ever, though. But apart from that, always take it easy behind the wheel. Mental as well as physical exertion can be especially tiring. You may have been overdoing it recently. Slow down.

15. THURSDAY. Sensitive. Keep mum! This is not a time for doing anything to fan the flames of rumors and gossip that are already rife. People who confide in you must not be let down. Try to deal with work that you can handle more on your own. These are the kinds of jobs that you will find easier to concentrate upon. You should also find them more profitable. Virgo people cannot afford to be too skeptical, especially of their own intuitive powers. You may be right on target with your hunches. Romance is likely to be playing an important role in your life today. Those of you who are dating for the first time should be especially pleased at the outcome of such affairs. You may be discovering love at first sight.

16. FRIDAY. Fortunate. People whom Virgos scarcely know, or those whom they may not have seen for some time could figure largely in events today. You may be offered a lucrative job. You will be pleased if you have the chance to branch out in a wholly new direction. This will be especially true if it means that you can make more use of your artistic talents. Valuable advice is likely to be forthcoming from people older than you yourself. Listen to the voices of experience as you can learn a great deal from such sources. These could save you a lot of hardship and perhaps loss of capital simply because you made many wrong decisions. Interviews with influential people can go especially well.

17. SATURDAY. Challenging. It looks as if you will be quite a busy beaver today. There is likely to be plenty going on in the social scene alone. This could keep you busy from dawn to dusk. But that does not mean to imply that you will not be able to squeeze in some work. To do so, you must be prepared to get out of your bed somewhat earlier than usual. You will have more determination to achieve a lot. Virgo people should find that they are fortunate enough to be in the right place at the right time. You may even get offered a new job that would give you the chance of promotion and a higher salary. Your services will be greatly valued by people who have recourse to them.

18. SUNDAY. Rewarding. Coupled with what took place yesterday, this should turn out to be about the best weekend of the year so far. You will be in a good mood as well as a confident one. Your feelings will be more easily conveyed to other members of your family. Virgos are likely to be happiest and most successful when attending to matters that keep them within their own home. Gardening could be a favorable endeavor and catching up with other outdoor jobs will keep you from lagging behind. Write letters to friends abroad who will undoubtedly be pleased to have your latest news and views of current events. A word in the ear of influential people can make all the difference.

19. MONDAY. Frustrating. You will start out this day feeling somewhat lethargic. After your productive weekend you will simply not feel like getting anything together. You must be self-disciplined. It is important for you to make a start as early as possible. Do not put off boring jobs to later in the day. If you do, you will almost certainly not get them done at all. Questions of security and protection will be a source of worry to the Virgo. You should probably be checking up on insurance matters. Make sure that you are fully covered where it counts. This is the wrong day for asking that favors be granted by people in positions of authority.

20. TUESDAY. Erratic. Virgo workers are almost always factual in matters connected with their jobs. But this is a time when it will be all too easy to make mistakes. You should check and double-check all accounts. Errors made now will not be easy to rectify at a later date. Your emotions will play havoc with you. Be careful that you do not upset the people who are close to you. You might do it by showing doubt about how they feel toward you. Avoid being taken in by glamorous people or situations. You may feel that there is easy money to be made, but this is entirely unlikely to be the case. You know that all that glitters is not gold. Evening is a time when you will have to exert self-discipline.

21. WEDNESDAY. Mixed-up. Your company is likely to be in demand today. There will be a number of invitations offered to you to go out, and some of these will be very enticing. But you must not start galavanting about the town when there is so much work to be done. Do not put off until tomorrow what you could really handle today. There will be some difficulties connected with getting jobs into operation at your place of employment. They are those that would require any sort of team effort. Handle only matters that you can deal with on your own. Some Virgo people may be feeling down in the dumps today. They will find that the best way to cheer themselves up is to get together with one or two pals.

22. THURSDAY. Frustrating. There is no point in pushing yourself too hard today. Make sure that you tackle the jobs that have to be done, however. This definitely is not the time to try to press influential people to support your new projects. You would be butting your head against a stone wall if you were to expect financial support to be forthcoming. Employers are not likely to be particularly bothered by the performance of Virgos today. You may even find that you finish work early and are able to attend to personal matters. Friends may land both themselves and Virgo people in hot water over questionable financial matters. Do not lend or borrow money. It's an easy habit to get into.

23. FRIDAY. Easygoing. All should be quieter today for a change. You will have the opportunity to think over problems related to household expenditures. Go over your accounts. You may find that there are one or two unpaid bills that you have overlooked. These should be settled now before interest is added. Make sure that you get a clearer idea of exactly how much money you have in your bank account. Look into insurance and income tax matters. You can afford to take things easy at your place of employment and to work at a pace that suits you best. There is not likely to be any pressure placed on you from superiors at this time. Today might be good for starting on new diets.

24. SATURDAY. Uncertain. The week comes to an end with you feeling that there is still quite a lot for you to achieve. If you do not have to appear at the office or store you should turn your attention to jobs in and around the home. Make sure that you tackle minor repair work before it becomes a major job, especially if it is outdoors. You may be able to save yourself quite a lot of money by doing work yourself that could otherwise become expensive. If you call in a professional builder or repairman, you might get a shock. Health may be somewhat below par and this will be another reason for taking things easy. Make sure that you are getting all the vitamins and nutrients your body needs.

25. SUNDAY. Enjoyable. The prime requisite today is for good company that gives you a lift. Mix with people who are as quick thinking as you are because your active mind will be working overtime. This is an excellent period for tackling artistic projects. You can work on these in conjunction with others who are on very much the same wavelength as you are. Today would be favorable, too, for taking loved ones on outings, especially children. You may visit out-of-the-way places, as you will enjoy any welcome break and changes of scenery. Virgo thoroughness in dreaming up entertainment plans will insure the maximum pleasure possible for all those involved.

26. MONDAY. Misleading. Do not count your chickens before they are hatched. You may receive some news through the mail or over the telephone promising you money. But you are not likely to receive anything extra today. Do not go on a spending spree. This is not the right day for buying any luxury articles for the home, especially if they are not absolutely necessary. The situation regarding legacies and inheritances may not be as clear-cut as it first appears. Knuckling down to jobs usually performed by others is the simplest and the quickest way to overcome delays. But financial miscalculations may have unfortunate consequences. Always check and double-check these. A quiet evening will suit you.

27. TUESDAY. Uncertain. Loved ones will be able to offer you some sound financial advice. Older relatives should be consulted if you have any cash-flow problems. It would be best to take a loan from a member of the family if you need it. But first, of course, be absolutely certain in your own mind that you can live up to any obligations as to when you will be able to pay it back. There will be quite a rush on in the morning at your place of employment. But do not resort to panic measures. You will not have any trouble in getting along with co-workers at the office or store. But you may find that you have to devote some of your lunch hour to catching up with affairs that simply cannot be left in abeyance.

28. WEDNESDAY. Challenging. This will probably be the best day of the week for furthering business developments and expanding operations. You may be able to make a handsome profit from a recent venture. Travel will bring you particularly good results. People in other towns and cities will be open to suggestions that you make. Traveling salespeople among you should be able to increase profits, especially if you are working on a commission basis. It would be a good move to join forces with people who share similar ideas with you. You could engage in a concerted attempt to make the world a better place in which to live. You will have particular concern for the underprivileged.

29. THURSDAY. Sensitive. People at or from a distance will not like it one little bit if you try to pressure them. You must cool it and put out of your mind any idea of trying to achieve too much too soon. Keep your artistic plans that need financial backing under wraps for the time being. You should concentrate more on routine jobs even if you do find them a bit of a bore. There will be a somewhat dull atmosphere at your place of employment today. Time is likely to hang rather heavy for the Virgo person today. Loved ones' reading or studies may make it difficult to discuss matters about which you would like to clear the air. But hobbies could become a major source of income if pursued with determination.

30. FRIDAY. Tricky. It will be extremely difficult for you to exert self-discipline today. You will have to exercise strict control. Even your New Year's resolutions that you have stuck to diligently thus far will be easy to break. Friends could be a bad influence. Do not mix with people who tempt you to put work to one side. Your boss may be watching your progress with more interest than you realize at your place of employment. You can gain recognition for endeavors in the artistic field, however. This just happens to be an excellent time for actors, writers and sculptors born under the sign of Virgo. Tax or insurance people may easily get figures wrong. You should go over accounts for yourself.

31. SATURDAY. Profitable. Look for one of the best days that you have experienced for quite awhile. Much that you have been trying to achieve during the past week and month is now likely to bear fruit. You will be able to clear the air with a loved one with whom you have not been getting along too well recently. You can speak your mind to this person in a diplomatic way and he or she will be pleased to know exactly where they stand with you. Researching business ventures that you want to embark on in April in greater depth will be rewarding. Virgos can gain excellent reputations for their skill in handling other people's money for them. Romance can give a great deal of pleasure and contentment.

APRIL

1. SUNDAY. Mixed. In the main, this will be a very happy and carefree day. You should be able to relax in the company of your close family members. Loved ones will be easier to get along with and recent frictions can be sorted out amicably. Virgo people should have every reason to feel more self-confident about what the future holds in store. It may be that you will get an unexpected call today. If so, it could make all your future career prospects appear much more encouraging. But you should be the first to admit that your own happiness and fulfillment are far from sufficient. There may be a good opportunity today for visiting friends. They may have been having a bit of a rough time of late.

2. MONDAY. Tricky. However friendly and charming people are, you must be on your guard this first day of the working week. Do not allow yourself to be duped into backing schemes in which there is an element of risk. Get-rich-quick plans should be judged on their merits alone. Virgos may not be putting two and two together. Financial affairs may be reflecting inconsistencies. But the day is favorable for launching advertising and publicity campaigns. Influential people will be obliging and cooperative. You will be encouraged to go further with your original ideas. Short trips can turn out to be most productive later in the day. These could be either work-related or connected with personal business.

3. TUESDAY. Demanding. Do not allow problems to come crowding in on you. You must not resort to panic measures today, especially where finances are concerned. Keep your cool. Handle income tax and insurance matters in a clear-cut manner. Do not allow yourself to be rushed into signing new contracts. It is important that you work at a pace that you find suitable and not at the dictate of others. This will be a difficult day by any standards. There will be problems connected with home and family affairs for you to straighten out, as well as those at work. Secrets should be kept strictly to yourself. People at a distance will be difficult to get hold of. Arguments at work can flair up into something serious.

4. WEDNESDAY. Confusing. Virgos should try to stand back and see things in perspective by all means. But they must avoid losing contact with the people immediately around them. Do what you can to build up a feeling of cooperation and understanding between you and your co-workers. This is a period for planning new starts that can be made later in the week. Hesitation on your part could result in missed opportunities. Loved ones may be a little troublesome. You will have difficulty in getting your mate to agree with your financial ideas. Early hours, especially, contain the possibility of arguments. Give ground on minor issues and bend over backward to be reasonable.

5. THURSDAY. Confusing. Keen as you may be to make a new start, this is a day for acting with prudence. It does not appear to have been a particularly good working week for you, so far. But nevertheless, you must not allow this fact to sway you in attempting to force the pace. Influential people will be helpful as long as you do not go over their heads. Do not try to make decisions that are not really yours to make. Virgo men and women may be tackling romantic problems from the wrong angle. Charm and flattery are unlikely to produce the desired results. Do not try to win the affection of others by wearing your heart on your sleeve. Your feelings that you might be selfish are not realistic.

6. FRIDAY. Rewarding. Stretch to your full capacity. There will be excellent opportunities at your place of employment to put yourself in line for promotion. Get through as much business as you can, even if it means staying on the job past quitting time. Virgo people will have a lucky break today. They should be sure that they are in a position to grasp it when it comes along. It is essential to make the right impression on people who matter. Propositions or opportunities received from an unlikely source can prove to be worthwhile. This is a good period for original, inventive and imaginative work. It is also favorable for travel. Friends will prove to be especially pleasant companions.

7. SATURDAY. Excellent. Virgo-born people are likely to end this week on a highly optimistic note. Not too much will be demanded of you today. There will be plenty of opportunities to catch up with jobs that you should have completed earlier in the week. You will have the comfort and the security of knowing precisely where you stand. You should have some good chances for getting your ideas across to influential people. Your stock appears high at the moment in the eyes of those who matter. Place freedom of thought and freedom of action above other values. They are vital to your well-being, and not only in the material sense. Romantic associations can be placed on a more stable foundation.

8. SUNDAY. Frustrating. There are many plans that you would like to put into action now. This is Sunday, however, so it is not the right day to make a start. It would be advisable not to contact influential people in the privacy of their own homes. Superiors will not be at all happy if you bother them with business matters. These could easily be discussed during the working week that will be starting up for you shortly. This will be one of those irritating days when you will be disturbed constantly. Loved ones will interrupt you if you are trying to catch up with your letter writing and your accounts. Virgo people will be all too easily disconcerted by trivial matters. You might be better off just having some fun.

9. MONDAY. Changeable. You will find this an up-and-down sort of day. Do not rely on promises made by your boss. People who have authority over you are likely to reverse themselves quite a few times. You must learn to depend upon yourself quite a bit more. However, almost every situation you are in at the moment will have a reason for it, so try to learn from experience. Proceed steadily to achieve the best results. Even if you think things could go a little quicker, do not try to force the pace. If you do, you will only succeed in becoming frustrated. This can be a particularly auspicious day for romance. Secret hopes and dreams will have a much better chance of being fulfilled sooner than you think.

10. TUESDAY. Satisfactory. You will be anxious to get on with your outstanding work. Your mind will be working fast and furiously. Jobs that require speed of thought will be easier to handle than routine ones. They will also be easier than anything demanding physical effort. Use your imagination. Do not be afraid to put artistic ideas to the test. You will be pleased to discover that you are surrounded by people who also wish to keep things going at a fast pace. You will get generous treatment at the hands of others. Be prompt in accepting work-related and social invitations and other gestures of goodwill such as membership in a club. Try to keep personal spending down, though.

11. WEDNESDAY. Successful. This will be a pleasant enough mid-week day. See what you can do, though, to cut the corners. You are quite likely to have a fairly large number of odd jobs to deal with that could take you rather a long time. Electrical equipment and gadgetry can save you labor costs. Be more of a handyman or do-it-yourself type. There are many little jobs that you can handle in and around the home. If you try doing them it will cut out the need to call in a professional who would be expensive. Appeals against decisions that you feel were unfair are more likely than not to be successful. Today is good for winning over people's confidence. But Virgos may be getting their facts wrong.

12. THURSDAY. Manageable. You are probably overreacting. A story that you receive second- or even third-hand may have been blown up out of all proportion. This is one of those days when you should act on facts and facts alone. You need to be more patient and to let people do things more their own way and in their own time. Trying to tell others how to handle their jobs will probably make them angry. You are really only trying to be helpful, but even so, they will resent interference. Speeding can be dangerous. Be sure that you obey the highway code at all times. Do not risk putting yourself on the wrong side of the law. Check your car for faults before setting out on any long journeys.

13. FRIDAY. Uncertain. For the superstitious Virgos among you, you will feel that Dame Fortune is not smiling in your direction today. This supposedly unlucky day could be heavily loaded with problems for you. Many of them are likely to be minor ones so you must try to take them in your stride. Whatever you do, don't allow yourself to be overcome by them. It can be difficult for you to know how to deal with domestic situations. The first priority is to ensure the comfort of your mate or spouse. Attempts at redecorating the home may meet with the disapproval of other household members. Objects tend to look more attractive in shop windows. Beware of so-called good buys.

14. SATURDAY. Pleasant. You will be glad that you have the chance to get some peace and quiet today. It looks as if you have had a fairly hectic time of it over the last few days. It would be a good idea to slow down the tempo of your life somewhat. Try to work out exactly what you have achieved in concrete terms. This will be a fairly relaxing beginning to the weekend, though. Trips that you make for pleasure with other members of the family should work out rather well for you. This is a favorable time for tying up the loose ends of jobs that you do not want to be bothered with in your spare time. Virgos will feel much happier for getting such affairs out of the way.

15. SUNDAY. Fair. Coupled with what took place yesterday, this should turn out to be a pleasant and fairly relaxing weekend. There is not likely to be a great deal of pressure placed upon you. It may be necessary, though, to make a duty call connected with an older member of the family. However, you will be pleased to do what you can to make someone happy who has always put your interests first in the past. This is an excellent day for entertaining employees or other influential people. Tabulating the results of research work to be submitted to superiors during the coming week would be very worthwhile. Children may get into trouble with the authorities and may need extra disciplining from you.

16. MONDAY. Mixed. Loved ones can make issues of their own independence and self-sufficiency. You must give more freedom to members of your family if you want to avoid serious conflict within the home. If you do not allow more give-and-take, you could be heading on a collision course. Perhaps you have been overprotective? Reason is not one of the things that people close to you are likely to be swayed by. Get on with your own affairs. Business should be attended to promptly. It is important that you go all-out to make the best possible impression on people who matter. Entertainment plans that you had been looking forward to this evening can be turned upside-down.

17. TUESDAY. Difficult. It may be necessary for you to slow the pace down today. You must give the kind of attention to details that you know you should. You may well discover that you have attempted to cram too much into your schedule today. It is all very well to take on new jobs if you can handle them. But little success will be achieved if you cannot complete them to your own and to everyone else's satisfaction. The need to take on extra responsibilities can interfere with your spare time. Pleasure plans may have to be postponed or even canceled altogether. Dealing with romantic problems will require a lot of tact.

18. WEDNESDAY. Rewarding. There will be no extra pressure exerted upon you. You will be in the happy, if unusual, position of being able to work at your own speed. Use your new-found freedom to show influential people just how responsible you can be. Someone who could help you with your career may be under the impression that you cannot handle responsibility. Now is the time to prove that person wrong. An increase in earnings appears to be in the cards. You should be feeling a little more secure about the financial future. Take advantage of a lucky break that occurs sometime about midday. There should be a good chance for small firms to put pressure on the management of larger businesses.

19. THURSDAY. Disconcerting. There may be more work for you to get through at your place of employment than you had realized this Thursday. It would be best to leave yourself more time to deal with all these chores. You must make as early a start as you possibly can. Influential people will be expecting a lot more of you. They may be watching your performance a lot more closely than you realize. This is not a period when you should underestimate anyone. You simply cannot afford to take time off for chitchat or gossip. Communicating with people at or from a distance may leave some doubts or suspicions in your mind. It is vital that you check all facts and relevant information for yourself.

20. FRIDAY. Sensitive. Perhaps you are pushing yourself too hard these days. Your desire to be a perfectionist can be carried too far. Make sure that all of your attention to detail is really required. Overwork can make you tense, not to mention tired. It may not be possible to make an important journey that you were planning. Just let people at a distance know in plenty of time if you are not going to be able to show up as expected. This would be a good time for obtaining professional advice on business affairs. Some Virgo readers may be thinking about branching out in an entirely new direction. They should be rather pleased at what they now hear. Finalize contracts and agreements.

21. SATURDAY. Fortunate. Push full-steam ahead. Go all-out to finish the usual chores ahead of schedule. It is important that Virgo people who have a deadline to meet finish their work on time. Do not allow friends to influence you to ease up. It is important that you tie up any loose ends at your place of employment as early in the day as possible. Later on, you will have ample opportunity for getting on more intimate terms with loved ones. Teamwork enterprises can produce especially good results. Virgos' aptitude for knowing what other people are thinking and feeling can be an especially good asset. The day will be favorable for reading and study.

22. SUNDAY. Excellent. Counting your good fortune yesterday, this would appear to be one of the most successful weekends that you have enjoyed so far this year. You will find that loved ones are more sympathetic to your long-term aims and desires. This is the right day to discuss openly and frankly any financial problems that you may have been keeping to yourself. The morning would be a good time for banishing past memories and letting bygones be bygones. Now would be a good time for turning over a new leaf in romantic and matrimonial relationships. You will be able to come to much closer terms with someone from whom you may feel you have been drifting away of late.

23. MONDAY. Tricky. Virgo-born people may find themselves out of their depth. It is advisable to make a cautious start this first day of the working week. Influential people will be expecting a great deal from you. Do not claim to have knowledge or facts at your fingertips that you do not have easy access to. You might very well find yourself tested and wanting. In research work or other investigation, there is a greater chance of your being led astray. Do not allow yourself to be influenced by people who have the gift of the gab, but little else going for them. People may resort to underhand methods in an attempt to get hold of your money. The computers of banks may fail to register special requests.

24. TUESDAY. Mixed. Your home life may be somewhat unsettled. You will be eager to get away from the domestic environment. Turn to an older friend for advice. Someone whose opinion you respect may be able to see the situation more clearly than you yourself. Your mate or partner will be unpredictable. But this is a favorable day for shopping expeditions and for buying in bulk. You should be able to save yourself quite a lot of money by shopping at the big malls usually found in built-up areas. Articles imported from distant places should be of especially good value. Virgos will be keen to search out interesting new reading material in bookshops. Extra effort may be required to get things finished.

25. WEDNESDAY. Sensitive. This is likely to be an out-of-the-ordinary kind of a day. Virgos are advised to hold their ground. Do not allow impatient people to force sudden changes upon you. You are absolutely correct to proceed with caution today. Your own conviction that your aims and goals are worth fighting for should not be allowed to falter. In-laws may admit their errors, but you should not try to score points on people for admitting that they were in the wrong. You will have to be extremely tactful with your mate's relatives. Do not do or say anything that would leave you open to misunderstanding. Virgo people should let neighbors have their say and not prejudge them.

26. THURSDAY. Manageable. You must relegate pleasure to the back of your mind now, at least until you reach the weekend. This is not a day when you should try to wriggle out of your responsibilities. You may be feeling tired and rather bored with the kind of duties that you have to perform at the moment. If you do not push yourself harder, however, you could find yourself looking for another job. Do not allow yourself to be influenced by friends who have more time on their hands than is good for them. Try to place trading ventures on a more stable foundation. Distant government or customs officials can grant definite assurances. Continued efforts and exertion should lead to a good performance.

27. FRIDAY. Demanding. Planning for the future is best left for another day. It is not a period for idle daydreaming either. There are plenty of jobs for you to attend to here and now. If you are realistic you will become aware of these early on. You may be making excuses to yourself in order to allow yourself more leisure time. Get off to an early start. Do not spend a great deal or any part of the morning period sitting around doing little that could be considered constructive. Concentrate on the present and what needs to be done. Routine affairs and activities should not be neglected, however dreary and repetitious. Nothing too ambitious should be attempted unless you are certain you can handle it.

28. SATURDAY. Inactive. You may have to catch up with some account work that has been piling up rapidly. Quite a lot of it accumulated during the week and some goes back for the month. Put some time aside today for jobs that you can handle on your own. These will probably require a good deal of concentration.

This is a day when Virgo people are advised to play things and events by ear when it comes to pleasure and entertainment plans. If you make arrangements to go out early in the day, you may well find that subsequent plans have replaced earlier ones when the time comes to go out. The impetus required for launching new business ventures may be lacking.

29. SUNDAY. Happy. As long as Virgo people do not raise their expectations too high, they cannot be disappointed in today. This will be a pleasant enough one, as Sundays go. But it is not a time when you should be aiming to get more new business ventures launched. Your best bet now would be to attempt to get to know influential people a little better and on a more personal level. Home entertaining would be well received by your friends. You will not find it terribly expensive to have a few people over for drinks or for a bite to eat, such as Brunch. Deepening and strengthening romantic involvements is starred as April comes to an end. You should be feeling more secure about a relationship.

30. MONDAY. Useful. Today appears to offer quite a promising start for the working week. But it is important that Virgo people should steer clear of debt. Do not launch business ventures that are highly speculative. You should not borrow money unless you can be absolutely certain about how you can pay it back. Virgo parents should give more time and attention to their youngsters. This is also a period when more time should be devoted to loved ones and to that of mutual acquaintances. Influential people may stretch the rules at your work place. This will enable you to break off from work a little earlier than usual. Vacation leave may also be extended. If shopping, keep your eyes peeled for bargains.

MAY

1. TUESDAY. Productive. You start off the month not entirely sure as to how to exploit your talents. You may feel that there are certain new areas in which you should begin to work. You are not quite certain, however, just how to go about it. Perhaps it would be a good idea to consult with friends of yours who are on the same kind of wavelength. This is probably one of the best days for approaching influential people to ask that favors be granted. You will find that your boss is more open and amenable to your plans. Your ideas for making changes in the way routine jobs are handled at your place of employment are acceptable. Homelife may present some problems first thing.

2. WEDNESDAY. Easygoing. There will be ample opportunities to catch up with accounting work. You should have been able to take care of it last month, but somehow didn't. Income tax and insurance affairs must not be left to chance. Meetings with bank managers and other professional people should go rather well. Some interesting and useful facts could come to light. People who you work alongside will tend to be rather slow today in their reactions. So it probably would be best for you to deal with jobs that you can handle on your own. Evening will be a good time for discussions with loved ones. You are anxious to straighten out some of the problems that have been souring your relationship.

3. THURSDAY. Challenging. You will be in a highly optimistic mood today. Not a great deal is likely to be demanded of you. You can count on the kind of jobs that you are required to handle being well within your capacity. Your relationship with superiors will be very much improved. There will be opportunities for you to place yourself in line for some sort of promotion in the not too distant future. Virgos can break out of their cocoon. You will be surprised at the extent to which people will wish to be of help to you. New friends can be made who will be helpful to you in a professional way, as well.

4. FRIDAY. Rewarding. This will be a good day for everything connected with sports and travel. If you are competing in a favorite sport you should fare particularly well. This will win the appreciation and the approval of your teammates. But exciting business plans should be held in abeyance for the time being. This pertains especially if you are asked to back new schemes and commit quite a lot of your savings to whatever the proposals are. Virgos should be able to make a success of whatever they put their minds to. Their ability to go into matters in great detail while maintaining an overall sense of perspective can be unequaled. This is a good day too for acting as arbitrator or a go-between.

5. SATURDAY. Satisfactory. Now you have reached the end of still another week. You would be wise to take stock of the progress you have been able to make over the first few days of this month. You should be rather pleased with the way you have been able to lay the foundations for future moves. You will probably want to make some in the not-too-distant future. They will be likely to bring you in quite a lot of money. There may be early fights with loved ones, but on the whole this will be quite a good day for romance. Fix up an evening out with your mate or partner who may have reason to feel rather neglected.

6. SUNDAY. Confusing. There may be a number of invitations that you have to choose from this week. You will be asked to attend quite a lot of functions, parties and social gatherings. It would be best not to spread yourself too thinly. You could easily become exhausted if you spend a great deal of time traveling from one place to another. Virgo people may be overreacting where money is concerned. Children should not be made to feel that nothing they say or do is to be taken seriously. Entertainment and recreation may involve you in too much expense. This is not a particularly good day for travel. There may be some trouble with government or customs officials.

7. MONDAY. Difficult. You simply will not be in the mood to carry on with your work. If you have quite a lot of routine tasks to attend to it will be especially true. Because of your present attitude it will be all too easy to make mistakes if you are handling accounting work. Try to slow down a bit. Do not be tempted to take time off by friends who do not have regular jobs. After all, you do not want to end up unemployed like them. People's suspicions will be hard to put to rest. You may feel that you have to earn the respect and the trust of people who you work alongside. Do not do or say anything that would fan the flames of gossip. Put yourself in the place of these people and you will realize why.

8. TUESDAY. Successful. You will be traveling more than usual today. Matters connected with your work are apt to take you to distant places. Be prepared for the unexpected. You should find it easier than usual to cope with any new responsibilities that are thrust upon you. If seeking to further creative enterprises, go out of your way to obtain professional advice. You do not want to risk your savings until you can be absolutely sure about what kind of scheme you would be investing in. Virgo people should speak in person rather than over the telephone. Advertising should have a remarkably beneficial effect on your business profits.

9. WEDNESDAY. Erratic. Confusion is likely to overtake you this morning. You may find that a good deal of pressure is being brought to bear upon you. You will also have a conflict of loyalties to cope with. There will be pressure from loved ones that may stop you from getting on with work. Loved ones will not understand about the amount of time you have to spend away from home. You have to earn enough money to pay bills and all of your dependents benefit in a roundabout way. Head-on collisions will be difficult to avoid. The ability of Virgos to concentrate will be adversely affected. You may get the uneasy feeling that you are not able to keep on top of your work. Do not allow that to persist.

10. THURSDAY. Lucky. Today will be outstanding for bringing important matters to a head. You should go all-out to straighten out situations that have been simmering in the background for some time. But you must not try to hurry chores that you would really prefer to be rid of. Influential people will want to question you closely if you are trying to get their approval. You need that for your new schemes that would require some sort of financial backing. It's a good time for putting down new roots. Virgos may discover a new sense of belonging and security. It is favorable for responding to the implicit and unspoken desires of loved ones. Tact, combined with firmness, should be effective in dealing with legal problems. People at or from a distance should provide you with some interesting new facts or information.

11. FRIDAY. Mixed. Virgo people should not worry too much if they are not able to finish work loads before they take a weekend break. You must not rush yourself as this would leave you wide open to the possibility of making mistakes in paperwork. You will probably get the chance to take little jobs home with you at the weekend. There you will be able to cope with them in your own time and at your own pace. This need not be a difficult day for any Virgo person. As long as you do not allow yourself to get in a spin about events that have not even taken place, you'll be fine. Loved ones are possibly not being very honest when it comes to money matters. If you have to discuss this, be tactful and do not get angry.

12. SATURDAY. Sensitive. This can be a good day for home entertaining. Ask people to your home if you owe them favors. Do not forget acquaintances who have shown you a lot of kindness in the past. This would also be the right time to contact family members with whom you have had silly arguments. Show that you are big enough to be the first one to offer the hand of friendship. Simply say that you are sorry. You will not lose face by such actions. Rather, your standing will rise even higher in the eyes of others. Casual romantic liaisons can end as suddenly as they began. Business partners know what they are doing. They probably will handle difficult people effectively.

13. SUNDAY. Demanding. Getting overexcited can easily lead to disappointments. You should not expect too much from today. In fact, the call of duty is likely to be far stronger than you would have imagined. You would like to get out and about for a change of scene. But if you ride roughshod over the desires of your family you are most certainly going to end up in hot water. Children will need special care. Do not try to turn them off with stories and excuses. What members of the younger generation will be demanding from you now is truth. You are undoubtedly going to have to change your relationship with offspring. It might be the only way you are going to keep things on a friendly basis with them. Friendship and romance simply will not mix.

14. MONDAY. Buoyant. You will be raring to go this morning. It appears to have been a somewhat frantic weekend for you. Now you want to come to grips with the kinds of jobs that can bring you in a lot of extra money. What is more, you should be able to do just that. You will notice that your relationship with superiors has very much improved. You will also find it is much easier to get your original ideas across. It will be one of those days when Virgos can astound even themselves with their own creative talents and inspiration. The day is also favorable for putting more exertion into hobbies and other spare-time activities. Mates and spouses will also be more efficient and accomplished. The atmosphere at home should be electric.

15. TUESDAY. Normal. You will not be likely have a great deal of energy at first. But you should be able to fulfill your duties in a quiet sort of way. Get on with the kinds of jobs that would not require you to expend a great deal of physical energy. You should slow down the tempo of your life. Go over accounts. You may have been having difficulty in getting done with income tax matters. You should be able to find new ways to get around the problems that have been bothering you. Home life may be rather dull, but you will be relieved that there are no serious arguments or differences of opinion to cope with. This evening will be favorable for cooking at home rather than eating out. Make a special dish and enjoy a leisurely meal.

16. WEDNESDAY. Misleading. Do not believe all that you are told. Stories may come to your ears about easy pickings to be had. But you would be wise to investigate the details of such schemes a good deal more closely before you decide to put any money into them. The health of loved ones may have been something of a worry for you. It should begin to show some definite signs of improving now. You will be very pleased that people are not looking to you quite so often to do things for them. But you want to be very careful about how you fill in your leisure time as you could be somewhat prone to extravagance. Influential people will tend to be more reliable than is usual, however. This may prove to be of great importance for you if you had hoped to ask for assistance.

17. THURSDAY. Frustrating. Virgo employees may have some difficulty in deciphering instructions. You may find that your boss's writing is rather difficult to piece together. Do not be afraid to ask questions of superiors. This is better than muddling along when you are really in the dark. Though people with whom you come into contact will be helpful, it is unlikely that any real progress will be made. You will find that you are very much on your own. So it will be entirely up to you as to how you cope with this sort of situation to achieve the best possible results. Deal with business matters in a thorough, organized way.

18. FRIDAY. Excellent. This will probably be one of the best days of the month so far. You must just do what you can to ensure that you are not overly extravagant with money. Try to keep your spending down to reasonable proportions. There seem to be new and exciting areas that you are moving into now. These are areas in which you will be able to make more use of your natural talents. You may perhaps even be able to make a good deal more money than heretofore out of what has been little more than a pleasant hobby to date. Closer liaison with business colleagues would be a good idea, especially when it comes to drawing up plans for the future. Socializing would be a great way to wind up a busy day.

19. SATURDAY. Difficult. The week comes to an end with you having mixed feelings about the progress that you may or may not have made. It would definitely seem to have been one of those mixed weeks. What you have gained on the upswings you have most decidedly lost on the downswings. But you must be patient. It seems vital that you try to make some sort of comeback with savings. Do not spend too much money on unnecessary pleasure or entertainment. Mates or spouses may give their Virgo partner a rough ride. Partners will change their minds constantly about plans for going out. Influential people may wish to be treated more as equals than superiors at work. Go slowly, nevertheless.

20. SUNDAY. Disconcerting. Do not do any business today. Relax and take things easy. The kind of work that you have been attending to seems to have taken a great deal out of you. This is true especially if they are jobs that require you to involve yourself in manual labor. Put domestic issues and personal problems in the back of your mind. Just come to grips now with work that you are anxious to conclude. Do not allow relatives to monopolize your time. If Virgos have financial miscalculations they should not try to hide the fact. What children have to say may be disturbing because it is so much out of character. Questioning their judgment, though, is only likely to make them angry.

21. MONDAY. Sensitive. This is the first day of the working week, and it is important that you get off to as early a start as possible. There are sure to be many little jobs that you must attend to that were left over from last week. There are also many new and exciting projects that you would like to make a start on in conjunction with others. Virgo people may suddenly develop an interest in subjects that previously held no attraction for them at all. Today will be favorable for deepening romantic involvements. It is especially true of people whom you work alongside. Just be sure that your personal life does no get too tangled up with career matters. In such cases, both work and private life usually suffer.

22. TUESDAY. Fortunate. Virgo people may have more of an idea about what their future holds in store for them than others around them. Therefore, it is important for you to follow your own intuition. Do not listen to good friends and associates, however well-meaning they may be. Get away from the domestic environment as early in the day as you possibly can. There will be good money-making opportunities open to you. Friends may come up with some speculative ideas that would be well worth your taking a calculated risk on. Do not allow yourself to be deterred by other people's fears and doubts. This can be a good day for taking a brief holiday before work begins in earnest.

23. WEDNESDAY. Rewarding. This could be one of the best days that you have experienced so far this week. Possibly, it could prove so for this month. The day will find you in an up-and-at-'em mood. You will have many new ideas for streamlining jobs that have become boring and commonplace. This is the time to go all-out to make a good impression on people who matter. Try to show your boss that you are now ready to take on that promotion you want. It has been dangled like a carrot before your nose for all too long. Obtaining professional advice should give Virgos more confidence in handling legal matters.

24. THURSDAY. Exciting. You should perk up considerably at some news. It will come through unexpectedly and should give you quite a boost. An upsurge in confidence is indicated. You will be feeling a good deal happier and more contented about your future career and work prospects. What will also appeal to you today is the lack of interference from family members. There had been complaints about the additional amount of time you may have to spend away from home. This can be a successful day for new beginnings. Get out and about more than you have been doing. Visit people who are in a position to enable you to reach the goals that mean so much to you. But it should be a last resort.

25. FRIDAY. Demanding. All the important work should be tackled as early in the day as possible. If you leave it too late you are likely to find you are unable to come to grips with it. By then you will become snowed under with more mundane jobs. People with more influence will insist that you attend to those first. Do not allow yourself to be pushed around by older family members who try to pull rank on you. Once you have decided on a positive course of action, you should stick to it come what may. Your mate or partner may offer you especially good career advice. You should always listen to people who have good intuition and whom you know to have your best interests at heart.

26. SATURDAY. Mixed. Expect a fairly uneventful Saturday. If you have made arrangements to see friends, be absolutely sure that you do not let them down. Friendship is not something that should be taken lightly. People who have been kind to you in the past will be very upset if you do not seem to care much about leaving them at loose ends. Romantic partners may attach exaggerated importance to matters of personal independence and self-sufficiency. Business financial procedures should be kept constant and not revised in midstream. People at or from a distance could become close friends, in time. The afternoon is good for participating in club or group activities. But some of your colleagues have no sense of fun and take everything seriously.

27. SUNDAY. Satisfactory. Like yesterday, it will be fairly uneventful. Leisure activities will be pleasant if not especially stimulating. Do not try to force the pace. Avoid any entertaining that would cost you more than you know you can afford. You may have a truly generous streak, but you must not allow people to take advantage of it on occasions. Do not throw money around that you have not yet earned. Remember that a bird in the hand is always worth two in the bush. Virgo people may have some doubts about whom they can absolutely trust. These doubts, unfortunately, may turn out to be well and truly founded. The time is favorable for putting more work into study and academic efforts. Virgo people can afford to speak their minds where loved ones and finances are concerned.

28. MONDAY. Productive. You will have plenty of energy at your disposal this first work day. It is therefore important that you channel it in a constructive and positive way. A more subtle approach than usual may well pay off when you are dealing with influential people. Remember the old adage about not putting all your eggs in one basket. This is a time for playing a hand close to your chest. Do not talk about your imaginative ideas with others until you have them fully formulated. They could otherwise be easily stolen from you. Influential people will tend to be more cooperative if they are caught with their guard down. Being known as an active sponsor of charitable organizations may make the good name of the Virgo-born person even better. Dealings with people who wield power behind the scenes should work out favorably.

29. TUESDAY. Disconcerting. You could be in for a number of disappointments. This is not a day for putting all your eggs in one basket. Don't even consider counting your chickens before they are hatched. From information at hand, it is reasonable to assume that some advantage, probably a financial one, is coming your way soon. But you could be overly optimistic, so do not start spending money until it is actually in your hands. Domestic problems, more than probably connected with health, could affect your judgment in an adverse way. Listen to the suggestions of people who admire you. A young person at your work place will make some lively remarks and also suggest some innovative ideas. Try them out, they might be good.

30. WEDNESDAY. Exciting. Get an early start because it will be important not to waste a second this day. You will have more matters of importance to deal with than usual. The troubles that are likely to have dogged romantic relationships throughout this month will undoubtedly be over. It could be a case of off with the old and on with the new where your romantic life is concerned. Many of you could be about to embark on an exciting new love affair now. You will be happier in your own mind and in your own heart than has been the case for some time past. Virgos can derive special pleasure from contemplating what the future holds in store for themselves as well as for the people who are closest to them. Dreams that you have are likely to be reassuring, if you can believe in them.

31. THURSDAY. Sensitive. It may be a special anniversary of somebody you know today. Even if this is not the case, a birthday or wedding celebration may be coming up soon. Perhaps you should buy a card and a gift now to be sure that you do not forget it when the actual day arrives. You may not feel in the mood for work today. But there will be any number of jobs that you should attend to. Account work is always important. Update it before the merry month of May comes to a close. Virgo people may need to rehearse speeches beforehand. Otherwise they could find themselves somewhat speechless when the actual occasion arises. Inlaws can be unpleasantly critical, even pointlessly so.

JUNE

1. FRIDAY. Confusing. You will probably not be feeling like your old self today. This is a difficult period for getting things going. One of the main problems will undoubtedly hinge on the necessity to clear up matters that were left over from last month. There will probably be a number of outstanding bills still to be paid. Some attention to your own accounts will most certainly be deemed necessary. Problems can also arise unexpectedly in connection with taxation and insurance payments. Research projects that you were hoping to launch may turn out to be more expensive than you first thought. You might find it necessary to review your budget. Don't risk being overdrawn in your bank account.

2. SATURDAY. Tricky. You will find that a bit of a rush will be necessary today before a weekend break. See if you can clear up all the little jobs that you would like to be rid of before you go. If you can do it you will be well pleased with yourself. Loved ones will be helpful. You should not even think twice about enlisting the aid of people who are prepared and willing to assist you. Virgo people should make sure they know what they are buying before they spend any of their money. So-called bargains may not be all that they are supposed to be when you get them home and examine them. By then, it will probably be too late to get a refund.

3. SUNDAY. Demanding. Virgo people will probably be feeling unduly pessimistic. You will no doubt be feeling the strain of the last few days. Make sure that you get a complete break from work and worries. Do not permit forceful personalities to direct you. You do not have to involve yourself in pleasure and entertainment arrangements that do not really appeal to you. You should not be having such glum thoughts about artistic ventures that you have only recently started with. It is far too early to write off ventures that are still in their early stages. Ambition on your part can easily be mistaken for greed. Virgo people's children should be taught not to be too cynical. It is not a desirable trait.

4. MONDAY. Mixed. It will be rather difficult for you to move into top gear today. There will be opportunities there to make progress with financial matters. Whether or not you will be alert enough to grasp them is another matter. You will have to be very much on your toes to beat your competitors to the punch. Charm and flattery are unlikely to help you to make substantial headway. For once your kindly ways and your good manners are not likely to stand you in very good stead. Virgos may be embarrassed that they have nothing to talk about with their romantic companions. The need to travel may demand temporary separations from loved ones. Some companies permit wives to go on business trips.

5. TUESDAY. Useful. There will be some slight improvement in your affairs today. In fact, this will probably be the best day so far in June. It seems to have been a rather difficult start to the month for you. There will be opportunities at your place of employment to move forward, although, no doubt, rather slowly. The methodical ways of the Virgo-born person will stand them in very good stead with influential people today. This can be a lucky day in many ways. The more you put into it, the more you are likely to get out of it. Important new contracts can be made. Casual acquaintances can sometimes turn into close and kind friends.

6. WEDNESDAY. Excellent. You can count on a really first-class day. This is a time when you should channel any probable upsurge in energy. You must direct it in a positive manner to gain the most benefit. Carry on with work that is at hand. There is a good chance that you will be able to make new starts. Stick to jobs that are likely to earn you quite a bit of money on the side. This is a day recommended for signing long-term agreements and contracts. It will also be good for dealings with people in the entertainment or theatrical business. Romance can open up entirely new horizons for Virgo men and women.

7. THURSDAY. Easygoing. You will have the chance to take a breather. It will be very pleasant, and unusual, for you to slow down the tempo of your life. You will be able to spend more time dealing with the smaller details of jobs you have only recently started. You may have thrown yourself into these with a great deal of energy, but perhaps too little forethought. Loved ones will be helpful. Try to find the kind of jobs that you can deal with from your home base. Concentrate on those that will save you quite a lot of unnecessary traveling. You will be able to tie up the loose ends of business matters. Go over your accounts. Try to get a clearer picture of your financial standing in its totality.

8. FRIDAY. Mixed. Be extremely cautious if you are doing business with distant people. Be careful about what you agree to. Wait until you have an opportunity to study contracts and other documents first-hand. Do not place too much faith in the promises of people you have not dealt with in the past. This is a day for sticking to tried and trusted, conservative methods. Family life will be unsettled. In-laws may criticize a recent decision you made regarding future security. Routine work should continue smoothly without interference from authority figures. Associates will be helpful. Property sales or developments may require government approval, probably State or Township.

9. SATURDAY. Difficult. This week comes to an end with your feeling that you could perhaps have achieved rather more than you have. But there are times you are altogether too critical of yourself. This is a tricky day for signing contracts. Although you may be keen to tie up the loose ends of business agreements, you may not yet be able to do so. Do not be too pushy. Stick with your intuition because it will not play you false. Financial transactions, especially, should not be rushed. Loved ones should be carefully consulted before you make any moves that could involve their long-term security. Taxation on spare-time earnings may be heavier than you had imagined.

10. SUNDAY. Pleasant. Virgo people cannot afford to beat about the bush. You should lay your cards on the table. It would seem that you have been keeping certain emotional feelings bottled up inside of you. Wherever there are assumptions about matters frequently taken for granted, there is a risk of misunderstandings. Speculative opportunities may not be nearly as worthwhile as they are dressed up to appear. You should not dip into money that you have earmarked for paying regular bills. This is not to back projects through which you could lose all of it in a very short space of time. Reading and study can bring you quite a lot of pleasure.

11. MONDAY. Uncertain. Virgos may be trying to make gambling an exact science. They should realize early in the game that it is not possible to eliminate totally the element of risk. There are certain activities to which this applies and gambling is a sure one. You should not allow yourself to be talked into backing the schemes of other people. The exception would be that you believe in them yourself 100 percent. Hesitation can lead to financial loss. You must decide at an early stage what is best for you and the long-term security of your loved ones. Only then can you act according to your judgment. If there is a sense of uncertainty, it would be best to keep away altogether.

12. TUESDAY. Mixed. Do not try to be too clever. Keep all business dealings open and aboveboard. However enticing an offer may be, you must not go behind the back of your superiors. Concentrate on work well within your capacity. If you chance your luck, losses could well be incurred. Those of you who have the opportunity to work from your home base will probably fare the best. Seek a peaceful, calm atmosphere when studying and planning ahead. Romance will brighten your leisure hours later in the day. Singles could meet someone new and exciting this evening. There may be pleasant trips in the offing for some of you. You may have to start working on reservations.

13. WEDNESDAY. Fortunate. You will have more energy than usual at your disposal. The only important thing is that you must be sure you channel it in a positive and constructive manner. Do not allow yourself to be led astray by people who have more time on their hands than is really good for them. Make sure that you employ your natural talents to their capacity. Go all-out to get the backing of influential people for your new schemes and creative ideas. Friends may show the stuff they are really made of. They can be scrupulous in keeping their promises and honoring their assurances. Travel in your local vicinity can lead to the realization of some of your secret hopes and wishes.

14. THURSDAY. Uncertain. Friends can easily turn into lovers. You may find that you become drawn to a person physically whom you may have known for some time. It happened without your even being aware that you had any such feelings toward the person. You may now see him or her in an entirely different light. But there is a greater risk of misunderstanding the intentions of business colleagues. Closer liaison in teamwork enterprises is essential. The signing of important business agreements would best be postponed. Virgos are probably at a disadvantage. This is a favorable time for breaking with tradition. Find a good excuse for giving mates or spouses a special treat or surprise.

15. FRIDAY. Productive. This will be a favorable time for formalizing new partnership associations. Virgos will achieve more with the assistance of helpers than they could possibly have accomplished by themselves. You should be able to look at the legal aspects of some business matters. It will be to your advantage to consult with experts in various fields. Bankers, accountants and perhaps tax authorities may be able to give you the benefit of their professional expertise. Professional advice could be obtained free of charge as it may well be all a part of the service. Influential people will probably be concerned with protecting their interests.

16. SATURDAY. Satisfactory. Virgo people can find themselves up to their necks if they let their curiosity get the better of them. This is a day for sticking to your word. Do not ever make promises that you may not be able to live up to for whatever the reason. People may try to tempt you to make investments. But you will probably discover that anything speculative you have been asked to put your savings into has some hidden loophole or catch. Check everything out carefully with your accountant or lawyer before you make any major alterations. Mixed motives are only likely to result in chaos and confusion.

17. SUNDAY. Difficult. Unfortunately, this day of rest will leave Virgos little time for either rest or relaxation. Much as you would like to take it easy and slow down the tempo of your life, it just may not be possible to do so. Mates or spouses could start to pressure you over financial matters. It may also be necessary to part with more money than you had realized if you are going to placate your opposite number. This is not a particularly easy day for dealing with loved ones generally. Virgos with children who have reached the awkward age will be hard-pressed to be reasonable and not to lose their temper. Attractive or glamorous situations could turn out to be deceptive.

18. MONDAY. Frustrating. Today will be very like yesterday in many ways. You will once again find that you are at the mercy of other people's whims. You may feel that you are not getting the chance to fulfill yourself or your potential. You will just have to grit your teeth and bear it. There just doesn't seem to be much chance of your altering the way things are at the moment. A pipe may spring a leak. Drainage or sewage systems could be in need of major repair. This is a sensitive day for all financial transactions. You may find that bank managers and accountants are extremely difficult types to deal with. But the morning is helpful for furthering negotiations with large business firms.

19. TUESDAY. Useful. A more intuitive approach to study or self-improvement endeavors is likely to prove the most productive. Virgos can become skilled in reading between the lines. You should listen to people whose opinions you have always trusted, as well. You may be able to learn from the mistakes of others. You can thus avoid making the same ones yourself. You may find it easier to judge people's feelings not so much by what they say as from the way they act. This should be a favorable period for trying to further overseas business development schemes. But you must be cautious with your money above all. Investigate carefully all new propositions you receive. There may be hidden clauses.

20. WEDNESDAY. Enjoyable. As long as you do not invest today in anything in which the risk factor is great, all will be well for you. Go all-out to impress superiors at your place of employment. A truly good performance on the job can bring you a great deal nearer to that much coveted promotion or salary increase. An elderly family member will need your assistance. Do what you can to help this unfortunate person in any way that you can. It is especially important not to neglect elders who may spend rather a lot of time on their own these days. They could feel unwanted and unloved, and need reassurance. Virgo business people can afford to press their claims more forcefully. It cannot hurt.

21. THURSDAY. Exciting. Routine work should be going along much more smoothly now. This should make it possible for you to turn your attention to personal matters. They will give you some outlet for your natural and creative talents. This is also another favorable day for romance. Your love life appears to have been moving along very well of late. There will be a chance to make a relationship that means a great deal to you far more stable and manageable. Greater harmony with loved ones will also tend to affect all of Virgo's daily dealings with other people, as well. New romantic attractions can be formed by younger students at colleges or other places of higher education.

22. FRIDAY. Tricky. Relations with employers or other influential people can take on an entirely new aspect. They may well turn into personal friends. The day could be good for obtaining official clearance for new business financial proposals. The early part of it is the best period for getting official agreements signed. You may find that you begin to fade fast from midafternoon onward. That makes it important for you to get as early a start as possible. There could also be pressures building up on you at home. Sponsors can be found to back humanitarian or altruistic ventures. Loved ones may be sulky and deliberately uncooperative. If you can't win them around, let them stew awhile.

23. SATURDAY. Manageable. Friends may be having parties or else have good reason to be celebrating in some other, similar way. A good time should be had by all. You may be asked to play a major role in the fun-seeking activities. There could be some romance in the air, as well. But it is important that you handle carefully all matters connected with your work and business first thing.

They must not be put to one side. This can be a favorable day for travel and for mixing business with pleasure. You may be having a working lunch with several people who can help you in some way with sound financial advice. Children may be feeling a bit sorry for themselves.

24. SUNDAY. Buoyant. It should be one of the happiest and most carefree days that you have spent for some time. You will find that you are able to get on extremely well with the people whose company you are in. It applies to all, whether they be friends, relatives or business associates. There is likely to be quite a varied program today and this will be just what the doctor ordered. It's also a day when secret romantic hopes and dreams will have a much better chance of coming true. These could quite well be involvements with people at or from a distance. The importance of sharing intellectual or self-improvement interests with loved ones can hardly be overestimated.

25. MONDAY. Disturbing. The end does not necessarily justify the means. This is a bit of information that you should remember well today. Virgos may find that their escape route is cut off. It may be necessary to face the music. It would not be a good idea to try to take any shortcuts. It will be favorable for out-of-court settlements. If you get in the hands of lawyers, you may find that expenses begin to soar and matters really do start to get out of hand. It may be in your best interest to be more of a realist. Save face and get out while you can still cope adequately. Friends may have suffered a stroke of bad luck. It will probably be Virgo's duty to help them out insofar as is possible.

26. TUESDAY. Erratic. You should get a good chance to obtain interviews with people who operate away from the public eye. You may find that meetings with people which take place in the strictest secrecy work out well. They may even be better than ones that keep everything open and aboveboard. But it might be best to give yourself a few days to think over what has been proposed to you. Do not sign contracts or documents connected with real estate or investments if pressure to do so is being put on you. It may be best not to entrust secrets to loved ones just for the time being. In romantic relationships, Virgos may find themselves back at square one. Depending on personal feelings, this may be fine.

27. WEDNESDAY. Rewarding. It looks as though you are on somewhat of an all-out roll now. It would be a good idea to make all the hay you can while the sun shines! The Virgo-born person will have an excellent opportunity to show off the less well-known side of his or her nature. They can safely let their hair down without causing a panic. People will find you entertaining and very amusing. You are quite likely to be very well received at any party you attend. In fact, you will be very much in demand socially. The time is good for capitalizing on artistic, creative or inventive abilities. Vacation leave may be unexpectedly extended. This is sure to create excitement.

28. THURSDAY. Profitable. Look for another fun day! But, at the same time, it is important for you to stick to what you know best. Make the most of your talents that you feel confident in exploiting. You will have a good opportunity to mix business with pleasure in an extremely relaxed setting. Although you will not be hard-pressed, much that will be of benefit to you and yours can be achieved. Tie up any loose ends of business that have been left undone. Do not leave paperwork unfinished. Now is the time to sign new contracts. It would be pointless to hold out any longer for better terms. You might even lose the deal entirely. Later today would be good for giving children the encouragement they need.

29. FRIDAY. Upsetting. You may well feel that co-workers are ganging up against you. Virgo people should check all facts for themselves. You might quite well find that you have been using out-of-date information for your financial calculations. You may have to review jobs all over again without being able to earn any extra money. It will be extremely difficult for you to get anything new off the ground. Homelife will also be somewhat upsetting. Differences with loved ones over financial problems cannot be solved easily. Romance will not be happy. Chasing after someone who has obviously cooled down toward you is pointless. It will only make you look foolish in front of your group.

30. SATURDAY. Demanding. Friends may land both themselves and their Virgo acquaintances in trouble with the authorities. Do not do anything that would in any way be likely to infringe upon the law. Even if it were meant only for a laugh, it will not appear so funny if you are brought before a judge for it. Today can bring a repetition of many of yesterday's problems, although they are not likely to be quite as pronounced. The difficulties that you encounter today will probably be in a much milder form. It is essential that Virgos know precisely where they stand in all financial affairs and dealings. Friends can be downright unfair and unreasonable with their requests or demands.

JULY

1. SUNDAY. Sensitive. You will have some difficulty with your immediate family. Virgo parents with teenagers may be confused about the best way to exert discipline. Domestic bliss would appear to be unobtainable just now. All around, this will be an extremely sensitive day. Virgos must watch themselves and the way they react very carefully indeed. Curiosity must be controlled. Seemingly harmless enough questions can set off a train of unfortunate consequences. Partners and spouses may be overspending. Any attempts to try to stop them and make them see reason can only lead to quarrels. Friends will not fall in with your plans for pleasure even though they may have agreed to them previously.

2. MONDAY. Satisfactory. You will be rather pleased to get back into the weekly routine. You seem to have had a rather troublesome and not entirely happy weekend. You will doubtless feel only too happy to come to grips with outside matters. These will take you out of range of any domestic crisis that you may have been facing. Travel is likely to work out rather well for you. Virgo people should get their priorities right. They should definitely not worry too much about trivial considerations. You may have a mental blockage which prevents you from remembering something. Check with your engagement book so that no important engagements can slip your mind. Today should be helpful for signing business financial agreements.

3. TUESDAY. Demanding. Be very careful about what you sign. You are usually a fairly cautious kind of a person. But this might be one of those days when you slip up. You could easily jump into a new deal when you would be putting up a lot of the financial backing. Do not do so without going into all details as you should. Friends may be very persuasive, but you should go over accounts in detail. Do not just listen to words, however eloquently they are strung together. If you look at things in the right way, this is most certainly a period when you can grow rapidly in experience and understanding. It will be favorable later for contacting or visiting friends whom you have not seen for a long time.

4. WEDNESDAY. Happy. This should be a tip-top day. This month seems to have gotten off to a somewhat difficult start. It appears, however, that you came back with all cylinders firing. It would be a good idea to write down important events. Then list the lessons that you have undoubtedly learned from them for future reference. Writing can also be a useful protection against self-deception. Virgos may have to express their thoughts coherently to realize they are wrong. This is a much happier day for romance. A difference with your mate or partner will be easier to iron out. You should be able to go out and enjoy yourself tonight without having to spend too much money.

5. THURSDAY. Disconcerting. Some Virgos may be living in the past. You are quite likely to come in contact with a person or a group of people who are much younger than you. You may meet some in your own age group. All of them seem a lot more with it than you. They are aware of the way things are shaping up for members of the younger generation. You may well find that you are shaken out of some of your complacency by this. It should be good for you. You may also have difficulty in coming up with some answers to very pertinent questions that are brought up. Influential people will not be impressed with off-the-cuff answers. Some serious misunderstandings can arise with business ventures.

6. FRIDAY. Easygoing. You will be rather pleased that you have the opportunity to take a bit of a breather. The working week should end on a relaxed and easy note. In fact, you may be able to take off from your place of employment early to get some personal matters finished up. Whatever the case, you should use constructively any extra spare time that you find you have. Even if it only means you will get in the shopping, that's a plus. Do anything that will save you precious free time on Saturday. That's when you will wish to give free rein to your own desires. There will be greater opportunities for mixing business with pleasure later. But try to keep the accent on having a good time.

7. SATURDAY. Sensitive. It appears as if you have had a bit of an upside down beginning to the month of July. This is a time when you should be attempting to bring some order back into your life. Thrash out some problems that have been upsetting you in the romantic area. Have a heart-to-heart talk with your mate or spouse. You will only gain respect from people close to you by stating exactly what is really bothering you. Travel with friends may open up exciting new vistas and horizons. Advertising or publicity may attract sponsors for causes that you feel are very worthy.

But certain members may not be toeing the line, and can be neglecting their responsibilities. You may have to correct this.

8. SUNDAY. Frustrating. You will not be able to get any cooperation today. Your mate will be unpredictable. Control your temper and do not act out of character. Family members may not intend to be trying to rub you up the wrong way. Your time will not appear to be your own now. You may have to answer to the calls of duty made on you by older relatives. You will be more aware of your responsibilities to your parents and kin than ever. It may be difficult to find anyone to share your sense of enthusiasm for an artistic venture that you would like to make some money out of. If you try to go it alone there will be a feeling of anticlimax. You are caught in a trap that is at least partly of your own making.

9. MONDAY. Slow. Gather yourself together. Try to get finished up with little routine jobs. This is one of those days when you should go over accounts. Get a better understanding of the current financial situation in its totality that you find yourself in. Some Virgos may have to spend more time at home dealing with the domestic chores. They should attempt to get ahead with them, however much of a drudge they may be. Virgo people may be very much left to themselves today. But you will like it that way as you do not need any outsiders to assist you. You are able to come to grips yourself with what you know you have to. A sense of pride can be derived from cooking that allows you to be artistic.

10. TUESDAY. Rewarding. Loved ones may come up with some especially sound career advice. You should listen to what your mate or partner has to say, especially. This is not a time for going against the tide of opinion. Do not allow yourself to become too much of a stick-in-the-mud. You may be able to bring your creative talents to bear on your regular job, with excellent results. You should certainly be able to catch the eye of your boss or superior. A more flexible attitude should help you to overcome professional problems. This might be a good chance for projecting a more attractive, even glamorous, public image. Friends can be made among people in the business world, a smart move for you.

11. WEDNESDAY. Mixed. A mixed sort of bag seems to be in store today for people born under the sign of Virgo. Caution is advised. Do not jump headfirst into any new deals in which you would be putting up a good deal of the financial investment. Wait until you get a clearer picture as to exactly when you would be able to get some of the supposed profits back. Allow your usual Virgo caution to be very much in evidence. This is not to say that you should not ever take calculated risks. Just make sure that the odds are stacked on your side as much as possible. Friends will not like to be pressured into helping you with personal matters. They may want to give their time to help you with causes.

12. THURSDAY. Productive. Partners in teamwork enterprises may be able to teach you Virgos a useful trick or two. You are fast learners, if nothing else. So you are always interested in anything that will save you time and effort. Only, however, as long as you are able to get the job well done. The day will be good for furthering imaginative or creative work. You may be able to use some of your spare time in more meaningful ways than you have been doing of late. A more indirect and subtle approach will tend to be the most effective when it comes to the handling of legal affairs. Influential people are likely to be friendly and helpful. Loved ones may be concerned with their careers.

13. FRIDAY. Disturbing. Friday the thirteenth is unlucky for some, they say. But you must not allow this to get you down just because you may be feeling superstitious and vulnerable. It will be genuinely difficult to decide upon the right approach. This will apply in personal as well as in business matters. It would seem that you are open to an awesome number of pressures. It is vital that you make sure you can indeed live with any decisions you make. They will surely affect the future of you and yours. Speculation should be avoided. You are not likely to come out the winner if you attempt to gamble in order to build up your weekly take-home pay. Social commitments may interfere with romantic ones.

14. SATURDAY. Tricky. You appear to be working under some sort of pressure at the moment. Be aware of whatever it is that is playing on your nerves. You should tread very cautiously when it comes to making any important changes, especially those of a financial nature. Virgos are unlikely to find they are the only people who are encountering difficulty this weekend. This fact, however, will probably be of little consolation to them! It is not a good idea to look a gift horse in the mouth. Quite the contrary, this would be the best way of losing influential friends. Listen to influential people, by all means. But remember that you will have to live with the decisions that you make.

15. SUNDAY. Sensitive. Virgos should not take the law into their own hands. This course of action not only would be futile but it could also be dangerous. If you consider that people are breaking the law, you should inform the correct authorities. You must allow them to act according to their rules. If you attempt to interfere in such situations yourself, you could find that you arouse the anger of the police force and end up in court. The financial side of the management of groups, clubs or societies may not be above suspicion. This will be a good day for deepening romantic involvements. Any meetings that take place between you and your loved one should produce harmony.

16. MONDAY. Useful. The morning period today may be a somewhat sticky number for you. It will be difficult to get new ideas off the ground then. In fact, it might be to your advantage to use the time for other matters. Up to midday, attend to jobs that you should have taken care of before you left for your weekend break. Influential people may be difficult to track down. Do not set out on long journeys unless you have definite appointments with specific people. Otherwise, you may discover that such trips are a complete waste of time and money. Friends can take remarks the wrong way. People's secrets must not be betrayed.

17. TUESDAY. Successful. It could probably be one of the best days that you have experienced for quite a while. It would appear that you have more energy and driving force at your disposal now. Virgo people should have reached the conviction that their aims are indeed attainable. Influential people will signal guidance for you. You can thus make moves on your own. You will also have greater confidence that they will receive the nod of approval from above. You may be assured of convincing confirmation of your hunches or suspicions. Contracts with publishers are likely to be extended. This is a starred day for making long journeys. Friends who live at a distance may have some valuable contacts.

18. WEDNESDAY. Excellent. There is no doubt about it. This will be the best day of the month for you so far. Virgo readers who have not taken a summer vacation as yet may be planning one now. You might be able to finesse a trip at a bargain price. You would be very pleased at the savings it would enable you to make. Romance is starred, especially for the footloose and fancy-free. Secret negotiations at your place of employment can result in the confirmation of some very lucrative deals. It is worth your while to operate away from the public eye. This could be a good time for pulling strings behind the scenes. People who are sick or being cared for are most likely to appreciate a visit from you.

19. THURSDAY. Uncertain. Very little is apt to go terribly wrong today. But you are quite likely to be feeling a sense of anti-climax after all the excellent things that happened in your life yesterday. There will be a somewhat subdued atmosphere at home. You will probably prefer to get out and about quite a lot today. It applies especially if you are able to make trips in connection with your work. One very important thing is that you will not want to get sidetracked. Be sure you do not have any truck with those people who would only waste your time. In business, it will probably be better to appeal to people's emotions just now, rather than to their reasoning. But that is a bit unusual.

20. FRIDAY. Mixed. This will be a pleasant day for romance. There will be opportunities to get closer to people to whom you are strongly attracted. You may not have known them for very long, but you can rectify that. Virgo readers who are involved in long-standing partnership arrangements would do well to speak their minds. Simply clear the air of any silly little misunderstandings that may have arisen. People may be spreading malicious rumors about you. It would be in your best interests to confront these gossipmongers and nip any gossip in the bud. Shopping could reap some good results. Go hunting where the bargains are most likely to be found. Get out and about more.

21. SATURDAY. Sensitive. You will be feeling a little tense today. It will be difficult for you to relax completely. You may not enjoy whatever pleasure and entertainment are available at the moment. Members of your family will probably be rather subdued. It will be difficult for you to discover what they are really thinking. It would be best not to probe into loved ones' affairs, though. More mutual consideration will be helpful. Allow more give-and-take to enter into your life. Disagreements with friends may come to a head. But both sides should realize that this is only a passing phase. They should not take matters too seriously.

22. SUNDAY. Uncertain. Trouble has been brewing for some time between you and your in-laws. It could reach a pressure point now. There are likely to be discussions going on that you find difficult to cope with. Some of the people involved may be going over the past. You probably feel that this is a most futile process. Virgos may become discouraged about the future. You should try to steer clear of people who have often had a depressing effect on your spirits in the past. Try to learn from previous mistakes. It is up to Virgo people to make happen what they want to happen. It should be good later on for all forms of recreation and entertaining. Check over the list of those friends whom you may owe.

23. MONDAY. Lucky. You may be feeling quite pleased that you have survived the rather strenuous weekend. It does not seem as though anything catastrophic took place on Saturday or Sunday. But you will be in the mood to get new business deals going, running on well-oiled wheels. Virgos will be the first to appreciate that they have reached a turning point. Ties that have been binding you in the past and holding you back can be broken. But first it will be necessary to learn the lessons that the past has to teach. There might be a good chance for rereading old diaries or records. Spare time should be used for doing what you can to help people less fortunate than yourself. There are always people who need help.

24. TUESDAY. Exciting. Carry on the good work! You should be able to combine business and pleasure to your great satisfaction. Take influential people out for a drink or for a working lunch. The day is starred for getting information from bank managers, accountants and stockbrokers. Make sure that any money you have on deposit is earning the best possible interest for you. This is also a pleasant day from the personal angle. Romance looks well starred. Some Virgos may have been going steady for quite some time. They may now decide that the time has come to make such relationships more permanent. Either moving in together or getting engaged are possibilities. Take a novel approach.

25. WEDNESDAY. Difficult. A few Virgos may have been overindulging themselves of late. They should face up to the fact that they are not in as good shape physically as perhaps they should be. Remember that if you are not physically fit, it will affect your temper at home. It will also tend to make you sluggish at work. Get on the scales, then face up to reality. If you are overweight, you will have to go on a diet and start with some light exercise. But do not overdo it. Nothing will be achieved in this area of your life by rushing things. You will be alert at your place of employment during the early part of the day. The period up to lunchtime is when things are most likely to go your way.

26. THURSDAY. Mixed. Friends and loved ones are not likely to hit it off. Be very careful before you invite a new associate home for a meal or a drink. Try to think of the mood that will exist on the domestic scene. This is not a time for trying to shock people. Nor, for that matter, is it a time to try to show them a different side of your personality. You should be trying for the easy options for the time being. Take shortcuts for now and settle for anything that will give you a peaceful time. A different approach to influential people may be worthwhile, however. Try to get your boss to appreciate that you have many natural talents. It might profit them to put some of them to use more fully.

27. FRIDAY. Tricky. Financial issues may not be as clear-cut as they seem. There appears to be a friend or relative who would like to give you and your projects some needed financial support. But you may both find that it is not at all easy to accomplish. You will see when it comes to thrashing out with accountants how this could be done. It may be that money that is tied up cannot easily be touched. It could well bring the tax man down on you like a ton of bricks. The voice of conscience may contradict the natural instinct for survival and self-preservation. Children may not be telling you the whole truth.

28. SATURDAY. Useful. With the week and the month coming to an end, this would be a good day for taking a look at what you have achieved. Sum up your career during the past three or four weeks. Then decide where you intend to go from here. Do not neglect paperwork. If you have some spare time on your hands, give an hour or two over to answering correspondence. Loved ones will show total understanding if you lock yourself away for a couple of hours. Go over the amount of money that you have been spending on household things. Try to make cuts that all the family can participate in. Virgos should not push their luck too far when it comes to making savings, though.

29. SUNDAY. Mixed. An influential person whose brains you would like to pick may not be available when you need him or her the most. Virgos should not reveal information that could fall into the wrong hands. Do not divulge secrets to secretaries or personal assistants. Promises made that the information will be passed on to where you want it to go are unreliable. It might be best for you not to be quite so impatient. You must try to give more time to domestic issues today. Do not neglect your obligations to your loved ones. Children may need the guidance of the Virgo parent more than ever now. Today would be good for all forms of creative work, but especially for poetry and other forms of writing.

30. MONDAY. Disconcerting. Don't reveal all of the cards that you have up your sleeve when discussing new business deals. It is best to play a very close hand. That is something Virgos are pretty good at, anyway. This is a time when the left hand should really not know what the right hand is up to. But this is a good day for extending contracts or agreements that are already existent. The day is helpful for breaking the ice and making friends with people who have only been casual acquaintances to date. This will be a sensitive day for romance. Try not to break dates or break your word in any other way to people with whom you are deeply involved. You do not want your motives to come under suspicion.

31. TUESDAY. Ordinary. Keep speculative instincts in check. Do not follow the advice of friends. Tips that are given to you are likely to cause losses. Do not dip into reserves to back harebrained schemes. Remember, this is the last day of the month. It would be wise to hold back from making any important changes in the way you handle your career matters for the time being. Virgos may have to subordinate their own interests to those of the family unit. Your feeling of not belonging anywhere is probably only temporary. The advice of parents or other family members may be more valuable than Virgo people are willing to admit. Children may leave the days of their fantasies behind.

AUGUST

1. WEDNESDAY. Fortunate. This midweek day sees you in fine fettle. As this is the beginning of another month, you will be raring to go. First, you will be keen to make new starts with projects that you had planned on earlier. You had intended to get rid of these some time ago before the summer was out. The attitude of influential people will be a boost to your confidence. For one thing, they will encourage you to be more creative. Virgos may win some new admirers now. Among these will be people who will be able to do them a lot of good in the future. It will be as a result of the contacts that they have. Secret romantic hopes and dreams are likely to move a step nearer to fulfillment.

2. THURSDAY. Easygoing. Lots of little odd jobs will keep you meaningfully occupied both at home and at your place of work or business. Virgo readers who have the chance to slow down a bit should take advantage of the easygoing conditions. Some of you may even be able to take the day off. This would obviously apply more to the self-employed and the homemakers among you. It would, of course, exclude those who work definite shifts. Virgo people are not likely to be confronted with any difficulties that they cannot find answers for. Today would be good for capitalizing on artistic or creative skills. It could also be helpful for looking more closely into speculative propositions.

3. FRIDAY. Uncertain. Virgo people may be looking at things through rose-colored glasses. Deal in facts and facts alone. Do not try to twist things to suit a definite point of view. You will only make life more difficult for yourself if you do not face up to certain facts now. Some of them will undoubtedly seem a little unpalatable. But that's life! Children's actions may be hard to predict or understand. Youngsters will be making some unexpected trouble for Virgo parents. But you should try to take what is probably only a phase well in your stride. Romantic affairs may contain some misunderstandings or confusion. Do not be afraid to state your wishes or desires; this can help everyone.

4. SATURDAY. Upsetting. Marital differences will flare up this morning. Any progress that you may make with work that has to be done in and around the home will be painstakingly slow. You will have some difficulty in concentrating. This will certainly not be made any easier by the number of interruptions that you have to put up with. Domestic affairs are likely to cut into the schedule that you had prepared for yourself. Be careful when traveling. If you are behind the wheel, make sure that you do not break any of the highway rules. Whatever Virgos may be doing today, there will be a good chance that they will be wishing they were doing something else. Make up your mind to change things.

5. SUNDAY. Demanding. You may want to discuss your salary with your boss. It would be wise to wait until tomorrow afternoon, when the working week is well under way. What it would be most unwise for you to do is to bother him or her too early. That mistake alone could result in a negative reaction to your request. This is not a day for hurrying or rushing any important decisions. You may feel that you are running down a blind alley as far as your future work prospects are concerned. But you must ask yourself what you would like to change to? Virgos may not be feeling in the best of health. Routine duties and commitments will appear to be very difficult chores. Quarrels with loved ones are likely.

6. MONDAY. Disconcerting. You have experienced what appears to have been one of the most difficult weekends you have encountered for some time. So you will probably have some difficulty in mapping out a plan of campaign for today. It might be best for you to mark time with jobs that do not require you to push yourself too hard. It seems unlikely that you will have nearly enough of the stamina required to make any new starts with creative ventures. This is one of those days when you are likely to feel that all of your efforts are simply not appreciated as much as they should be. Obsessive thoughts can make concentration rather difficult. Influential people are not inclined to be sympathetic.

7. TUESDAY. Sensitive. Virgo people should press on with their work regardless of the obstacles that they may feel have been put in their way. This is not a day for sitting around moaning. You will have good opportunities to make more money through working overtime. What you must avoid is speculation, or the company of people who make you feel lazy. Steer clear of friends who seem to have much more time on their hands than is good for them or good for you. Influential people are unlikely to be very fair, but yours is not to question why today. You may feel that someone who has a superior position to your own may be out to get you.

8. WEDNESDAY. Satisfactory. You may be blamed for other people's errors, but don't worry too much. When a superior goes over the details of the work, it will become obvious that you have been falsely accused. You will then be exonerated of any blame. Influential people will probably have to apologize to you. You should accept such apologies magnanimously and not try to make capital out of it. A series of flukes can help you in your desire to make progress with teamwork activities. Today would be good for clarifying legal issues. Professional advice can be well worth obtaining. Virgo people should try to be faster in their responses. This evening could be ideal for catching up with reading.

9. THURSDAY. Rewarding. Things do not seem to have run very well for you so far during this month. But this will be a much better day than you have had lately. You will have more driving force and energy at your disposal. This may mean that you can come to grips with many of the jobs that you have fallen behind with. There is likely to be more money to be made and that alone will give you a boost and perhaps encourage you to push yourself. This is one of those happy days when many things that have been burdening you will sort themselves out. It is a particularly auspicious day for romance, favorable for Virgos who are considering getting married or engaged. You will feel closer to your mate or partner than has been the case for some time past.

10. FRIDAY. Confusing. Do not change around any of the work that you have completed earlier in the week unless you get a definite directive from your boss to do so. This would be a wrong day to take on more authority than has been invested upon you. You will not get much praise for initiative. Your best bet today would be to deal with jobs that you cannot be criticized for. Wind up the loose ends of any office jobs. Get caught up with your correspondence. Write letters to people in faraway places especially. By doing so, you might be able to save yourself the expense of going on a journey. Gambles are unlikely to pay off, perhaps because there is a greater risk of deception.

11. SATURDAY. Tricky. There could be serious differences of opinion with members of your family. It will not be simple to get loved ones to agree to the financial plans that you wish to put into effect. The chances are that your mate or partner will think that you are simply being tightfisted. They will find it hard to understand why you feel it is so necessary to be a little careful. But this is not the right time to reinvest mutually held funds. Hold down spending merely for pleasure. Curb feelings of jealousy and suspicion because such negative emotions will usually be destructive. Avoid becoming overly emotional. The health of children may be a cause for concern. Try to spot a problem early.

12. SUNDAY. Mixed. This is not a day for crossing swords with people in authority. You should keep your more way-out opinions to yourself. Any ideas that you come up with for changes in the way regular work is handled are likely to create a very frosty reception. It would be best for you to stick to your regular activities on this day of rest. Forget anything connected with the routine affairs of the working week. Distant government or customs officials can be obstructive. But the day is favorable for entering into untrodden territory if it is connected with artistic work. Creative talents can be developed far more expressively. In romantic associations all can be and should be forgiven.

13. MONDAY. Erratic. Virgos may be trying to run before they can walk. Do not hurry tasks that require a lot of attention to details. If you gloss over mistakes, you may get away with it in the short term. But you will not be able to get over it for a long period of time. Some day soon, what you do is almost certain to be checked and then come under very close scrutiny. You must choose your words with more care when dealing with superiors. This is especially true when it comes to writing correspondence. Travel can be tiring. There could be holdups both on the roads and on the regular train and bus routes. Don't get yourself worked up over delays because it won't change anything but your temper.

14. TUESDAY. Difficult. Get your priorities right. The best way to avoid confusion today is to work out a plan and stick to it. Do not allow yourself to become ruffled by people who appear to be living on their nerves. The best way to make a good impression on your boss is to show that you are able to keep your cool while those around you blow hot. Try to clear up any confusion that still exists in your mind with regard to business and career affairs. Seek clarification from influential people, if necessary. Personal likes and dislikes should not be allowed to intrude into the making of professional decisions. Interviews are not likely to be a great success, no matter how you relate to them.

15. WEDNESDAY. Excellent. You are entering into a more positive phase now. Of course there may be a few setbacks. But you will be pleased to know that the general trend would appear to be upward for quite a long time ahead. What you must remember, though, is to avoid rushing anything. More haste would most definitely mean less speed. This is a favorable day for attempts to pull strings behind the scenes. All in all, this will be an excellent working day. From start to finish you will be able to make noteworthy progress. People will be helpful. Investment matters and career ambitions are starred. You should be feeling very pleased with yourself.

16. THURSDAY. Difficult. Friends may be gossiping about you. You will be very annoyed with such people. They seem to have little more to do with their time than to be rumormongers. It would be best to stay clear of such pettiness. You will find that there are many things that you can get on with yourself. You will not even have to call on the assistance of those who have proved themselves to be somewhat two-faced. It would be a good idea to set your standards very high today. Electrical equipment may save time and labor, but it may also result in the loss of that personal feeling of accomplishment. Humanitarian ventures or organizations may be jeopardized by internal conflicts and rifts.

17. FRIDAY. Productive. Use this day to concentrate on jobs that do not require a great deal of outside assistance. The morning can be a good time for placing advertisements in the media. If you are counting on selling something, it would be a really good idea to run an ad. If you run it in your local paper, you may be surprised at the very large response you will get. You will find that work requiring more attention to detail will be much easier to get through. Loved ones will not interfere and you will have the chance to plan your day as you see fit. Business financial negotiations should make some definite headway. But money should not be borrowed unless it is absolutely necessary.

18. SATURDAY. Challenging. Do not let up with your creative work. You will have the chance today to finish off an artistic job. You have devoted quite a lot of your time to this special interest of late. There is not likely to be any pressure on you today. This will result, of course, in your being able to work at a much faster pace as it will be unlikely that you will be inhibited in any way. Virgo people may notice a new feeling arising inside themselves. But they may possibly have trouble in pinning it down at first. It can be a new sense of self-assurance and self-confidence. You will have a greater idea of your own true worth so you will have no need to try to convince others of it.

19. SUNDAY. Changeable. You may be feeling rather restless. Perhaps you have been giving a lot more attention than usual to your work. This could have made you very itchy to break out. But it would be a good idea to start the day slowly. Do not accept any invitations to go out until midday because you seem to be in a changeable mood. So if you do make definite appointments first thing, you are likely to want to wriggle out of them later on. Perhaps it is the fact that you are waiting on an important decision until Monday. Knowing what is going on behind the scenes could be partly to blame. Compassionate or charitable impulses that you may have could be misinterpreted.

20. MONDAY. Fortunate. This could be a very good beginning to the week at your place of employment. Some welcome news may come through. You may not achieve all that you had been hoping for as a result of some very delicate negotiation. But you should certainly be able to live with the result of what has been agreed upon. Reviewing the recent past should show Virgos clearly where they have gone wrong. With that knowledge, they know how they can avoid repeating the same errors in the future. There may be a good chance for attempting to find sponsors for charitable or other worthwhile causes. It is worth obtaining the official seal of approval before launching any untried ventures.

21. TUESDAY. Exciting. You appear to have gotten off to a good start this week. Yesterday was an excellent beginning, it would seem. Today you will have the opportunity to build on the worthwhile results that you have already achieved. Try to get influential people to back your artistic schemes. If this will not be with money, it could be by affording you the opportunity to make use of the good contacts they have in other towns or cities. Calculated risks would seem to have a good chance of reaping rewards for you. Reports received from unofficial sources may save Virgo people from having to go through normal channels to obtain their information. This could expedite their work and save time.

22. WEDNESDAY. Rewarding. This is the third in a cycle of good days. You should be very well pleased with conditions both at home and at your place of business. Loved ones will show greater understanding and sympathy if you are kept at the office or factory longer than usual. It may be possible to delegate some of your domestic responsibilities to a member of your family. Older relatives will be more cooperative, too, especially in-laws. Ideas that come to Virgos in the morning would be well worth noting down. This might be a good time for gathering information and obtaining advice. Equally, Virgo people's advice on subjects in which they are experts will be greatly valued by others.

23. THURSDAY. Uncertain. Continue with any work already under way within the home. This will be a bit of an anticlimactic day after what has been going on of late. It will do you good to slow down a little, though. Get your feet back on the ground by concentrating more on routine matters. Be sure that you use your spare time constructively. Do not do anything that would waste physical or mental energy. See to the needs of your family. You may have to put some of your free hours at the disposal of others. You are advised against putting money down on purchases that you have not seen with your own eyes. If they turn out to be inferior in quality, you might lose the payment.

24. FRIDAY. Difficult. Some health problems suffered by your mate may necessitate your calling in a doctor. You may have to cancel some important engagements because of conditions at home. Virgo people may be forced to pay for other people's errors. Or you can be made to pay for your own errors down to the very last cent. People are unlikely to be in a forgetting or forgiving mood. Do not be in too much of a hurry to rush through business. You will not achieve your aims if you are aggressive with influential people. There will be difficulties with romance. Loved ones are not likely to be in the mood to see things your way, even if they know in their minds you are right.

25. SATURDAY. Sensitive. This can be a pleasant enough day as long as you look on the brighter side of things. Do not be glum or keep going over mistakes. You are probably powerless to do anything about them, anyhow, for the time being. You should definitely try to build up a more confident outlook generally. You are not likely to have any difficulty in getting along with your loved ones. A recent tiff that involved you and your opposite number will be easier to unravel, especially if it was over money. But Virgo people must watch their tempers. They could easily get out of bed on the wrong side. Influential people will be helpful and sympathetic this evening. But don't ply them with sob stories.

26. SUNDAY. Manageable. Virgos may be fussing too much. Just because you want everyone to have a good time you could tend to overreact. Remember that this is a Sunday and you want to do a bit of relaxing yourself. It seems that you have had quite an eventful week and you need to unwind. Seek out the company of people with whom you are at ease. Try to avoid people who make you feel ill at ease. Do not go to formal functions where you would feel you had to be on your guard for most of the time. In romance, it is important to relax and let things take their course. Silence can communicate more than words. Your favorite forms of self-expression will give you an anchor for your thoughts and feelings.

27. MONDAY. Mixed. There continues to be a restless atmosphere on the domestic front. Married Virgos may find their spouse unpredictable and demanding. It will be difficult to get a positive answer on any important issues that you wish to sort out. Health could be another problem. Doctors' bills will be higher than you had budgeted for. Once you knuckle down to work, your worries will ease somewhat. Influential people will do a lot more to ensure that working conditions are comfortable and harmonious. A journey this afternoon could bring you in some extra money. Addressing correspondence to the wrong person could bring you some embarrassment, not to mention delays.

28. TUESDAY. Quiet. This is probably going to be a very uneventful day. You are not likely to have a great deal of driving force in any case, so it is probably just as well. You should attempt to get something constructive achieved, though. It might be a good day to go over recent bills and bring your accounts for the month of August up to date. You could also use part of the day for writing letters to family and friends who are abroad. Do not lose touch with people who you always got on very well with, but have not seen for quite awhile. Where business is concerned, you seem to have planted the seeds of what you wanted to sow.

29. WEDNESDAY. Enjoyable. Now is the time to push hard to get your propositions accepted by relatives. Your positive attitude will give close family members the confidence to follow your plans. Do what you can to make the future more secure. Seek areas where cuts in spending can be made. Today is favorable for setting up home with loved ones. Virgos are advised to keep their sense of indecision to themselves. Asking other people's advice will only tend to make them more confused than before. It is a good time for obtaining the assistance of influential people in turning creative enterprises into commercial propositions.

30. THURSDAY. Mixed. A close friend is likely to ask you a favor. Unless this would put you to considerable inconvenience, do your best to oblige. Romantic partners can act in an impulsive and reckless way. The solution of children's problems cannot be brushed under the carpet any longer. They may require some drastic action on your part. One-time gambles are unlikely to lead to success or financial gain. Recognition or fame can unexpectedly attach itself to Virgo people. Loved ones may be looking to you to take the lead and to show the way ahead. You can afford to act with a good deal more confidence now. You appear to be self-sufficient and to know your way around.

31. FRIDAY. Uncertain. This month comes to an end with your perhaps feeling a little worried about loved ones. Your pangs of guilt may be quite exaggerated. You really cannot and should not go around trying to take responsibility for everyone. It is important to know when to be serious and when to relax and enjoy yourself. There are unlikely to be any new difficulties cropping up at your place of employment. Youngsters should not be treated too harshly. Older relatives can be very helpful if you feel unsure about what would be the best way to act in the matter of discipline. Today could be favorable for signing pending agreements. Even Virgos should see that the time of hesitation is past!

SEPTEMBER

1. SATURDAY. Mixed. It is just as well that this first day of the month falls on a weekend. You will have the opportunity to get finished with routine chores and organize accounts and paperwork, etc. You will then be able to make a fresh start with new jobs when the working week unfolds. Continued perseverance with routine occupational activities will impress your boss. You will be able to prove your worth by showing that you have the staying power to see boring work through to a satisfactory conclusion. The day will be favorable for you Virgo bosses to locate and deal with sources of labor unrest. But this evening you could become easily discouraged. You must try to keep your spirits up.

2. SUNDAY. Confusing. You seem to be in a bit of a neurotic state. You must relax. This is, after all, a day of rest. You should not take on any additional responsibilities that will make you feel uptight or tense in any way. Too much rushing about will merely result in exhaustion. If you do attempt to do any work connected with your regular job, be sure to do it very carefully and thoroughly. Otherwise, it may not be appreciated at all. Cookbook instructions may be either impossible to follow or just plain wrong. This is no time for experimentation in the kitchen. Neighbors can be a nuisance. Explanations would be best left until another day.

3. MONDAY. Misleading. Do not allow negative feelings to affect your performance on the job. It is important that you try just as hard as you can to make a good impression on key people. They are probably in a position to do you some real good. Superiors will be helpful, too. But that would only apply if you show that you are keen to get on. You cannot expect promotion to be presented to you on a silver platter! Too much rushing about could merely result in exhaustion. Just make sure that you get your priorities right. People's ungratefulness may merely add fuel to the fire of Virgos' feelings of not being appreciated. Loved ones may be immersed in their own problems, in a world of their own.

4. TUESDAY. Satisfactory. Some improvement is indicated today. You will find it easier to get on with other members of your family and to communicate meaningfully with them. Try to sort out any financial problems that have been worrying you. Women Virgos should try to make an effort to cut down on the amount of money that they spend on shopping. Keep your eyes peeled for the bargains. Buy summer produce which should be plentiful and reasonably priced now. Exciting progress can be made in teamwork and cooperative endeavors. There might even be some important breakthroughs. The best way to obtain respect and acknowledgment is for you to give the same generously to others.

5. WEDNESDAY. Sensitive. This midweek day will find you very wrapped up in your own affairs. It is true that you have many small problems to sort out that concern you and you alone. But still and all, you must not be selfish or appear cold and indifferent to the feelings of other members of your family. You should make more of an effort to see things from the others person's point of view, as well. This is not the greatest time for entering into new agreements. It would be in your best interests to postpone the signing of important documents. Only when you have had the chance to study them at your leisure, and to obtain the advice of a professional person, should you sign.

6. THURSDAY. Uncertain. Virgos' belief that everything can be rationalized and worked out logically may lead them astray. You could be dealing with some highly strung and very emotional people now. You will not necessarily be able to get them to do and see things entirely your way. You will only be able to solve your current problems by allowing more give-and-take to play a part in all relationships. It is best to seek out people with the requisite experience who can be of assistance to you. But later in the day, you should be able to increase pressure on large business firms or corporations. Today would be good for putting more time and exertion into research projects.

7. FRIDAY. Sensitive. You may find that you have certain legal matters to attend to. Out-of-court settlements can save time and money, as well as avoiding unwanted exposure.If you are in the public eye at all, you must do all that you can to maintain a very low profile. What you should want to avoid most of all is attracting any unsavory publicity. This is a good period for charity work. It is equally good for doing more to be of assistance to people who are less fortunate than you are. Children may need a lot more attention. Youngsters may also need firmer control from Virgo parents. There is always the possibility of their becoming involved in brushes with the law. Do not carry grudges.

8. SATURDAY. Useful. Investments may not be yielding the interest expected of them. It might be a good idea to have a chat with friends who know something about buying shares, building up a portfolio and the stock market in general. There are people who will be willing to give you good advice about such matters. That could mean you can change your investments to some advantage for yourself. It is favorable for communicating ideas or suggestions to influential people. Superiors will have more time to listen to what you have to say. This is a happy day for romance. You should try to get finished with work matters fairly early today. Then you can let your hair down and enjoy yourself.

9. SUNDAY. Pleasant. The more time that you can spend seeing to the needs of members of your family, the better it will be. Try to make this a typical family day. There will not be any necessity to spend a great deal of money to get the most benefit the day has to offer. It might be best, though, to keep your own relatives and in-laws separate for the time being. The family of your spouse or partner and your own family may not have met before. It would probably be best to postpone this until a future date. This is a day when you might possibly have some difficulty in bridging gaps that could exist between them. Virgo people may have trouble expressing themselves on paper. Letter writing will be tiresome.

10. MONDAY. Ordinary. This will be a reasonably successful kind of day from the career point of view. Slow and steady progress can be made. But this is not the right time to try to make any new starts. Influential people will be rather busy with their own affairs. They should not be troubled now with new ideas that you have come up with. It does not matter that you are keen to get your creative projects off the launching pad. Virgo business people may be trying to achieve too much too quickly. It is important not to tread on the toes of your colleagues. It would be good, though, for pinning people down and obtaining definite commitments from them. These could be either personal or business-related.

11. TUESDAY. Satisfactory. You do not seem to have the necessary energy or drive to make that important new breakthrough. Long journeys made in an effort to drum up support for your creative ideas are not likely to work out very successfully for you. It will be difficult to arrange to see influential people in faraway places without appointments. You must make definite appointments to see them before you set out on your trip. Virgo people should not look for personal glory or recognition. You will do best working in conjunction with colleagues. Remember, a task shared is a task halved. Virgos' intuition could be a reliable guide at the point where reasoning must break off. Don't fail to test it.

12. WEDNESDAY. Mixed. Expectations could be disappointing. Some money that you were hoping to receive by today may be delayed for one reason or another. Some Virgo people were probably expecting a lump sum payment. But they may find now that it is held up for some sort of official inquiry. You will undoubtedly have a lot of red tape to deal with. It will also be difficult to get hold of people who have the necessary authority to change such situations. You may have to be patient even when that patience has reached its breaking point. Secret hopes and wishes are quite unlikely to be fulfilled. Romance will be stormy, with the outcome unpredictable.

13. THURSDAY. Disconcerting. Virgo people can be mystified by the attitudes or remarks of friends. People may be leading you up the garden path. It will be difficult for you to ascertain whether this is intentional or not. Be careful about getting involved romantically with a person who has recently broken off a stormy relationship. You may find that you are merely being unwittingly used to help a person forget about a past sorrow. Members of the opposite sex may just want to be with you because of what you personally have to offer as a person. But it could be somewhat more complicated than that. Speculative propositions could be attractive, but deceptively so.

14. FRIDAY. Easygoing. You may be feeling emotionally drained. It would be a good idea to slow the tempo of your life down somewhat. Take it easy. You should not assume any additional responsibilities. If it is possible to knock off from your place of employment a little earlier than you usually do, that is exactly what you ought to do. This should not be an especially demanding ending to the working week. It can be quite delightful, depending on the company that Virgos happen to find themselves in. New friendships can be formed which might be important for the future. Today is helpful for attending to minor business affairs.

15. SATURDAY. Sensitive. The week ends with many of your hopes and dreams remaining unfulfilled. But you should not be too depressed about this. There are many things that have happened this week that augur well for the future. You ought to be looking at your affairs, both private and professional, from the long-term point of view. Virgos, more than almost any other sign, should realize the futility of rushing matters that demand time. Trying to squeeze unnoticed through the back door will not work. Virgo people will be surprised at how gracefully they are able to express themselves and their intentions, if only they try. But one wrong step can give rise to scandal or malicious gossip.

16. SUNDAY. Rewarding. This will be one of the best days that you have experienced all summer long. Virgo people will be delighted that they are able to benefit from privacy. In romantic relationships, it would be an especially good idea to spend more time alone with your loved ones. Do not allow friends to put pressure on you to involve yourself in activities which do not really appeal. Remember that this is your day of rest. It is very important that you spend your time as you see fit. It would be a good day for catching up with imaginative work. It will give you the chance to express the creative side of your nature. You will also be able to catch up with your personal letter writing.

17. MONDAY. Fortunate. A reasonably good start can be made to the working week. But this is a better day for attempts to set up deals than for trying to clinch them. Do all in your power to get into the good books of your superiors. You will be able to do very little to make progress in your career without the active support of influential people. This is an excellent day for Virgo readers to go on shopping expeditions. You will be able to pick up some excellent bargains at end-of-summer sales that are going on now. Virgos may at last be able to afford that special treat for themselves for which they have been saving up. They will also be able to continue to express themselves with grace and charm.

18. TUESDAY. Challenging. This is an important day from the money-making point of view. You should be prepared to work longer hours now. There will be good opportunities to earn overtime and bonus payments that should not be passed up. Virgo people are likely to play as seriously as they work. Business can be mixed with pleasure to some advantage. This is a good period for entertaining influential people. For sports people and athletes, this can be an excellent day for stepping up training. Your prowess at competitive activities will be much admired. Perseverance in hobbies or creative endeavors will be rewarded. Virgo parents should give their offspring the full benefit of their experience.

19. WEDNESDAY. Pleasant. Virgo-born people cannot afford to change course in midstream. Once you have decided on a positive course of action, you must stick to your guns, no matter what develops. It is important for you to build up an atmosphere of mutual trust and understanding between yourself and your associates at your place of employment. You cannot back out of projects that you have committed yourself to even if you can see the possibility of financial loss. You must not allow colleagues to be left holding the bag when you are just as responsible for the present situation as they are. Today would be favorable for raising funds for charity. It would be good for marriage proposals, too.

20. THURSDAY. Difficult. Do not purchase goods that only have a relatively short life span. Do not try to be penny-pinching by accepting shoddy merchandise. It would be best to live well within your means rather than buy inexpensive copies of well-known products. It is essential to keep all financial dealings aboveboard and fully documented. Virgos may be becoming too attached to their material possessions. Listen to what your mate or partner has to say. Some sound advice may be offered to you by close family members. It is certain that you would not get this from any other source. Older relatives will also be on hand to give you assistance, if required. Their experience makes it valuable.

21. FRIDAY. Inactive. You are undoubtedly keen to make progress in your work. But you are likely to find conditions at your place of employment somewhat slow-moving today. This will be a fairly uneventful and unexciting ending to the working week. Influential people will be pleasant enough, but perhaps a little too reticent for your liking in their approach to new ideas. If you want to get anything creative launched, you are probably going to have to do it alone. Virgo-born people who are looking for distractions or amusements are likely to be disappointed. Routine affairs and activities should be carried out, however boring they may be.

22. SATURDAY. Exciting. Several tempting opportunities are likely to crop up today. They will afford you the chance to increase your income and therefore your wealth. You will probably have the time to give more attention to your regular job than is usual for you on a Saturday. You will be delighted to rise to any new challenges. You should be able to get out and about more. You will enjoy travel as it would appear that you have been frustrated in your efforts to see people living at a distance of late. You can afford to be more of an adventurer and chance your luck. Virgo people will have their wits about them and will be able to penetrate any smoke screens that people try to put up.

23. SUNDAY. Quiet. Slow down a bit now that you have a day of rest. You should try to relax and unwind. It might be a good idea to get away from familiar surroundings. Some Virgos may find it hard to leave housework alone if they stay within the limits of their own four walls. Take a trip into the country. Visit friends or relatives who have been out of sight for all too long. You will also enjoy yourself if you have the chance to attend informal social functions. There you will have the opportunity to mingle with people from walks of life different to your own. You may have been worrying unnecessarily and to no avail of late. There would be a good chance for keeping abreast of neighborhood news.

24. MONDAY. Erratic. What Virgos have done or accomplished of late can stand them in good stead with influential people. You may not be too happy with the situation at your current place of employment. If this has been the case for some time, it might be good to arrange meetings with prospective employers. But it is important that you do not make any changes until you are satisfied you are right. Be absolutely certain that you can ensure future economic security for you and yours. This is not a time for throwing caution to the winds, something that Virgos do not like to do in any case. People may repay previous acts of generosity or kindness. This could be rewarding to your morale.

25. TUESDAY. Misleading. You may be a little disappointed with today. You seem unable to make the progress that you were expecting and counting on. Virgo people may be dwelling too much in the past. Nostalgia is one thing, but you must also try to move with the times. Remember the old days with fondness, but do not try to rekindle feelings and passions that have long since died. You will be wasting your time in an empty quest. Mix more with people younger than yourself who have new ideas. Family or household members may oppose some of your plans. Do not be too stubborn; be willing to accept compromise solutions. Some Virgos may lack a sense of belonging.

26. WEDNESDAY. Sensitive. Finding backers or sponsors for speculative ventures may not be as easy as you had first expected. People may not be quite as keen as you had hoped when it comes down to the crunch of handing over money to further creative or artistic ideas. You will have to rely on yourself more than ever. This should strengthen rather than weaken your resolve, though. Influential people in the theatrical or entertainment world can be tightfisted when it comes to money. You may not be able to demand the high wages you had hoped for if you are an actor, singer or dancer. Today would be a good one for handling correspondence. The world of show business is frequently rough.

27. THURSDAY. Tricky. You will not have an easy time understanding your mate, or possibly your date. Loved ones will say one thing and mean another. Emotions can be vague, undefined and confused. Virgos may be lacking in confidence when it comes to exhibiting their skills or expressing themselves. Joint activities will not be satisfactory. Single Virgos may find that their sweethearts have been concealing something. There is also a greater risk of deception in financial affairs. Getting out and about more can be useful for obtaining up-to-date information. Virgos should not shut themselves up in the proverbial ivory tower. What you don't know could hurt you more than you might ever know.

28. FRIDAY. Erratic. The more important work that you wish to tackle should be completed before midday. If you leave prime jobs to one side early in the day, complications may develop. These could stop you from getting back to the important ones successfully. After lunch you will find it difficult to track down needed helpers. If you are thinking of purchasing any real estate, get a surveyor to go over the property before you make a down payment. Excessive optimism could be a drawback. But this is a particularly favorable day for romance. Virgo charm can be irresistible, making it easier for you to form new romantic attractions. Guard against becoming known for playing fast and loose.

29. SATURDAY. Mixed. Do not be so willing to accept things at face value. Family expenses will increase. It will be hard to keep within a strictly defined budget when it comes to weekend shopping. You are likely to find that there are always extras to buy when you are in the big department stores. Virgo parents are likely to find that youngsters keep making additional demands. This is a good day for putting in some overtime to boost your income. Employers may grant not only bonuses but also permanent raises. Productivity-related pay schemes can help to boost employees' incentive and efficiency. But if you are taking loved ones out this evening, you may have to dig deeper into your pocket.

30. SUNDAY. Demanding. Curb a desire to splurge. The only problems that are likely to arise this day of rest will probably be of your own making. Slow down the pace a little. Do not be in too much of a hurry when making decisions that could affect your future financial security. The morning can be a tense and possibly stressful period for Virgos. You may be demanding too much of yourself or letting other people expect too much of you. You will be held to promises, so do not make them unless you are absolutely certain that you can deliver the goods. Distasteful chores should be left for another time if possible.

OCTOBER

1. MONDAY. Rewarding. The working week and the month of October get off to a fairly promising start. You ought to have a fair idea by now of what your priorities are. What is just as important is how you plan to go about achieving them! Associates will be helpful. Teamwork would be your best bet for getting odd jobs out of the way that have been dragging on for all too long. Legal problems can yield to unconventional solutions. The whole week could be favorable for original and inventive work. Homelife will be happy and more contented. Loved ones may spring surprises on you. But don't worry as they are likely to be ones that meet with your approval! Even if not, they are not apt to be gross.

2. TUESDAY. Sensitive. There are likely to be some difficult situations to overcome at the office or store. Internal conflicts may make it almost impossible for you to continue to make the progress you appear to have been able to keep up recently. Your best bet today would be to deal with jobs that do not require outside assistance. It would not be advisable to confront people head-on with whom you have differences. Virgo business people must be careful that they do not neglect their marital affairs. Those Virgos who are involved in the advertising business should find this a promising day. Original ideas are likely to get the nod of approval from superiors. This would boost both morale and reputation.

3. WEDNESDAY. Misleading. Career and professional affairs will require more tact and diplomacy. Be careful about treading on other people's toes. The situation at your place of employment may be more sensitive than you realize. It would be best not to speak your mind or shoot your mouth off to certain people. They may well be inclined to gossip or pass information on in a more colorful way than you have expressed yourself. Continue to push on with jobs that do not require the support or assistance of others. Romantic partners may oppose your financial plans. Upon reflection, you may find that their opposition is fully justified.

4. THURSDAY. Tricky. Virgo people should not demand more from others than they expect of themselves. This is a day when you may be setting yourself up as a judge. But it would be silly of you to be too harsh with friends and family. Loved ones who come to you for advice should be given renewed confidence. Emphasize the good points that people have rather than pointing out their deficiencies. This is a sensitive day for handling other people's money or property. You may think that you are helping others. However, you are likely to come in for a good deal of criticism if you make changes in investments without first consulting with owners or partners. Influential people can become difficult.

5. FRIDAY. Demanding. Do not talk about original ideas that you plan to put into operation in the not-too-distant future. People who hear you may be in touch with competitors. Virgos should keep mum until they have achieved their objectives. Do not allow yourself to become involved in gossip. What you say may be misinterpreted. The more you can mind your own business and deal with your own affairs, the better it will be. You may have some difficulty in getting into top gear, but you must not give in to lethargy. Virgos may have a lucky break later in the day, so they should keep their eyes open for the main chance. People in authority can be incompetent, leaving undone what they strictly should have done.

6. SATURDAY. Satisfactory. Loved ones may be difficult to understand. Do not be overly critical of other members of the family. You should not set yourself up as any judge of morality. If you do, you could find that some recent actions of your own will bring you in line for some heavy criticism. You may not be going about it the right way for winning the confidence of others. Demonstrations of force and power can be countereffective. It would be best for you to take a more subtle approach with people who may be opposing you. Mates or spouses will be more sympathetic. Professional experts can indicate ways of getting around the law. But be careful; don't risk your good name.

7. SUNDAY. Enjoyable. This will probably be the best day of this month, so far. You should be able to please yourself as to how you fill in your time this Sunday. You will probably have the opportunity to mix business with pleasure which will give you quite a lot of satisfaction. It is likely to be worth your while to spend quite a lot of today dealing with business financial affairs. You should be able to get through any jobs that you have to deal with on your own fairly quickly. If you handle work early in the day, it will make pleasurable activities all the better when you come to them later on. New ideas that come to mind should be written down.

8. MONDAY. Erratic. Your confidence should be riding high today. It would not be a good idea, though, to go plunging headfirst into schemes for which you would be expected to put up most of the capital. Allow that Virgo caution for which you are quite well known to be more in evidence. Do not permit yourself to be influenced by people who seem to be trying to carry you along on the wave of their own enthusiasm. Virgo people must try to express themselves in a way that everyone would understand. Ideas that you thought you had originated may, in fact, have been copied from someone else or read in a book. Written agreements may not be worth very much.

9. TUESDAY. Fortunate. This day starts on a quiet note, but you should not worry about the lack of action in the early part. This rather slow-moving period will enable you to deal with certain minor jobs that you will be only too pleased to get rid of. This can be a fortunate day for financial affairs. It may be that you will get hold of some extra money in the way of bonus payments. People who owe you may settle a long outstanding debt. Winning people's confidence and goodwill will be easier. A telephone call that you receive could boost your confidence. Original ideas will be more acceptable to people whose support is essential. An old friend may come back into your life and you will be very pleased.

10. WEDNESDAY. Tricky. The money side of any arrangements that you make this midweek day must be clearly understood, especially in any close associations. Misunderstandings or wrong assumptions can have unfortunate consequences at a later date. People who resort to flattery as a way to win you around should not be trusted. You have a vivid imagination so be sure that you put it to good use. There is a greater risk of deception than usual in romantic affairs. Your love life may be in a bit of a mess. Someone who you care for quite a lot may be playing with your emotions and leading you up the garden path to a certain extent. Children may not be as innocent as they try to make out.

11. THURSDAY. Happy. Go over your accounts and settle outstanding bills. Financial matters should not be shunted to one side. There may still be debts from the summer that you have not settled in full. It would be best to try to get a clearer picture of your financial situation. You may think that you are better off than you really are. Be sure that you are putting enough money to one side from your take-home pay. You will need it to pay the heavier winter bills that will be coming in a month or two. You should start to plan now with the future very much in mind. This is a very happy day for personal affairs. Secret hopes and wishes may be fulfilled. Travel can be helpful for furthering private matters.

12. FRIDAY. Pleasant. This is a period when you should be taking the initiative. Friends with powerful personalities must not be allowed to influence the way you handle your career. Regular work may not progress as smoothly as you may have hoped. Your immediate boss may find fault with a job that you recently completed. You just might have to do some of the work all over again. Do not rise to the bait and get involved in arguments that you have no hope of winning. It's a good time for pinning down evasive people and extracting from them definite answers. This can be an exciting day for romance. Loved ones will be more agreeable than they often are to your plans for seeking pleasure today.

13. SATURDAY. Rewarding. That special personal touch will be all-important when you are dealing with influential people. Virgos should do or say something pleasing that will make this an especially memorable day for superiors. You are very good at organization. So you are certainly likely to hear your praises sung for any pleasure and entertainment that you arrange. You may even be in the mood to do a little home entertaining. Just be sure that if you do ask people back to your place, you pick your guests very carefully. You must be sure that there would be no clashes of personality. Quick thinking on your part can lead to financial gain, if not immediately, then some time in later years.

14. SUNDAY. Fortunate. Coupled with what took place yesterday, this is probably going to be a very interesting and valuable weekend. You are likely to have more than one tantalizing invitation to choose from. Your day of rest will certainly be anything but dull. All in all, this will be a most exciting period for Virgo men and women. Travel will be pleasant. You may be able to meet people whom you have long admired. Some of you may be getting more involved in second-string jobs or hobbies that can bring you in extra money. Virgos are likely to become more aware of their strengths and this will help them toward obtaining greater self-sufficiency. Children should be encouraged to be independent.

15. MONDAY. Fortunate. You will have plenty of driving force at your disposal today and an abundance of original ideas. So you should be able to get off to a good start with business affairs this Monday. This is a favorable day for all attempts at self-expression. Influential people will boost your confidence by showing more interest in your innovative suggestions. Writing and similar forms of artistic endeavor will be particularly favorable. The kind of jobs that you wish to handle will require a certain amount of solitude. You should find that friends and family are therefore more understanding and sensitive to your desires. Later in the day, it will be favorable for the search for pleasure.

16. TUESDAY. Demanding. Virgos may be going about making money the wrong way. You must be more cautious about what you invest in. Any get-rich-quick schemes that are suggested to you are likely to turn out to be anything but that. You must be careful that you do not put more money into ventures that are speculative than you can really afford. Do not use any of it that you have earmarked to pay regular bills. Do not allow yourself to be pressured into signing long-term contracts or agreements. Maintaining your financial independence will be difficult but crucial. Romantic partners may blame Virgos for what is not really their fault. Quarrels can be unnecessary and upsetting.

17. WEDNESDAY. Sensitive. Do not take any risks, especially with finances. Do not follow other people's advice either, without checking the facts for yourself. Serious losses may be incurred if you act on hearsay. Stand up for what you believe, even if arguments arise as a result. Be strong-willed. When out shopping, you should keep your eyes open for bargains. You may be able to save quite a lot of money through buying in bulk. Bargaining can be successful in knocking down prices, especially for goods that are bought in bulk. But any increase in salary should be saved or invested wisely. Matters at your place of employment will move ahead satisfactorily. Resist a sudden whim this evening.

18. THURSDAY. Challenging. It will be a favorable day for implementing and sticking to new financial resolutions. You should be able to enlist the support of loved ones for your plans to put more money to one side. It will be easier to be self-disciplined if you find there are other people who agree in principle with your ideas as to the best way to divide your earnings. Today will be good, too, for submitting ideas or projects to the scrutiny of influential people. It will also be favorable for replacing worn-out possessions with new ones. Pay raises may be earned. You should not have any difficulty in taking up challenges if they afford you the opportunity to show off your artistic talents.

19. FRIDAY. Erratic. Relatives may have a stroke of bad luck. You could be required to go to the assistance of a member of your family who is having troubles and misfortune. It looks as if quite a lot of your time today will be spent seeing to the affairs of people who are less fortunate than you. Advertising campaigns can be expensive as well as unsuccessful. You will never be able to buy success. Entries in newspapers may be put in the wrong column or there could even be errors in typesetting. Anything that you have paid for in advance will be difficult to get credit for. Virgos should not take complete or comparative strangers into their confidence immediately. Good for trying a different tack in written work.

20. SATURDAY. Rewarding. You will welcome a banner ending to the week. Many of the things that you have been attempting to achieve should now come out right. This is an important day, and spare time should be used meaningfully and constructively. Virgo people will have a clearer idea of what they want out of life, and even more important, they will know how best to go about achieving it. By seeing difficulties as challenges, rather than as causes for despondency, they cannot help but do themselves a favor. You may finally be able to overcome fears or inhibitions that have been haunting you. Loved ones can be instrumental in aiding the process. Don't flag in your quest.

21. SUNDAY. Excellent. A happy and carefree day appears to be in store for you people born under the sign of Virgo. Many of the things that you have been trying to achieve in your private life can be worked out now. You should not have to stray very far from your own home to obtain the best that this day has to offer. This is an excellent time for home entertaining. Virgos will make ideal hosts or hostesses. The day is especially good for entertaining influential people and for getting to know them on a more informal basis. Financial negotiations could be conducted most profitably in the cozy surroundings one's own home can provide. Today is favorable for handling official correspondence.

22. MONDAY. Mixed. Reviewing your progress of the last few weeks is sure to add to the self-confidence and optimism of Virgo people. It should be possible to continue building up your reserves. Try to avoid extravagance. Remember that you are probably going to have to dip into savings soon, in any case, in order to pay for some of the heavier winter bills. People whom you have known from your childhood may perform a special favor for you. This might be a good day for adding to collections of antiques or other valuable objects. But impatience could be disastrous. It is essential to wait for the right moment before you launch any new projects. Rushing anything that's so important is plain foolhardy.

23. TUESDAY. Buoyant. Pull out all the stops. This is the right time to make a concerted effort to round off financial transactions. Some of these may have been going on for all too long. Grasp opportunities to take the limelight. If you are going to get anywhere, you must be a bit more pushy. Luck will be on your side so you can afford to take a few chances now. Secret agreements will be useful. An influential person may take you into his confidence. This is a good month for setting up home with loved ones. Your good vibes will be helpful for putting the finishing touches to creative or artistic work. The value of your property can be increased by doing some repairs.

24. WEDNESDAY. Tricky Virgo people must try to keep calm. Your nerves could be on edge and this could cause you to speak out of turn. You may well be acting out of character if you do not keep a very tight grip on your emotions. Do not allow yourself to become flustered as it will be impossible to make the right decisions if you do. People may resort to unconventional tactics in order to try to confuse you and get you off your balance. There is a greater risk of deception in speculative affairs. This is not the right time to take unnecessary risks with your hard-earned savings. Children may be getting up to some tricks. It does not pay to leave them alone for any length of time.

25. THURSDAY. Sensitive. You will have an opportunity to do a good turn for a loved one for whom a hospital could be involved. During the morning, a simple word or statement may clarify a major issue. Look after your own physical well-being with more care. You may have been burning the candle at both ends recently. Indications are that you need to exercise more control over your diet. Do what you can to relax frayed nerves if you are feeling uptight and tense. Do not accept invitations to go out on pleasure jaunts casually. There could be some doubt as to how you will be able to get home again afterward. Parties at a distance are not likely to live up to expectations.

26. FRIDAY. Confusing. Health may continue to be a problem and it might even stop Virgo-born people from doing what they most want to do. You must watch your nerves. Seems that you have been working yourself up into a bit of a high-strung state. Virgo parents may have been worrying rather a lot about youngsters. If you are feeling under the weather, you should not hide the fact from superiors. Love letters may fall into the wrong hands. Think twice about committing your personal and private feelings to paper. Neighbors may provide you with a fascinating challenge. Unconventional methods of transport and communication can save you valuable time and money.

27. SATURDAY. Useful. A great feeling of cooperation and understanding is likely to prevail at home. But it is important to foster the feeling that Virgo people declare their interests openly. It would be best for you to stop beating around the bush. People will admire you for your honesty and your attitude that no punches are pulled. This will be an opportune moment to discuss the financial situation. You may be able to come up with useful ways for making extra savings. You will be able to demonstrate now that you mean what you say. Call a family powwow. Ask loved ones for ideas for savings on weekly necessities. Do not exclude youngsters as they may come up with some useful ideas.

28. SUNDAY. Easygoing. It would seem as if you have had a fairly action-packed week. You will be pleased to have the opportunity to slow down your tempo somewhat. Make this a typical family time. Do what you can to bring happiness to your nearest and dearest. Loved ones will be easy to get along with. You should not have to stray very far from familiar surroundings to obtain the best that this day has to offer. There is not likely to be very much going on socially that would excite you or interest you, in any case. Virgos should try to get some extra rest, especially if they are feeling a bit below par. Routine chores may be a bit of a drudgery, but they will require surprisingly little effort on your part.

29. MONDAY. Mixed. Much more effort should be made to improve the value of your home. Readers who do not have to attend a regular place of employment should busy themselves around their home or apartment. Be more of the handyman. Do not call in a professional workman when there are chores that you can easily handle yourself. You have merely to apply your talents correctly. Closer liaison in business partnership activities will help to prevent emergencies from arising. Do not allow confusion to overtake you when it comes to handling your accounts, especially income tax matters. It would be a good idea to talk over financial problems with your bank officer or your accountant.

30. TUESDAY. Fair. Professional advice will be more beneficial than listening to friends. In fact, it would be best not to confide too many secrets in your close associates. You will regret it if you put money on horses or any kind of game of chance. Virgos can gain important new insights by trying to put themselves in other people's places. Influential people may be willing to stretch the rules. You should have no trouble in getting along with superiors. Special favors are more likely to be granted. Chance encounters with people whom you meet while traveling can lead to the forming of new romantic involvements. But this is not a particularly favorable day for distant travel.

31. WEDNESDAY. Difficult. The atmosphere at home is likely to be tense. It will not be easy for you to see eye-to-eye with your close family. You may even be accused of not taking your responsibilities seriously enough. You will find it especially difficult to understand the stance that your mate or partner is taking at the moment. Trying to stand up to large business firms or organizations can be doomed to failure. It may be too late now to back out of business mergers. If handling other people's money for them, instructions must be followed to the letter. The result of research work may prove that theories were incorrect. Mysteries are likely to remain unresolved.

NOVEMBER

1. THURSDAY. Mixed. Bills may be received today for work that was never carried out. You may have to spend some time going through accounts and files to prove your point. Certain people could be trying to get money out of you that is not due to them. You will have to be constantly on the alert for fraud and deception. Children need discipline, needless to say. But this should be accompanied by a clear explanation of why you are doing so. Youngsters must understand why you are taking such a stand. Chance encounters with influential people can lead to new friendships. Social affairs that you attend are likely to go rather well. Loved ones will prove their worth beyond all question.

2. FRIDAY. Demanding. Backlogs of boring jobs will have to be finished up. This will be a difficult day for making any new starts. Loved ones will be demanding more of your time and attention. It will be difficult to concentrate on jobs that require a calm and peaceful atmosphere. Virgos who criticize others may find themselves on the receiving end of a whole string of accusations. It would be best to take more of a live-and-let-live attitude rather than voicing your disapproval of associates. At your place of employment, you should steer clear of people who seem to want to spend more time gossiping than working. Time should not be wasted over splitting hairs. Look at the broader issues.

3. SATURDAY. Fortunate. The week comes to an end on a brighter note. It would seem that you were starting to get rather frustrated by what took place during the first couple of days of the month. Today will see you with good opportunities for making more progress. For a start, the atmosphere at home will be much better. Loved ones will show a greater willingness to fall in with your ideas for extra savings on the weekend buys. This is also a favorable time for breaking the ice with people at or from a distance. Journeys that you make today are likely to work out successfully. You should not limit yourself in any direction. There will be more opportunities for combining business with pleasure.

4. SUNDAY. Challenging. An upsurge of energy is indicated. Household chores that you have been putting off can be successfully tackled. You will be in an up-and-at-'em mood. Get on with jobs that you have been ignoring. Answer any correspondence whether of a personal or a business nature. Friends will be more congenial than has been true of late. Today should be favorable for using professional standing as a platform for promoting charitable and other worthwhile causes. There is no need to beat around the bush. But it would probably be best to approach people in private. When you have completed your tasks, you will be in the mood for fun. Accept any invitations to go out.

5. MONDAY. Useful. Routine matters should take priority. You are eager to make starts with exciting new ventures that could bring you in extra money. It is very important that you bring outstanding paperwork and accounts up to date. The morning is probably the best period for dealing with affairs that require a peaceful atmosphere. Do not leave income tax and insurance affairs until the last moment. Influential people may have a strange sense of fun. You could have some difficulty in comprehending the sense of humor of your superiors. The need for secrecy in your dealings with people in important positions can be crucial. Favorable for getting on more intimate terms with such contacts.

6. TUESDAY. Tricky. Business financial affairs may not be as simple as they seem. You may have quite a lot of explaining to do to people such as income tax authorities. Do not try to bend the law to suit yourself. In all matters connected with your earnings, it would pay you to be strictly open and aboveboard. One small error or miscalculation could have major repercussions. So-called friends may deliberately try to lead Virgos astray, but these are people who are not all they appear to be. Social functions can be disappointing. An evening out could be more expensive than you had realized. Charitable ventures that you would like to promote may meet with fierce opposition.

7. WEDNESDAY. Sensitive. People can be downright selfish. Associates for whom you have done a lot in the past may be unwilling to reciprocate your kindness. You will be surprised at the attitude of people whom you thought were your close friends. Small interests may be placed above larger considerations by your colleagues. You may find that you have to pay a rather large bill that you had thought would be evenly divided. You may even have to draw on savings reserves to cover your debts. Friends can easily become a financial liability. Virgos' secret hopes may prove to be unattainable after all. But the day is favorable for signing business financial agreements.

8. THURSDAY. Difficult. The day will be good for putting some extra pressure on people in the business world. Be pushy. Do everything that you can to win around people who have been sitting on the fence. This is a day when it will certainly pay you to put more effort into all of your activities. You will find that a few influential people are easier to pin down if you really try. This could be a favorable time for attempts at unearthing plots or the strategies of business competitors. But this is a sensitive day for romance. Love life will prove to be difficult. Sweethearts and partners will have very definite ideas that may run contrary to your own scheme of things. Flirtatious behavior can result in rebuffs.

9. FRIDAY. Disconcerting. You cannot escape from devoting a goodly portion of this day to the needs of others. Domestic problems will be worrisome. Married Virgos may find it impossible to avoid friction with their spouse. Do not attempt to make any new starts with business ventures. Lapses of concentration could cause influential people to doubt your reliability. A bad dream in the night may leave Virgos feeling slightly uneasy and off-color. It is a day when you will simply have to learn to do your best. You must realize that there is nothing else and nothing more that you can do. Even if the results are poor, this will really be no reflection on you.

10. SATURDAY. Difficult. You still seem to be one degree under par. It would be best to maintain a low profile. If you have any important routine affairs that you really must attend to, it would be best to get rid of them before midday. Later in the day, it will become harder and harder to concentrate. Correspondence should be double-checked as you may have addressed it to the wrong person. Influential people may be making unreasonable demands. Your relationship with superiors is likely to be somewhat strained. Later in the day is good for throwing your cares away and doing something exciting. Romance could be blossoming then. Forget the troubles of the week and decide to have a good time.

11. SUNDAY. Rewarding. Who you know, rather than what you know, will count for the most. Do what you can to contact as many influential people as you can. Some could provide you with information that would be helpful to your career. There will be an air of secrecy surrounding discussions in which you participate. Business and pleasure will mix in well. Attend social functions where you will have the opportunity to meet people from different walks of life. Virgo men and women seem to be in an especially perceptive frame of mind. Your intuitive abilities can astound people around you. Hunches are more likely to prove to be correct. A small sacrifice can lead to major gains, albeit by an indirect route.

12. MONDAY. Fortunate. You may need to make arrangements for long-distance traveling, especially so if you are involved in any foreign project. You may also be communicating with someone far removed whose advice would be extremely helpful. This could be an advantageous time to deal with legal problems. Virgo people will find that the pace will slow down considerably later on. You will have fewer business matters to deal with by late afternoon than you had thought. You will be pleased to give more of your time over to the affairs of family members as well as to other personal matters. This should be good for terminating money-making ventures while profits are at a peak.

13. TUESDAY. Productive. Influential people will be easier to approach than usual. This will be a pleasant day. You will welcome the easygoing pace. Virgo people who are studying for examinations will not have too much difficulty in concentrating. Knowledge that you are acquiring and storing up will be easier to retain. There is not likely to be any special pressure placed upon you. Business ventures can be made more lucrative. Today will be favorable for using your spare time to assist those not as well off as you are. It is especially true if you are attempting to raise funds for worthwhile charitable causes. But compassionate impulses can easily be misinterpreted by those who scoff at poverty.

14. WEDNESDAY. Demanding. Members of your family may become bothersome. Do not allow youngsters to pester you. Make sure that your mate takes a fair share of responsibility. Expenses at home will increase. Regular bills that come up for payment now are likely to be larger than you had anticipated. Speculation is not the way to solve your long-term problems. Virgos may develop an instant dislike for people with whom they are forced to have financial dealings. You may be too fearful of making mistakes. Hesitation can cause financial losses. Personal possessions need protecting against possible theft or against simple wear and tear.

15. THURSDAY. Buoyant. This day favors self-employed Virgos especially. Always staunch in upholding your ideals, your faith in them will be justified now. Important people who might assist you will be amiable. You will have no trouble in obtaining the support of people who are in a position to help. A change in the neighborhood can be especially welcome. You may get some new neighbors and find that you hit it off with them immediately. The day is good, too, for having new electrical equipment installed. Separations or estrangements can end in reconciliations. Mental or creative endeavors can lead to exciting breakthroughs. If you have to work later than usual, loved ones will be understanding.

16. FRIDAY. Erratic. This can be a good day for shopping expeditions. You will probably have to buy clothes for the winter for yourself or for other members of the family. With a little luck, you should be able to purchase the very articles that you have been searching for at extremely reasonable prices. But Virgos need to plan their day with more care. They should avoid unnecessary and expensive traveling and exertion at all costs. Children may be especially grown-up in their attitudes and actions. But attempts at persuading people in the business world to agree with your concept of a project are unlikely to succeed. More patience will be required on your part when attending to long-term projects.

17. SATURDAY. Profitable. This will be an exceptionally good ending to the week. Business and pleasure can both be attended to. You may even be able to arrange something for an influential person that delights him or her. Your chances of gaining promotion even sooner than you has anticipated would now appear to be a distinct possibility. The earlier part of this day is favorable for interviews or discussions with people in authority. It may well be that it is your own well-being in the future that is under the microscope at the moment. It's favorable, also, for the handling of official correspondence. Virgo's ability to be in the right spot at the right time can ensure a place in the limelight. This is an auspicious day for romance.

18. SUNDAY. Mixed. Business and career affairs may be a touchy subject in the home. Certainly it would seem that you have not been paying enough attention to the desires of loved ones. Put some of your time aside today to attend to what your mate or partner wishes. Household members should not be left to do all the work. Make sure that you offer to lend a helping hand with domestic chores. It is not fair that your mate or partner should do all the cleaning up after other people. There will also be plenty of odd jobs to do on the outside of the house and in the garden. Today is favorable for contacting or visiting parents. More time spent at home will give Virgos the opportunity to find privacy.

19. MONDAY. Encouraging. Some good news that you receive through the mail or over the telephone is likely to cheer you up considerably. You are likely to make some financial gain this first day of the week. It may be that you receive some income tax rebate, or that a bill that arrives is less than you had anticipated. Travel can be helpful in tying up the loose ends of an outstanding business deal. You had hoped very much to clinch this matter before the last working week had come to a close. You will be able to function extremely well in unfamiliar surroundings and in dealing with newcomers. Young people will inspire you and may give you a new slant on old problems.

20. TUESDAY. Misleading. Loved ones may fail to do what is expected of them. In fact, you may have been expecting too much of family members. The more that you can rely on yourself, the better it will be for you. This is a better day for dealing with matters that do not require teamwork and outside assistance. You may feel that your mate or partner is exaggerating his or her need for independence and self-sufficiency to the point of absurdity. Romantic affairs that you embark upon without much thought are unlikely to offer you the sense of security or permanence that you seem to be looking for. Children should be kept away from electrical gadgetry. Conditions are too uncertain for speculating.

21. WEDNESDAY. Mixed. Brothers or sisters may be able to provide you with valuable information or advice. It would be best to turn to members of your family for assistance rather than confide in outsiders. This is especially true when you are dealing with personal problems. This will be a day when you need to exercise more self-control over your emotions. You could be inclined to feel a bit sorry for yourself. Do not give way to self-indulgent tendencies. This would be a good day for making new contacts in the business world. The day is also favorable for attending interviews with important people, especially if you are contemplating changing your job. Virgos seem to be having some luck.

22. THURSDAY. Fortunate. Employers may grant permission to Virgo men and women to do their work from their home base. New job opportunities can be received through the medium of parents or other family members. This would appear to be a promising day for those of you who have a particulalr interest in family businesses. You may be given more responsibility and the chance to prove that you have more talent than you have been able to demonstrate, to date. Occupational activities will give Virgos a greater sense of belonging and of participation in the group. Workloads finished ahead of schedule will win praise for you from superiors. There could be a reward in the form of a promotion.

23. FRIDAY. Disturbing. Some of you Virgos may have been hoping that you would receive some sort of promotion or other advancement in your career today. But this is likely to be a disappointing day for you. Influential people are not likely to live up to promises that are made to you verbally. Contracts that you were hoping would be clinched are not going to be offered as yet. Your boss will be busy with other matters. You may get the feeling that management is avoiding discussing certain subjects with you that are important to the future well-being of you and yours. But this is a good day for Virgo bosses to handle labor or personnel problems. You should watch your health though.

24. SATURDAY. Profitable. Virgos should keep their options open. This is not the right day for planning too far ahead. Loved ones will be making additional demands on you. The amount of time that you can spend on matters connected with your career is likely to be limited by conditions at home. Readers with young families should pay more attention to domestic issues. Try to make it up to your mate or partner if you have been spending a lot of your time away from your home base. But quick thinking can enable you to finish workloads by cutting corners. Today is favorable for attending to routine medical checkups. If you have been worried by minor ailments, you should have them treated now.

25. SUNDAY. Frustrating. Protect your health zealously today. Be quite sure that you are up to any sporting activity or other pastime that people urge you to try. Do not overdo. Guard against strain and exhaustion. Be well aware of your limitations and avoid extremes. This is not a good day to attempt to work. Avoid getting in touch with your boss or any other superior. You are unlikely to get cooperation from an influential person. Pay more attention than you do normally to the needs of close relatives. Brushes with the law should be avoided if at all possible. Fines for infringements of traffic regulations can be heavy, so drive extra carefully.

26. MONDAY. Manageable. You will probably do best involving yourself in the affairs of family members and friends. It would be more productive than attempting to sort out your own personal problems. But this will be a useful day for dealing with business matters. It is especially true if you are trying to reach long-term agreements regarding matters of a legal nature. An older person would be grateful if you were to drop in and pay your respects. Give some consideration to the lonely and the needy. Romance will be happy for Virgo singles. A secret wish could come true. Loved ones may find a suitable outlet for their unique abilities. There is always a market for work that demands special skills.

27. TUESDAY. Disconcerting. Researching current ventures and enterprises will put Virgo business people in a stronger position. You should look into the background of deals that have reached the point of conclusion. You may be able to streamline them in a way that will be more profitable than you had fully realized. You would be well advised to pay more attention to the small details of accounting and paperwork. Be sure that you have all the information you need at your disposal. Do not hesitate to get in touch with influential people who may be able to help you. Investment affairs contain an uncertainty factor. This evening you may find you are in the grip of circumstances beyond your control.

28. WEDNESDAY. Sensitive. Virgo people should act well within their capabilities. This is not a day for overreaching yourself. You may find that associates attempt to dominate you. Be careful about agreeing to invest capital in any projects that you have not been able to examine in detail. You should rely more on your own intuition rather than that of others. If you wade into unfamiliar areas, you are likely to find yourself out of your depth. Trying to solve mysteries is likely to be a waste of time. People may not be willing to answer your searching questions. It would be best to accept things as they are rather than trying to change them. But this can be a particularly reassuring day for romance.

29. THURSDAY. Successful. Today will be favorable for handling investment affairs. You may have meetings with accountants and trustees of estates. They could mean that you will be able to get hold of more capital to put into stocks and shares. Tips that you receive with regard to the stock exchange would be worth following up and examining further. The atmosphere at home will be better than it has been lately. This will probably be related to the fact that financial pressure on you is relieved somewhat. Today could be useful for handling correspondence with regard to taxation and insurance matters. Bankers may be able to help you with a short-term loan.

30. FRIDAY. Changeable. There will be quite a lot of catching up for you to do as the week and the month come to an end. Try to deal with affairs that you do not want to have hanging over your head when December gets under way. Helping charitable or other worthwhile causes can give Virgos a greater sense of fulfillment. But you must be prepared for the possibility that your compassionate urges may be misunderstood. Virgos may have more options than they think. They would be smart to explore all the possibilities of any moves that they can make. Use more imagination and do not limit yourself in any one direction. It is worth sketching the outlines of plans for the future.

DECEMBER

1. SATURDAY. Difficult. It looks as if you will have quite a lot of jobs to deal with connected with the week that is about to come to an end. It will probably be true, too, for the month that has already finished. You will feel that you are being held back and frustrated to a certain extent. But it would not be a good idea to attempt to make progress with new projects until you have completed what is currently on the agenda. Reputations should not be jeopardized through reckless or badly thought-out actions. Too much trying is likely to be counterproductive. Virgos may be putting more effort and exertion into what they are doing than is needed. Allow business affairs to develop at their own pace.

2. SUNDAY. Sensitive. Get your house in order. This is an excellent period to deal with domestic issues. You must try harder to be of assistance with problems of others family members. You can't help but feel some sort of responsibility for these people. Write letters to relatives in faraway places. Catch up with your personal correspondence that may have been neglected. Entertaining influential people at home may not be such a good idea. Mixing professional and private interests can have unfortunate consequences. Family or household members may land themselves in trouble with the authorities. It may be left to you to straighten out this situation.

3. MONDAY. Tricky. This month does not seem to have gotten off to a very good start for you. This will be a difficult day for making progress in business. Superiors at your place of employment may not come forth with the help that you may have been promised. Friends' schemes or suggestions may be even more crazy than they seem. This is not a day for gambling or speculation, especially as a means to supplement your income. Anything for which you would be called upon to put up capital, and for which the outcome is uncertain, should be avoided. Electrical equipment may cause you more trouble than it is worth. Humanitarian ventures may be jeopardized by disputes over policy.

4. TUESDAY. Deceptive. During this rather unsettled day you should not make any important moves without careful consideration. Do not get carried away on the crest of a wave. Make quite sure that creative projects do not become too expensive. Avoid speculation. Stay well away from friends who try to influence you to back their risky propositions. Failure to obtain the fulfillment of secret hopes and wishes can result in disappointment. There is a greater risk of deception in business financial affairs. Friends may become ill and you may have to go to their assistance. Quite a lot of your spare time is likely to be devoted seeing to the needs of others. This will put a real crimp in your personal plans.

5. WEDNESDAY. Exciting. This would appear to be the best day of the month so far. At last you will have the opportunity to put many of your new and original ideas into practice. Influential people will show a greater willingness to be of assistance to you. You will feel that you can now take people into your confidence. You will undoubtedly have good reason to believe that they really do have your well-being very much at heart. More money can be earned which can be put to one side. It will help to pay for the additional expense of Christmas that you are bound to feel quite soon. This is a helpful period for pinning down difficult people.

6. THURSDAY. Useful. Plots can be unearthed. You may find that associates at your place of employment now confide in you matters that have been kept secret. Today should be favorable for breaking with the past. Virgo readers who are starting out on new jobs or taking on positions at their old place of employment will feel renewed and invigorated. Superiors will be particularly helpful, especially if they are approached in private. But one or two people may be envious of the strides that you are making. Virgo people should take more of a live-and-let-live attitude and not worry more than is necessary. People who reappear out of the past may have useful contacts and provide you with introductions.

7. FRIDAY. Confusing. It looks as if you are down in the dumps once again. It will be difficult to pin down the reason why you are feeling depressed. It might well be that you are feeling tired and your nerves are on edge. Try not to take on more work than you can reasonably be expected to handle. Associates may not be pulling their weight. You are very conscientious and people may be taking advantage of this fact. Business competitors can make the going fairly unpleasant and rough for you. Virgos may find that their judgment is being hotly contested. It is important to try to remain more impersonal in professional and career affairs. Don't get involved in areas that are not your concern.

8. SATURDAY. Sensitive. The end of this week could see you with your work cut out for you. You are doubtless hoping to finish off some work that you may feel has been dragging on for all too long. It is best that you go along with your own judgment and do not pay too much attention to what other people have to say. Although advice that is given is likely to be worthwhile, it is likely to be way off the mark. It simply will not apply to your own particular situation. Virgo people should try to fight their own battles in their own way. They will tend to be more successful if they do so. Influential people may waste valuable time splitting hairs. But the day is very favorable for romance.

9. SUNDAY. Pleasant. It is important that you work out a definite plan for today. If you allow things simply to happen, you may find yourself very much at a loose end. Virgo-born people may discover that others are looking to them to supply a lead. It might be a good idea to do something completely different. You may not have been away from familiar surroundings for some time for pleasurable reasons. So it might be a good idea to plan a trip to the country. You will not necessarily have to spend a great deal of money to realize the best that this day has to offer. Calculated risks will have a better than usual chance of paying off. But Virgos should not become overly attached to possessions.

10. MONDAY. Disconcerting. It will be difficult for you to get back into the workaday weekly rut. You will be demanding a little more of life than simply attending to routine jobs. But it is better to trust what has already been tested and proved to be successful rather than trying out new ideas. Do not risk savings in speculative ventures. Departing from norms that have been laid down by others could get Virgo people into trouble. Do not do anything at your place of employment that could upset superiors. Accounts may have to be gone over again. Mistakes may be discovered in paperwork that have to be put right without further ado. Romantic partners can change their minds at the last moment.

11. TUESDAY. Mixed. Take advantage of an opportunity to right a matter connected with your family life. Do all that you can to repair broken relationships. This will be a valuable day for having conversations with loved ones. They could help to straighten out problems that may have become buried under the surface. At your place of employment there are also likely to be some helpful changes taking place. Employers may give bonuses or even permanent pay raises as a result of and reward for work that is completed today. Government grants can be obtained for home or property improvements. But elders will be killjoys. In spite of this, children should not be denied fun and amusement.

12. WEDNESDAY. Lucky. You will be able to get on with work that requires a great deal of concentration. You should not be disturbed or distracted in any way once you have begun your tasks. Studious pursuits ought to be attended to early on, though. Conditions are likely to heat up considerably later on. After midday there will be valuable opportunities for combining work with pleasure. This can be a particularly favorable day for romance. New attractions can be formed as a result of flirtations or chance encounters with people while you are traveling. Virgo charm can work wonders. Advertisements can lead to attractive offers. You may be selling an heirloom or rare books, and want top dollar.

13. THURSDAY. Uncertain. Christmas is not too far away now. So you should be thinking very much about how far you can go with your spending. There will not only be presents but also pleasure and entertainment during the forthcoming festive season. It might be a good idea to start to buy cards and presents now. Otherwise, if you leave it all until the last moment, you will have too much of a rush. Virgo readers who are working throughout the day may be able to do some shopping during the lunch hour. If not, they will have to do so after they finish at their place of regular employment. Virgo people are being too critical both of themselves and others. It is best to give people the benefit of doubt.

14. FRIDAY. Useful. Correspondence should be brought up to date. Come to grips with backlogs of paperwork. You will find that there is plenty to keep you meaningfully occupied today. Virgos who have the chance to spend more time at home will be able to get done with tasks that they have had hanging over their heads for some time. Carry out repair work yourself. For those tasks that you feel you cannot handle on your own, you should call in the services of a professional person without further delay. It's a good time for extending contracts with agents or transport people themselves. People at a distance may cause you some worry, either intentionally or unknowingly. Don't hesitate to tell them so.

15. SATURDAY. Rewarding. This would be a very good time to resume operations suspended during the last few days. Try a fresh approach with people whom you have been unable to contact. It applies also to those with whom you have been making unsuccessful overtures. Picking up the threads of the past should serve a particular purpose today. An investment that has been stagnant for some time may show a new lease on life now. This is also a favorable day for bartering and exchanging goods. It will be useful, too, for last-minute Christmas shopping. Be sure that you have sent Christmas cards to friends and relatives who always remember you at this time of the year.

16. SUNDAY. Excellent. All in all, this will be an excellent weekend. Coupled with what took place yesterday, you should be well pleased at the favorable turn of events. The atmosphere at home should be bubbling with pleasure and excitement. You and your loved ones are likely to be getting very much into the Christmas spirit now. It will be a day when the old and the new can blend effortlessly and beneficially. Starting up with work again from the point where it had been left off, due to interruptions that had occurred, is recommended. Parents or other family members may be able to provide useful introductions to influential people. Virgos have more experience than most to fall back on.

17. MONDAY. Easygoing. This will not be a very important period. You will be grateful that the pressure is taken off you to a certain extent. This will be a quiet and peaceful day. You will be able to take a breather before the Christmas season gets into full swing. This would be a helpful day for tying up the loose ends of work and business. There are some especially vital matters that you do not want to have hanging over your head during the next week or so. You will not be required to exert yourself overly much at your place of employment. You should be able to work at a pace that suits you best. Now is favorable for putting the last-minute touches to pleasure plans that you will be involved in fairly soon.

18. TUESDAY. Tricky. Check up on the state of your bank account. You may find that you are not as well off as you had at first thought. People may be taking advantage of Virgos' kindheartedness. You may want to help friends in distress, but the best way may not be with monetary handouts. You will not find the atmosphere at your place of employment will be the easiest in which to operate. Children may not be telling the truth. You will not want to be too harsh on youngsters at this time of the year. Nevertheless, it may be necessary to discipline them for their own good. There is a greater risk than ever of estrangements and separations from romantic partners right now.

19. WEDNESDAY. Difficult. Think about the future. If you have not yet taken out an insurance policy or joined a pension fund, do so now. This is especially applicable to younger Virgo people. Christmas is now only just around the corner. You are quite likely to spend a lot of this day making a list of people to buy presents for. If not that, you will be actually out shopping. This task you are likely to find rather tiring what with all the people and traffic. Do not make any important switches in your career. You may feel that loved ones are being rather cold-hearted and unyielding. Do not splurge on objects or a pedigreed pet you could easily do without.

20. THURSDAY. Frustrating. This will be a frustrating period. You will be in an eager-beaver mood, but there will be little to keep your active mind fully occupied. You will probably find that the pace at your place of employment will be far too slow-moving for your liking. You would much rather be out and about, putting the last-minute touches to your Christmas arrangements. Virgo people may be rather slow off the mark where romance is concerned. Someone whom you fancy strongly will also be rather keen on you. But perhaps you will not be intuitive enough to see the signals today. People who operate behind the scenes may break their word. Others' careless actions could cause accidents.

21. FRIDAY. Demanding. This is likely to be the third in a cycle of somewhat difficult days for the Virgo-born person. Nothing terribly vital is likely to go wrong for you. But you may just feel a little frustrated that you are not making the kind of progress you expected. It does not seem as though the happy Christmas that you were hoping for will materialize. Loved ones will be difficult to pin down if you were hoping to go on joint shopping expeditions with them. Try to do your best at work today. There may be one or two important rush jobs on. Influential people will be keeping an eye on you to see if you pull them off. Although it will be a little hard, you must try to exercise more self-discipline.

22. SATURDAY. Pleasant. Get out and about. It is vital that you make an early start with your shopping. Go over your lists of goods that you need to buy, especially of the perishable variety. This may well be your last chance to get such things before everything shuts down for Christmas. Check your Christmas card and present list. Make very sure that you have not forgotten someone who always remembers you at this time of the year. Success in teamwork enterprises may lead to fame and public recognition for those who are attending to job and career matters today. This is a favorable time for the making wills and signing other legal documents. Recreational activities can provide a good opportunity to make friends with influential people.

23. SUNDAY. Tricky. Watch out that you do not accept more invitations to go out than you could reasonably expect to handle. In fact, it might be a good idea to limit your visits to other people's homes to the very minimum. There will be quite enough for you to come to grips with in the confines of your own four walls. Loved ones will be helpful. But only as long as you give more attention to their desires and do not allow them to feel neglected in any way. Do what you can to make it up to your mate or partner if you have not seen very much of him or her during the week that has just ended. For the single Virgo reader that is a greater chance of deception in romantic matters. Be on your guard and do not let yourself get swept off your feet in the excitement this week.

24. MONDAY. Enjoyable. Legal decisions made today by judges and other influential people will tend to be favorable from the Virgo's point of view. You may well have to go before the courts today. The decisions that are made will probably be better for you than you or your advisors had been hoping for. There will be many matters for you to attend to connected with Christmas. You may find that you get to bed later than usual. Many parties or gatherings that you attend are likely to go on longer than you would have anticipated. Offspring can make Virgo parents very proud. This is a happy day for family matters. Holiday leave may be reduced, rather to your annoyance.

25. TUESDAY. MERRY CHRISTMAS! Virgo men and women are likely to have that quiet self-confidence that always makes other people feel comfortable and at ease with them. You could be the one who shows the way ahead today. Others will be looking to you to come up with the ideas for the best way to have a good time. A certain amount of time is likely to be spent away from home. It would seem that you will be spending most of your waking hours in a domestic situation. You will have the chance to bring much pleasure to older people. There will be good opportunities for intimate get-togethers with people who mean the most to you in all the world.

26. WEDNESDAY. Pleasant. This will be another one of those days when you will be spending a good deal of your time with the family. It would be good fun to move around with your mate or partner and go to visit others. You certainly do not want to spend too much time sitting around doing nothing. You would soon get frustrated if you follow that line of inaction. Virgo readers who are attending to other matters not connected with Christmas may find that they are quite caught up in legal dealings. You may be making arrangements for the rental of property early in the new year. Childhood friends may get in touch. You will be surprised and delighted to hear from them.

27. THURSDAY. Manageable. Problems of children, most likely connected with finances, will be your main worry. This is a day when you will be counting the cost of Christmas. Perhaps you have laid out more money than you really meant to spend. Now you will be looking for ways and means to build up your reserves once again. Your mate or partner will be helpful and may come up with some ideas. These would be well worth giving consideration to. The first half of the day is the best period for approaching influential people with special requests. These are more likely than not to be granted. If Virgos try to look too far ahead they will only cause unnecessary worry for themselves.

28. FRIDAY. Fortunate. Problems of a romantic nature may have been worrying you over the holidays. But they will have a way of sorting themselves out now. You and your opposite number will find it easier to overcome silly little differences that may have been dividing you. It will be quite a good day for knuckling down to writing thank-you letters. It will be equally good for going over accounts that you do not want to have to deal with once the New Year gets under way. But Virgo people should avoid trying to cram too much into the latter hours of the day. You must put some time to one side for rest and relaxation. If you are impatient you will miss important things.

29. SATURDAY. Profitable. The week ends with your feeling very confident about the future. It would appear that you have decided at last just how you can make more of a success of your chosen career. When the New Year gets under way, influential people whom you approach are likely to be extremely helpful. Many of your talents will be appreciated. It will do you much good to realize that people whose opinions you respect are very much on your side. Some secret maneuvering can be especially lucrative in all business and professional activities. Opportunities received from unusual or unlikely sources may offer considerable possibilities for short-term gain. It will be easier for you to win people's trust.

30. SUNDAY. Demanding. Arguments within the home are likely to arise early on. This will be a difficult day for dealing with other members of the family, especially those who are in their teens. You will have to watch your own temper too. Be sure that you do not act like a juvenile yourself by being quick to lose your temper. Virgo people should not start a new project until they have brought outstanding matters to a conclusion. Using your own home as a base for business activities is not such a good idea. Family members may forget to pass on important messages. The more that you can rely on yourself the better you are likely to fare this first day of a new week. It may bode well for the year ahead.

31. MONDAY. Disconcerting. You are going to have your work cut out to finish your tasks on schedule. There will be many little matters that you will be wanting to finish off before the year comes to an end. You may have to spend more time than usual at your place of employment. Associates will not be as helpful as you would like. This will mean that you will have to rely on yourself rather than on team effort. Influential people may tend to overreact, and will therefore be much more unreliable. Promises of promotion may not be fulfilled. You will have considerable difficulty in knowing precisely where you stand. Try to have fun, anyway, when you welcome 1991 tonight!

October–December 1989

OCTOBER

1. SUNDAY. Deceptive. Plans will not go off today as you had hoped. This is one of those difficult days for finding pleasure and entertainment. Parties and gatherings that you are invited to are likely to be a complete waste of time and money. Even worse, they may be full of people who you find boring. Also, if you are going to be out late, be sure that you arrange to have transportation home. You certainly do not want to get stuck in some out-of-the-way place. Changes may be occurring in Virgo's immediate neighborhood which can be beneficial. It should be a good day for keeping abreast of local community news. This will be a sensitive day for money. Spending may get out of hand and you will have little to show for it at day's end.

2. MONDAY. Tricky. Virgos who have connections in show business will be delighted that they are able to make good use of them. Try to reach producers and people who direct shows and plays. If there is any casting going on, you may be able to get an audition. It is more than likely that there will be a part that is just right for you. New contacts can help to boost business profits. Virgos who are in real estate should be able to do very well over a deal that they are able to clinch today. But those who are in the public eye want to be very careful about attracting too much publicity. It is possible that it could be detrimental to them. You do not want to lose a job because of some unsavory gossip.

3. TUESDAY. Pleasant. You have had some fairly good opportunities during the first two days of the month. Nevertheless, there does seem to have been an underlying feeling that something you could not quite grasp was wrong. You may find a talk with your boss or some other influential person will reveal underlying causes that will help you to clear this issue up. Taken as a whole, this can be an especially pleasant and enjoyable day for Virgo men and women. Tasks that you usually shy away from will be that much easier to handle. You will derive pleasure from little things, as nothing of particular importance is likely to happen. Enjoy the break from the usual frantic pace and clear up any backlogs.

4. WEDNESDAY. Mixed. There will be a greater sense of warmth and contact with other people. Strangers will seem pleasant. Virgos who are making trips by train could form liaisons with people who become firm friends in time. They may even become romantic partners. You could be taking up a new hobby now from which you will derive a great deal of pleasure. In business, Virgo's power of persuasion can win them added cooperation and assistance. Some of you who have been going steady for some time may decide that the time is ripe for a proposal of marriage. But this is not a day for making any major financial moves. Sit tight and wait for a more propitious time.

5. THURSDAY. Easygoing. This will be a peaceful day. You will be able to draw your breath and take stock of your current situation. Try to persuade influential people to allow you to do a little experimenting on your own. You may be able to find ways to make dull, routine jobs more interesting. Virgos who are able to spend more of their time at home will be in a fairly relaxed kind of mood. There are not likely to be problems or major arguments with any of your loved ones. This would be an especially good day for getting on closer terms with members of the younger generation. They may have been acting somewhat distant and strange of late. The day will be useful for adding finishing touches to jobs.

6. FRIDAY. Difficult. Personal plans may have to be shelved completely. You must not put pleasure and entertainment before your work. If supervisors at your work place think you are coming in just to pick up your paycheck, you could soon find yourself out looking for another job. Virgos are not likely to have much success today in imposing their wishes on other family members. Some people in the house may fail to relay personal messages. That could cause quite an uproar under certain circumstances. Correspondence can be mislaid, particularly if it is incorrectly addressed. Children could begin to cause new problems for you. Try to get to bed early. Your nerves seem frayed and you need rest.

7. SATURDAY. Disturbing. Although nothing particularly wrong is likely to occur, your plans for today will not turn out as you would have hoped. Any ideas for making contact with someone you recently met and feel keen on are not likely to work out. But save those plans for later. You should turn to old acquaintances for socializing as they will be the most reliable. Virgo-born people cannot afford to be extravagant. You have to count your pennies and be extra careful. It is not the time to indulge in purchasing new clothes or even any articles of adornment. You might even have to restrain your generosity toward people who are in real need. Overindulgence will cause a sense of guilt.

8. SUNDAY. Fortunate. This should be a favorable day for implementing pleasure and entertainment plans. You should be able to get quite a lot of fun from today without having to spend a great deal of money. Judging by the current state of your finances, you should be pleased that you can cut down a little. Loved ones will make good company and will agree to any ideas that you have for trips. Perhaps a nice drive in the country would be a good idea; there could be fall foliage to view. Or there might be some place of historical interest you want to visit. Family excursions with the children can provide excitement and amusement for all. People you meet today may lead to compatible romantic associations.

9. MONDAY. Productive. After what appears to have been a restful and pleasant weekend, you should be raring to go today. You will get a chance to put some of your new projects into operation. This should mean that you can probably make more money from part-time jobs. The morning may possibly start off on a fairly slow note. But at least you will have the chance to get finished with routine jobs that you don't want to be bogged down with later in the day. Later on, the pace will pick up and the day will become more active. It will offer additional opportunities for winning bonuses or other financial rewards. The evening may provide a surprise in the way of a romantic reunion.

10. TUESDAY. Happy. This will turn out to be another prosperous day. You will be able to carry on with the good progress you have made so far. It might be a good idea to get up a little earlier than usual each morning. Some really energetic exercise could get your juices flowing and perhaps give you an extra charge. You would undoubtedly be more alert and thus more capable of quick action when it comes to making important decisions. Virgos' reliability and efficiency can win a place for them in the good books of their bosses or superiors. There is a very good possibility of earning a permanent raise in pay. Overtime will also be well rewarded. Influential people in business will be helpful.

11. WEDNESDAY. Productive. Virgos may win legal actions today. Or if you have been involved in litigation for some time, you might get a chance to settle on terms that will be advantageous to you. And it might not even be necessary to resort to the time and expense involved in going to court. Your legal advisors may be able to win a handsome settlement for you. This is not a day to be too pushy, though. Do not aim for spectacular results. Virgos should be willing to plod steadily along with their work that is already well under way. More collaboration on it may produce particularly good results. Business colleagues may have a stroke of good luck which will lead to increased profits.

12. THURSDAY. Confusing. Do not adopt a resentful or noncooperative mood because it will only hurt you. This is a day when you should try harder than ever to put on a pleasant face for people with whom you are doing business. Even if you do feel low, you should hide your emotions. You will find you have less leeway for implementing your personal plans and ideas. You might even be forced to make some major compromises. Loved one's feelings and wishes should not be neglected. If you are planning on going out for a business-related lunch, it is advisable to make a conservative appearance. Do nothing that might turn people away. You could lose the support and financial backing you probably need. Just let your natural Virgo charm work for you.

13. FRIDAY. Demanding. Maybe this is Friday the thirteenth, but nothing is likely to happen to you. It should not make you feel that fate is conspiring to create an unlucky day. Much of your destiny is in your own hands at this point in your career. You seem to have reached a crossroads where you cannot put off making a definite decision one way or the other any longer. It will need all of your Virgo powers of logic to make sure that you decide upon the correct course of action. This is a highly sensitive day insofar as joint finances or partnership funds are concerned. The irresponsible handling of other people's money can cause trouble. If it has been entrusted to you for investing, you must be very careful about choosing a reliable type of stocks or bonds.

14. SATURDAY. Difficult. You cannot be feeling too pleased over the way that things have gone for you this last part of the week. It is true especially where financial considerations are concerned. You will probably have to work fairly hard now. You want to earn some extra money to make up for some of the silly losses you have incurred. Perhaps there is someone to whom you loaned money who has not yet paid you back. For some unknown reason, it might be that this person is suddenly and conveniently unavailable. You may resent the obligations that are put on you by older people. But it is best to be patient and conciliatory. You probably do not want to risk hurting their feelings.

15. SUNDAY. Enjoyable. It's about time now that you felt a bit more cheery! You should be able to put last week's troubles behind you and forget them. Relax and enjoy yourself today in the company of good friends and family. It might be a novel idea to throw a little party in your home and brighten up your day. If you invite people early, you can enjoy yourselves without making it a late evening. This could also be a favorable day for travel. Even if trips are undertaken for business purposes, they could offer unexpected opportunities for combining work with pleasure. Today could also be an opportune time for starting to arrange plans for coming holidays. Or it would be equally good for a vacation.

16. MONDAY. Easygoing. There will not be much doing today, either at home or in your place of business. But you will probably be quite pleased that there are no important new jobs under consideration. You might have your hands full, anyhow, finishing up the details connected with some work left over from last week. This should have been done then, but was not. Influential people will not be putting any pressure on you. It would be a good day for improving your relationship with all people to whom you have to answer in some way or another. Virgos can always learn a great deal through reading and study. In-laws may be especially helpful in an unexpected way. You will appreciate this.

17. TUESDAY. Tricky. Do not overreach yourself with the boss! You want to be very careful about taking on responsibilities that have not been delegated to you. There are Virgos who earn their living as traveling salespeople on the road. They may have to make longer trips than usual with little chance of there being the incentive of extra pay. But this can be a helpful day for furthering business negotiations. You may possibly be putting pen to paper and signing major contracts or agreements. However, although the time for formalizing such agreements may seem right, the future might prove otherwise. Borrowing is inadvisable, whether from friend or family member.

18. WEDNESDAY. Disconcerting. Gambling can result in some especially heavy losses. You want to be very cautious about doing any speculating. Tips that come from proven sources may turn out to be worthless this time. You should concentrate more on making money through your job rather than the so-called easy way. This can be a somewhat uncertain period for Virgo business people. It would be advisable for them to accept all the official support and assistance they can get. Influential people can be helpful in getting rid of troublemakers. You should be grateful for any assistance they give you. These are just not the sort of matters that you should try to attend to yourself.

19. THURSDAY. Deceptive. So far, this does not appear to have been a very constructive or fulfilling week for those born under the Sign of Virgo. Unfortunately, very little is going to change today. Nothing is likely to go terribly wrong at your place of employment. But you will find yourself irritated by co-workers who will just not agree with the way you want to handle jobs. Try to avoid doing any that would require some sort of joint effort. Virgo men and women should also try to avoid raising their expectations of friends too high. Otherwise, it is entirely likely that they will be disillusioned. Business finances will be in a shaky situation.

20. FRIDAY. Productive. Some improvement in your fortunes is indicated for the Virgo today. It does not appear, however, that you will be able to make any major breakthroughs with new projects. This is too late a stage in the working week. But you should be able to put out feelers to influential people, at least. You might even get their early reactions to what you are trying to achieve. Publicity can prove to be especially successful. The returns on the investment and effort put into the work seem out of all proportion. However, Virgo business people may have to pay for financial errors out of their own pockets. With regard to your home, this would be a favorable day for buying necessities.

21. SATURDAY. Misleading. Friends may land both themselves and Virgo acquaintances in trouble with the authorities. Try to steer clear of associates who may be fun to be with, but who can act in an outrageous way. This could create adverse publicity that could damage close personal relationships and your future career prospects. Humanitarian or altruistic ventures may be denied official sponsorship or even permission. You may find it hard to understand why certain people are trying to stop you in your efforts to help others. Virgos who try to ingratiate themselves with influential or important people may experience a rude rebuff today. Plan for some kind of gala evening.

22. SUNDAY. Sensitive. It is important for you to choose your words very carefully. This is especially true when you are dealing with people whom you know from past experience to be both touchy and sensitive. You may have to spend some of your time seeing to the needs of older people, such as parents. You probably find it difficult to control your feelings when people ramble on, and perhaps keep repeating themselves. You must accept this fact and try to keep yourself in check. Jokes can easily be taken the wrong way, depending on your listeners. Not everyone has the same sense of humor, so be wary of what you say. Evening will be a favorable period for making it up to loved ones.

23. MONDAY. Encouraging. This will be a fine start to your working week. You seem to have learned quite a lot from the recent difficult experiences that you have been encountering. Both men and women born under your sign should be able to win the support and trust of influential people without too much trouble. Perhaps some work that you completed recently will be brought to the notice of your boss, with especially favorable results for you. Submit written work for the approval of superiors and publishers. Interviews for new jobs can go especially well. This is also a good day for the handling of official correspondence. But you should be careful about hurting the feelings of other employees.

24. TUESDAY. Productive. Push hard now to complete any important negotiations you had started on yesterday. It would be a very good idea to get contracts signed while the concerned people who are abroad can be contacted. This is a starred day for those of you who act on behalf of others. Agents, publishers and salespeople should be able to earn excellent commissions. You are likely to find that your services are much in demand. Calculated risks are more than likely to pay off, leaving Virgos with fewer fears about the future. Friends and close acquaintances can be a valuable source of inspiration and undying enthusiasm. Treat them with the respect and admiration they deserve.

25. WEDNESDAY. Mixed. This can be an unusually exciting day. But you will have to be wary about getting carried away on the wave of another's enthusiasm. This is especially true where risky investment schemes are concerned. But on a different front, it is vital that you do not dip into money you have been painstakingly building up. You have regular bills to meet, as well as increased ones during the coming winter months to consider. Influential people may push Virgos to develop their creative and inventive abilities to the full. Such people can be extremely helpful in unusual and unexpected ways. However, Virgo men and women could be feeling rather divided emotionally.

26. THURSDAY. Confusing. It would be best for Virgos to freeze major financial moves until they can get a clearer picture of the immediate future. Pretending to be able to predict that very accurately can prove disastrous, in any regard. But it is especially true where there is a lot of money involved. You should be making more effort to trim the domestic budget now. Cut out the foolish luxuries that appear to have become so very much a part of your life. Children's waywardness can be a sign that they require more attention and caring. Your health may be somewhat below par.

You would probably respond quickly to some extra rest. Others' health may also give you good reason for concern.

27. FRIDAY. Difficult. This is another sensitive day from the financial point of view. You must definitely continue in your efforts to trim the budget. Be far more forceful when trying to get your point of view across to loved ones. They seem to be taking a live-for-the-moment attitude toward life. Virgo people may tend to be subjected to pressures from others to make reckless or highly risky moves. You must be strong-willed and do what you know is for the best in the long run. You will have to face the music at some point if you continue to make excuses to yourself. It is likely that associates at your place of employment will go ahead with shady deals. If so, wash your hands of them completely.

28. SATURDAY. Uncertain. Friends may prove to be unreliable. Your plans for the day may get completely mixed up because they will let you down at the last moment. People may forget to tell you about cancellations of parties or other gatherings. You will have to be more self-reliant than ever. But this can be a good day for home and family affairs. You and your mate or partner may be able to save quite a lot of money. You can do so by going to the big discount warehouses to stock up on household goods by buying in bulk. Although the initial outlay may be quite large, you will save a considerable amount of money in the long run. Keep accurate records of all these financial transactions.

29. SUNDAY. Happy. At last, you will be relieved to set aside the problems and work-related responsibilities of the workweek today. This will be an excellent day for getting in touch with friends and family you have not been able to see during that time. Loved ones will be in an adventurous mood. It is quite likely they will dream up all kinds of bright ideas for having a good time on a modest budget. The Virgo sports fans among you may be able to pursue their favorite pastime. Get involved in anything that will take your mind off your problems. It is enough that you were wrestling with them all week. Besides, there is nothing you can do about them today.

30. MONDAY. Exciting. Any persons whom you meet today for the first time may turn into close friends. You might even be able to make a deal with someone you hit it off extremely well with right from the start. You will have an opportunity to make up for lost time. You can also attend to any of the irritating little jobs you were unable to get rid of last week. But get out and about, too. Try to make new contacts and gather information which would not normally be available to you. Virgos' well-known mental abilities are likely to be in peak form. You may even astound yourself with the accuracy of your thinking, reasoning and intuition. Virgos could play a new role in club activities.

31. TUESDAY. Routine. After the past two rather promising days, you appear to be in for a quiet spell. There is not any reason for alarm at this turn of events, far from it. It simply means that you will have a good opportunity to tie up your affairs for the month. Get your accounts into better shape before you close the books on October. Virgos are advised to concentrate on finishing up what has been half-completed. Use your time wisely in bringing transactions to a close. If you attempt to launch new projects, you will merely be taking on unnecessary burdens for yourself. This would be a good day for spending more time in the family circle. It will also be useful for contacting parents.

NOVEMBER

1. WEDNESDAY. Buoyant. Something that happens first thing today is likely to set you off on the right foot for this month. And from then on, you are not likely to look back. Perhaps you will receive a letter about a job you had applied for recently. One way or another, you will undoubtedly be feeling much more confident about the future than has been the case for some time past. Influential people will be rooting for you, too. They may be able to offer you some valuable assistance that enables you to leapfrog over competitors. Keep your ears open for tidbits of conversation. You may hear something on the grapevine that will mean you will be saved a journey.

2. THURSDAY. Exciting. Carry on with whatever is already under way. The only problem there might be for you today would be if you were to spread yourself too thinly. This is an auspicious day for home entertaining with a view toward aiding your career. Perhaps you should ask an influential person in for a meal or even just for a cocktail. Your mate or partner will be of help in insuring that things go smoothly and with a zip. Charm and a pleasant manner will be valuable assets to Virgo people. Gentleness and persuasion should help you to get associates to meet deadlines for you. It would be a favorable day for terminating financial agreements, and reaping the benefits.

3. FRIDAY. Sensitive. Romance will be uppermost in your mind, but you must not let it interfere with your work. You can make good progress on the job as long as you do not daydream. Nor must you allow personal issues to hinder you. But in leisure time, you will be able to deepen current romantic involvements. Quick thinking on the part of Virgo people can bring them in some instant money. Tips that are passed on to you are likely to be winners. But you should keep your gambling within reasonably strict limits and not risk more than you can afford. This could be a favorable day for dealings with influential people in the entertainment and theatrical world. But Virgo artists may lack inspiration.

4. SATURDAY. Slow. This is not a bad day on which to end the week. You will not be under any particular pressure, either of time limits or workload. This will mean that you will be able to tackle any little jobs that were left over from last month and from the first three days of this one. Loved ones will show greater understanding if you have to lock yourself away for two or three hours. You must do so in order to deal with accounts, the writing of letters and other desk jobs. But be very sure that you do not neglect their desires completely. Perhaps a trip to the countryside or some other special treat this evening would be the answer. Make plans to get together with close friends tomorrow.

5. SUNDAY. Harmonious. Driving will require extra care today. If you are planning on going off on a trip, be alert to the careless antics of so-called Sunday drivers. Do not speed, certainly, or break the law of the road in any other respect. The Police are frequently out in redoubled force, waiting to catch speeders and drivers weaving from lane to lane. Don't risk spoiling your little leisure time by being pulled over. Do not push yourself too hard with heavy manual jobs. Physical overexertion can have unfortunate consequences. This is a good day for getting out and about on secret missions. It would also be favorable for surprise visits to friends or relatives you have not seen lately.

6. MONDAY. Disturbing. This will not be a pleasant beginning to the working week. One of your problems would appear to be your attitude toward your work and your associates. It still will not be an easy matter at all to get team efforts launched. They will be more likely to founder first. People whom you try to influence will be uncooperative and even sullen. Virgo people will have to accept full responsibility today for their actions. You will no longer be able to plead ignorance in your own defense. Jealousy or envy by co-workers is uncalled for and should not be permitted to show itself. Try to be more loving and understanding with people who may feel they have been left out in the cold recently.

7. TUESDAY. Mixed. You would very much like to improve your knowledge of certain specialized subjects. But you will not be able to do so unless you are willing to exert more self-discipline in your leisure hours. Make your intentions clear to other members of the family. You are going to put a certain period of time aside each day for personal work. In this way, you will have no excuses for putting it off. Put more effort into teamwork at your place of employment. This is a period when partnership endeavors can reap rich dividends. Superiors must be treated with respect. Challenging authority could prove to be disastrous today. Actually, there are more subtle ways of making yourself heard and heeded.

8. WEDNESDAY. Harmonious. Virgos will benefit greatly from the kindness and generosity of other people. Some of you may have been feeling a bit down in the dumps recently. Today you are likely to get a telephone call out of the blue inviting you for a meal or to attend some type of entertainment. You will enjoy anything out of the ordinary very much today. Be sure that you show gratitude to people who may well have put themselves out a great deal on your behalf. An overcritical attitude could lose you friends. Do not offer your opinions, therefore, unless you are specifically asked for them. This is a favorable day for all matters requiring initiative and enterprise.

9. THURSDAY. Tricky. Your mind will be wandering constantly today. You will be in a restless mood unable to think clearly. Be careful at your place of employment. Your boss will be watching your performance with interest. You could ruin your chances of promotion if you do not show how responsible you can be. Try to show yourself in the most favorable light possible. Virgos involved in research or investigative work must try to avoid getting sidetracked by irrelevancies. If you allow your judgment to be influenced by emotional considerations, you may find yourself in deep water. Loved ones can be extravagant and may have to be persuaded to forgo costly whims.

10. FRIDAY. Mixed. On no account should joint funds or marital resources be used either for speculative purposes or without the consent of the other person. You may hear all sorts of rumors flying around today about a very good deal that you should try to horn in on. But this is likely to be nothing more than just so much hot air. Funds need to be protected. Do not dip into money earmarked for insurance policies or for paying rent or mortgages. Virgos who try to dig too deeply into the emotional problems of others could easily find themselves out of their depth. Today would be favorable for consultations with influential people. They are sensitive now to the problems of others and eager to help.

11. SATURDAY. Important. You will find that this is an important day. It is a particularly favorable period for Virgo men and women who can look ahead to a brighter future. They have no fear of having to make sacrifices to achieve it. Because what they will have to give up will be far outweighed by what they have to gain. So they will scarcely consider it as a sacrifice at all. Your relationship with your mate or partner today will be greatly improved. So joint decisions will be far easier to make. There are some Virgos who are not prepared to break new ground. This pertains in both personal affairs or creative endeavors.

12. SUNDAY. Easygoing. New romantic attractions may be formed with people whom you meet for the first time. You could get hooked by someone much older or younger than yourself. It might even turn out that you feel strongly attracted to a distant family member whom you have known for some time. Special invitations should be accepted, especially if you think you're going to meet people from different walks of life. It will do you good to get out of your rut and not be such a stick-in-the-mud. You might find some interesting people out there. Remember, variety is the spice of life. But Virgos may tend to be rather forgetful.

13. MONDAY. Misleading. Beware! You may only think that you have plenty of time to deal with certain jobs. You simply decided that these do not appear to require a great deal of attention to detail. But when you actually get around to doing them, you will probably discover that there is a lot more to do than you had thought. It would be best to make as early a start as possible with all routine matters, and especially desk jobs. Virgo folk should take the opportunity to rise above their petty emotional and practical difficulties. You must try to place matters in a broader perspective. You are failing to see the forest for the trees.

14. TUESDAY. Tricky. You will find this another rather tricky day. You may be fooling other people, and what is equally as bad, yourself! You must try to take more of a realistic approach to financial matters. Go over your accounts very carefully. You may discover that you have been going away over budget in certain areas. You will have to make adjustments, and perhaps some sacrifices, if you are going to balance the books for the month. Virgos will have to resist the temptation to escape into careers or occupational concerns as a way to get out of personal or relationship problems. Self-deception is but a dead end.

15. WEDNESDAY. Confusing. There is just no doubt about it. This will be one of the most worrying days of the month for you Virgos. Young or old, single or married, there are going to be problems. You would, of course, prefer to ignore them, but they simply cannot be brushed under the carpet. You must be prepared for the unexpected at all times. You may have to make alterations to your program, and at the very last moment. The actions or words of friends can catch you by surprise. Lack of openness and directness between romantic partners is likely to give rise to all sorts of misunderstandings.

16. THURSDAY. Sensitive. Quite a lot of your time today is likely to be spent picking up the pieces of what went wrong yesterday. Personal problems should be sorted out as soon as possible. But this will not be done if words become heated and tempers become frayed. Do not do or say anything that could possibly hurt your mate or partner. Such scars would take a long time to heal. Virgo people are likely to be feeling some delayed emotional reaction to the events of the past few days. Although you may have been detached at the time, such events or confrontations may now begin to take their toll. Friends will be supportive.

17. FRIDAY. Rewarding. You do not appear to have had the most spectacular of weeks so far. But today should see a big change and you once again will be back in the driver's seat. Influential people will be more sympathetic and helpful than usual. Your boss is likely to be aware of the pressures that you have had to cope with during the past few days. You will certainly enjoy any creative work that you are asked to handle. A romantic problem is likely to be resolved one way or the other. Whatever the outcome of serious discussions with your opposite number today, it is an important start.

18. SATURDAY. Disturbing. Nothing terribly wrong will be likely to occur today. Unfortunately though, what you were hoping would happen will probably not work out. A telephone call or a personal message from a loved one is not likely to come through. It would be best to make arrangements with friends early in the day. If you sit around waiting for one special person to call you, you could find you are left at loose ends. Go to parties and try to meet people who you hope can cheer you up. You have had a hard time of it recently, and you deserve to let your hair down and enjoy yourself.

19. SUNDAY. Happy. This can be a pleasant enough day for doing your own thing. Recreational activities will be enjoyable. It should go without saying that you leave any work you normally handle during office or factory hours until another day. You deserve a complete break. Try to make it up to loved ones if you have had any arguments or disagreements that could possibly sour the domestic atmosphere. Virgos are likely to be in a light-hearted mood. They will be only too happy to share this spirit with others. Later in the day, attempts to get the authorities to bend the rules may backfire. Today might be good for getting out and about.

20. MONDAY. Useful. This is a good day for Virgos to pull something rather special out of the hat. Do what you can to get ahead of your competitors in working situations. Play your trump card to gain advantage. Try to please superiors. Any projects that you have been working on alone should be shown to people who are in a position to give you some meaningful backing. They may also be able to assist you with the valuable contacts that they undoubtedly possess. Unexpected events can be turned to personal gain. Feuds with family or household members should be brought to an end, even if it means compromising slightly.

21. TUESDAY. Exciting. This will be one of the best days of the month. You may suddenly become aware that Christmas is not really very far away. Something will happen today, or someone will make a remark that will remind you that the festive season will soon be here. You are likely to be feeling rather more optimistic about life in general, and about one close relationship in particular. With your love life seeming to sort itself out now, many other things are likely to fall into place. Virgos will find that their popularity rating is boosted considerably. Chance encounters can lead to the forming of new friendships.

22. WEDNESDAY. Sensitive. There is nothing likely to go terribly wrong today. But you may feel that you are doing little more than just getting through the day. Nothing particularly exciting or dramatic is likely to take place, either at your home or at your place of work or business. Concentration may be a little difficult, though. There may be constant interruptions. This is especially true for Virgos who are attempting to deal with desk jobs. Superiors may grant pay raises or bonuses, but these are not likely to be on the scale that you had been hoping for. Virgo people should be sure to buy only what they want or need.

23. THURSDAY. Mixed. Quick thinking can enable Virgos to clinch lucrative deals with fast action. This is an especially favorable day for those who are involved in shipping, brokering and insurance. You should keep your eyes peeled for good opportunities. You may be able to pick up some unexpected new business. Social activity and work will mix well together. People will like your original way of doing things. It is important to show that you are truly a person whose word is their bond. This is vital if you are in the highly competitive business of buying and selling. Today will be favorable for the buying and selling of antiques.

24. FRIDAY. Easygoing. You will find this a fairly low-key ending to the working week. You are not likely to feel that you have to operate under any special pressure. This is a good day for housewives and mothers to get ahead with weekend chores. That would enable them to spend more time with loved ones. There is not any likelihood of there being any rush on at your place of employment. You will be rounding off old jobs rather than starting up any new ones. It may even be possible to get away earlier than usual and make a really long weekend of it. The extra time will be helpful for going through accounts and for paperwork.

25. SATURDAY. Enjoyable. You can probably count on there being quite a lot of activity today, and most of it will be to your liking. You may be traveling a little to see relatives or friends, for one thing. You should be able to spend more time on pleasure than on any business activities. But if it happens that you have a chance to get into some discussions in relation to your type of work, then why not? Loved ones will be agreeable, for the most part, to whatever your ideas and suggestions may be for this weekend. It would be wise, though, for you to make sure that your suggestions will really have appeal for your mate or partner.

26. SUNDAY. Uncertain. Do not push yourself too hard today. You are likely to be in for a fairly hectic ending to the month. You will undoubtedly need to have your wits about you in days ahead. You will need all the energy you can muster to cope with an ever-changing situation from tomorrow onward. This can be a tough day for Virgo people unless they avoid neighbors and friends who are both aggressive and bossy. You would do best to stick to your immediate family circle and try to have a quiet time of it. Even if your neighbors are in the wrong, it is wise to avoid provoking them, thus making enemies.

27. MONDAY. Tricky. You will not find this one of the best of starts to the working week. You may have been entertaining some high hopes of launching some exciting ventures. But because of a negative attitude of an influential person at your place of business, it is not to be. You will just have to shrug your shoulders and get on with the routine matters. The best attitude for you to take will be a philosophical one. Some Virgo shoppers may already be out looking for early Christmas bargains. And they may well be able to pick up gifts at very reasonable prices. But be sure that any articles you buy have warranties.

28. TUESDAY. Lucky. Today will bring about a complete reversal of yesterday's dismal trends. This will be a helpful period for all property and real estate transactions. You should be able to make a modest killing if you put the finishing touches on a deal now. This is a good time for doing business with real estate agents. Family or household members may be able to provide valuable introductions to people in positions of power and authority. Do whatever you can to advance yourself in your career through your good connections. Business and pleasure will definitely mix. Superiors will be impressed by the quality of work recently finished by Virgo people.

29. WEDNESDAY. Inactive. Take advantage of the peaceful conditions that today offers to catch up with your accounts. Finish off the little jobs that are connected with this month. Go through your files and rid them of outdated material. Make sure that you pay bills promptly. You will then have a clearer picture of your financial standing at all times. A midweek lull will give Virgo people the freedom to have more time to themselves. You may have an opportunity to indulge in a favorite hobby or pastime. Or you might prefer to take loved ones on a special trip. This can be an especially nostalgic day.

30. THURSDAY. Tricky. Virgos may feel a bit uncertain about how other people will respond when they take the initiative. You are usually a patient and careful person, and it would be best to stick to this role. In time, you will find out for sure how a certain someone feels about you. But it would be unwise to try to force the issue at this point. It might be best not to take any actions that have no precedent or may be viewed as too futuristic. It is important to maintain good relations with close friends and acquaintances, and not allow mutual enthusiasm to wither and die. Think up something novel in the way of entertainment this evening.

DECEMBER

1. FRIDAY. Happy. You probably have been approaching this month with some excitement and confidence. Many of the things that you have been planning so painstakingly to achieve during the last few weeks should be coming to fruition about now. Virgos who have been looking for a job that is different for some time may find that very niche. Look through the want ads in the newspaper. Some useful bargains can be picked up. If you are able to keep moving with the tide, you will also be able to benefit from other people's enthusiasm. Today will be favorable for all creative and artistic work. It is also the eve of a weekend.

2. SATURDAY. Quiet. This will be an easygoing day that is better suited to planning than to action. Many of your future hopes will rest on today's plans being carefully worked out. You should not leave anything to chance, especially not if it is connected to your job. If you work as a handyman, you must be prepared to figure out an estimate for jobs that you are planning to do for people. This should, of course, allow you a fair margin of profit while still making you less expensive than most of the people in your area. In this way, you will be building up business and goodwill for the future. There will be more opportunities for rest today.

3. SUNDAY. Sensitive. You will become easily upset by little things today. Remember, though, that you are not the only sensitive person around and that other people have feelings, too. Try to do more to satisfy the desires of your mate or partner. You may have been functioning well away from home. But you might not have been doing as much as you should have to keep loved ones happy and contented. This can be a good day for entertaining superiors and other influential people. You should be sure, however, that it does not take up the whole day. You must allow for some privacy in your domestic life.

4. MONDAY. Productive. The quick thinking and alertness, in general, of Virgo employees can bring them commendations or bonuses. The chances are, you are in need of as much additional money as you can manage to save at this time of the year. It will not worry you much at all if you have to put in a bit of overtime. Do everything you can to boost your earnings. Today is favorable for furthering property or real estate deals. Virgo real estate agents should be able to earn good commissions on the purchases and sales that they are able to finalize. This can be a good day for experimenting with new diets and cooking recipes.

5. TUESDAY. Useful. You are going to be having a busy time of it today. The work that you will be carrying out will be important for later. You are not likely to see the fruits of your labor for some time to come, though. Virgos who are self-employed may have to wait to be paid for services rendered. You will be likely to find yourself going to considerable expense due to travel. Collaborative and joint endeavors can produce particularly pleasing results. Business colleagues may have ways and means of achieving results that Virgos would have been incapable of alone. But influential people may be reactionary.

6. WEDNESDAY. Mixed. It will be another day on which Virgos will be likely to reap the full benefits of their own potential in teamwork and partnership endeavors. See what you can do to drum up support at your place of employment. You need it for projects that will save time and give you the chance to be more artistic. This day can be quite successful if you act with firmness and appear to know what you are talking about. Virgos who are involved in the world of advertising should be pleased by how many publicity stunts they organized came off. Virgos in love will find this evening is a particularly romantic time for dating.

7. THURSDAY. Disconcerting. Bank statements and invoices that you receive today are likely to give you a bit of a shock. It would be wise to go over the state of your finances in considerable detail. The chances are good that you are not as well off as you thought you were. There may have been some hidden expenses. Bills that come in will be far more expensive than you had budgeted for. It may even be necessary to reconsider the amount of money that you can really afford to lay out over the coming festive season. Virgo people are advised against changing course in midstream, as far as their career is concerned.

8. FRIDAY. Important. You are in need of a breather! Slow down a bit and relax. Take careful stock of the situation that you find yourself in. Allow that logical side of the Virgo character to get to work on your problems. You may have been tempted to resort to panic measures previously. All in all, this will be a fairly low-key ending to the week. You will be grateful that the pressure is off you now. Lack of any pressing demands can be taken as an opportunity for furthering routine activities undisturbed. Try to work out a schedule of the most important jobs that you would like to complete before Christmas.

9. SATURDAY. Challenging. Opportunities will arise that you may have thought you had missed out on completely. You will have to be ready to change your schedule for the day. You might have to act at a moment's notice if you are going to pick up extra profits. These could be all yours if you can beat your competitors to the punch. With more energy at your disposal, you will be in a gritty mood. You will not often, probably never, take no for an answer. This is an auspicious day for distant travel. Be prepared to make long journeys on short notice. Perhaps by doing so, you can secure interviews with influential people.

10. SUNDAY. Tricky. Your nerves and others' will be on edge today. It will be difficult for you to settle down to anything. You seem to have quite a lot on your mind. There are a great many steps that you would like to take in connection with your career. But you will be powerless to do so at this point. The influential people you would like to get hold of will not be available now, on this, your day of rest. You may also meet some opposition and hostility from some unexpected quarters. You will really get angry if people start to stick their noses into matters that you consider to be strictly personal.

11. MONDAY. Ordinary. Try to get as organized as you possibly can. Do the annoying little jobs now that you do not want to have to deal with later in the week. Then the pace will have picked up considerably and you might not have time. You are not likely to have much opportunity to make any major new moves today, though. This will be a favorable beginning to the working week insofar as professional and career affairs are concerned. Reputations can be built up on the basis of sound work and a name for efficiency and reliability. You may have the chance to get in some of your early Christmas shopping.

12. TUESDAY. Disturbing. Influential people can create problems. Superiors may conveniently forget about promises that were made to you last week. You may be required to work overtime, with very little chance of earning much extra money in the bargain. However, this is not a day to start looking for a new job. As much as you may feel exploited, you will have to swallow your pride. You must follow the dictates of people who have authority over you. Virgo people may be obliged to dig up past cases for official inquiries and investigations. This could lead to your getting behind schedule. Be sure you do not.

13. WEDNESDAY. Mixed. Women Virgos will be able to get ahead today. There may be a number of domestic chores to do that you should have completed as long ago as last weekend. But you simply have not been able to get around to doing them because of constant interruptions. However, the domestic atmosphere will be far more conducive to work today. It is particularly important for Virgo people to seek greater emotional stability and detachment. Otherwise, bouts of overoptimism and enthusiasm are likely to be followed by swings toward depression and self-doubt. Romantic arrangements may have to be canceled.

14. THURSDAY. Rewarding. This looks as if it is going to be the most positive day of this week so far. It is about time that Fortune smiled in your direction. Moreover, it is likely that she will be doing so again today. You may at last get repair work done around the home. Some problems that you have been enduring with the water system, the gas or the electricity can be worked out. Repair men may actually arrive at the time when they say they will. Loved ones will be more agreeable to your ideas for making budget cuts. It is important that you try to put extra money to one side for the additional Christmas expenditures.

15. FRIDAY. Confusing. The health of loved ones may be the cause for some concern. You might have to rearrange your schedule at work at the last moment. You will probably have to take care of the needs of someone who will be relying on you more than usual today. You might even be required to make one or more trips to a hospital or to a doctor's office in order to assist someone. This will be an especially sensitive day for romance. You may be wondering what is wrong with your mate or partner. He or she is likely to be in a worse mood than you have ever seen before. You will perhaps be upset, too, by the way they snap at you.

16. SATURDAY. Difficult. Virgo people will have to insist on precision and accuracy today. And this may very well make you quite unpopular, being critical of others' work. But if you do not adopt this attitude, and insist on its being maintained, superiors will hold you to blame for any errors. And these will probably not be of your making. So Virgos who have any kind of authority over others are going to have to be hard taskmasters, indeed. If you make your position known from the start, confusion and resentment will be less likely. Firmness with children should not be carried to extremes. Try reasoning with them.

17. SUNDAY. Sensitive. There will be only one more Sunday to go after this one before Christmas Day. So you are probably going to want to spend quite a lot of time at home. Putting up the decorations and giving pleasure to children will make time fly. But there will be problems in your relationships with close members of your family. There is no way you will not be able to iron these out completely. It will take you some time to build up the trust of a person who may have reason to feel let down by you. Tact and diplomacy will be crucial. Harsh words, spoken in a moment of passion, will lead to regrets.

18. MONDAY. Rewarding. This will be one of the most important days so far this month. There will be quite a lot for you to deal with at your place of employment. It is just as well that you are quite apt to have the necessary energy to deal with the rush jobs that are almost certain to come up. Hunches may prove to be correct. Go with your intuition, because it will not play you false. You will find it easier to plow through the usual number of problems this first workday. You should depend on your feelings, rather than relying on just plain logic. Today will be favorable for all artistic and creative endeavors.

19. TUESDAY. Tricky. Things may be getting to you today more than you would wish for. You doubtless feel that there is still far too much to do before you can safely believe that you're ready for Christmas. Virgo women, in particular, must not get themselves into too much of an uproar. Do not try to spread yourself too thinly. You cannot possibly do everything at once. Take care of one chore at a time and finish it. You will have to guard your temper with youngsters, as well as with older family members. It may be necessary to confront influential people at your place of employment. It is inevitable that a compromise will be made.

20. WEDNESDAY. Sensitive. Virgos must make it their duty to stand by their viewpoint. You can perhaps compromise in your actions, but never in spirit. Do try to manage difficult people with more charm, though. You may find that there are easier ways to get what you want than by an all-out confrontation. Taking an obviously antagonistic stand is equally as bad. It might be most helpful to give way on smaller issues. You can then score on those which really count for something. The health of romantic partners may have been giving you cause for concern. But it should now take a turn for the better. This will be a great relief for you.

21. THURSDAY. Disturbing. Virgos would be well advised to review their current financial situation. Do so before going off on any spending sprees. There are many people you would like to treat to expensive gifts this Christmas. But you do have to be sensible about this. If you get yourself into debt now, you could set all your plans back for some months to come. Don't forget to allow for that holiday you were planning for next year. Do not make snap decisions about spending money reserves you have been painstakingly building up. Make room for your natural Virgo caution. Don't be late for important appointments.

22. FRIDAY. Harmonious. Recreational activities can lead to some valuable introductions. You may meet important or influential people in unexpected places. This will be a pleasant day for Virgos who are finishing up work before Christmas, or starting vacations from school or college. Pre-Christmas office or school parties are likely to go very well and should turn out to be jolly occasions. There might even be a hint of romance in the air with someone whom you had only known on a formal level. This could be a favorable day for discussions with your boss. You are particularly anxious to turn creative enterprises into paying ones.

23. SATURDAY. Mixed. You may feel there will not be enough hours available to you today for all that you have to do. The important thing for you to remember is not to resort to panic measures. Last-minute shopping should be done in a practical and orderly manner. Make a list of the people who always remember you at this time of the year. And don't forget to send Christmas cards to people who live alone. They will be delighted to know that you still remember them. You may not have seen them face-to-face for quite awhile, but you have not forgotten them. Do not allow old friendships to drift away.